Dr. Ball is Associate Professor of Political Science at Hofstra University. His previously published books are *The Warren Court's Conceptions of Democracy* and *C[illegible]*
in Contempora[illegible]

HOWARD BALL

The Vision and the Dream of Justice Hugo L. Black

An Examination of a Judicial Philosophy

THE UNIVERSITY OF ALABAMA PRESS

University, Alabama

FOR MY NEWEST GIRL,
MELISSA PAIGE

AND FOR A GOOD MAN
BY THE NAME OF
SIDNEY BUDD NEIDELL

ISBN 0-8173-5165-5
Library of Congress Catalog Card Number: 74-22710

Manufactured in the United States of America

CONTENTS

Acknowledgments

I am grateful for the opportunity New College at Hofstra gave me, in the 1971 school year, to use two students as research assistants, Ms's Barbara Brown and Ruth Goldstein. I am equally grateful for the leave granted to me by the Hofstra University Board of Trustees in the Fall of 1972 in order that I might complete the manuscript. I also wish to thank the many former law clerks of the late Justice Hugo Black, and his personal secretary Mrs. Frances Lamb, who were kind enough to provide me with pertinent information about the Justice.

Thanks are in order for my wife Carol, who let me escape household chores—even on Saturdays—so that I could write. Thanks also to my three children, Susan, Sheryl, and Melissa, for having the good sense not to chase me to the office.

Finally, I most gratefully acknowledge the kind words of encouragement and the most knowledgeable words of wisdom from my good friend and colleague Tom Lauth. From the very inception of this project to the very end, Tom was an invaluable comforter and critic. To these individuals, and to my students who have argued with me about Courts and politics, I say thank you so much.

HOWARD BALL

Preface

This book is about a great man, the late Justice Hugo Lafayette Black. It is not the traditional biography of the man for there are many standard books on Black's life and career, in the Senate and as a member of the Supreme Court—and there will be many more to come. It is, instead, a biography of his convictions, an examination of Justice Black's "unwavering vision" of the law, of democracy, of, in a word, constitutionalism.

Justice Black was a true lover of democracy with a passionate devotion to the Constitution. Shunning commitments to popular, particular economic, social, or political causes and ideologies *except* his commitment to the Constitution, Justice Black's judicial thoughts and actions simply cannot be conventionally categorized as "liberal" or "conservative." For (given Black's allegiance to the words of the Constitution), before anything else and beyond misleading labels such as "civil libertarian," Justice Black was, in his own words, a "Literalist."

This is not to say that Mr. Justice Black had no doubts about the issues that came before the bench. He was, in his own words in a letter to the author, "always ready to change the [conference] vote if I reach the conclusion that my vote was wrong." Nor was he aloof from the very real problems raised by litigants in the cases before the Court; to the contrary he was a very empathetic Justice who understood the indignities the poor and the uneducated went through in the criminal law process. But this concern was tempered by an even greater concern for the maintenance of a constitutional Republic.

And so, even though Black felt, for example, that the civil rights movement served a "noble cause" and was a positive force in American life, its leaders could not violate the Constitution of the United States nor could they violate, with impunity, the laws of the State or of the Federal government. In a similar vein, Black voted to uphold many laws he felt to be *unwise yet constitutional*—the birth control case for example—while other Justices voted to strike these laws down. His reason for not acting was simple and profound: it is not for the judges to make or unmake what they think are ill-thought-out legislative acts.

One must assume that this self-imposed self-abnegation of the Justice did cause some problems for Hugo Black. But he had taken an oath to support the Constitution of the United States and he was committed to that oath one hundred and ten per cent. So if there were doubts and uncertainties, Black managed to resolve them before he wrote his opinions. And once the decision was made, once he finished weighing the arguments on both sides, once he wrote his opinion, he was fairly well committed to it. As one of his law clerks said: "Black did not sign an opinion he did not believe in."

The key to his decision-making process was the Constitution of the United States. It was Justice Black's "legal bible" and he always tried to act and judge in accordance with its rules and its guidelines. He, in his own words, "deplored even the slightest deviation from its least important commands."

In an age of head-nodders and standardization, Justice Hugo Black was an unconventional man. In an age where men, even men in the highest offices of government, lack commitment to principle, Justice Black was a man who was intensely committed to an idea. That idea was that judges, and most especially Justices of the Supreme Court, should not–must not–make laws but, rather, act in accordance with their limited powers outlined in the Constitution.

And Justice Black never wavered from that fundamental principle of judicial behavior. He was a most courteous, soft-spoken judicial "giant"; a man who appreciated his role as Justice of the Supreme Court; a man who was not afraid to act in accordance with the commands of the Constitution. This book is an attempt to capture the intense commitment of Justice Hugo Black to the Constitution.

HOWARD BALL

1

Black's Democratic Vision

How does one account for the profound impression Hugo Lafayette Black, Associate Justice of the United States Supreme Court for 34 years, made on the law? A legal admirer of the late Justice Black suggested that the answer lay in Black's brains, rectitude, and singleness of purpose: "He has exhibited to a singular degree...an intense moral commitment, concentrated through the focus of an unwavering vision, and brought to bear with an immense prowess."[1] Wallace Mendelson, scholarly critic of Justice Black, has said: "In a word, Mr. Justice Black is an Idealist. His wisdom is the wisdom of a great idea. He knows with Chesterton that the 'center of every man's existence is a dream.'"[2] And they are correct.

Reading and rereading his thoughts, in his many opinions and off-the-bench remarks, one is made constantly aware of the vision and the dream of Justice Black that propelled him to action. "Since the earliest days," Black once wrote, "philosophers have dreamed of a country where the mind and spirit of man would be free; where there would be no limits to inquiry; where man would be free to explore the unknown and challenge the most deeply rooted beliefs and principles."[3] Black's writings underline his belief that the American constitutional pattern is an effort to give effect to this dream; "to establish a country with no legal restrictions of any kind upon the subjects people could investigate, discuss, and deny."[4] His function, as criminal court judge, county prosecutor, United States Senator from Alabama, and, finally, Associate Justice of the Supreme Court of the United States, was to maintain the fragile reality of that dream—certainly to protect and foster it; more basically, to educate the people so that *they* could maintain, protect, foster, and live the vision.

Put simply, the "unwavering vision" of Justice Black was his love of a living, functioning, edifying, advancing democracy.[5] He saw in that form of governing the potentiality of the full flowering of positive man—love, trust, reasonableness, fairness, in a word, goodness. The purpose of this volume is basically to (1) outline the essential, salient characteristics of Justice Black's perception of democracy, and (2) then to examine the ways in which he gave life and meaning to his thoughts in the very many opinions he wrote while on the Supreme Court.

The Essence of Hugo Black's Democratic Vision

The "People"

Justice Black, wrote a former law clerk, "trusted in the wisdom and justice of the masses," whether they be lay jurors or voters, "more than the temporal power of individual mortal judges."[6] John Frank, another former law clerk, maintained that Black's faith in the people came from his early contact with Populism; that he became "saturated (with the idea) that the people had the right, through *their* government, to improve the condition of *their* daily lives."[7] Justice Black himself, in 1968, spoke of his "ultimate faith" in the judgment and the wisdom of the people.[8] This was simply a Jeffersonian love of the basic ideal of self-government: the people have the capacity to govern themselves without having anyone tell them (least of all the judges) what is best for them.

But this view is tainted with what another law clerk calls Black's "touch of Protestant pessimism."[9] According to Justice Black's long time associate, Associate Justice William O. Douglas, Jr., "Black knows that man's great capacity is the ability to err—to make errors because he sees only part of the facts, to make errors because he is often swept by prejudice or other emotions."[10] Black's optimism was tinged with the idea of fallibility, the idea that men were not omniscient and were not without greed and instinctive dislikes.[11]

Because of this fallibility of man, Justice Black could never emphasize strongly and passionately enough the "firstness" of the First Amendment freedoms of speech, press, association, and religion. Because Black felt that, in the words of his close friend, Edmond Cahn, the Bill of Rights was "directed toward values that lie beyond,"[12] because Black felt that full and open debate on public issues (guaranteed the people by the First Amendment) would clear out misconceptions and reduce the potency of the emotions, he was an absolute defender of these rights. Given his deep faith in the people, Black was confident that they would make wise choices *if* they were allowed to receive information. In his very last opinion from the Bench, Black said that: "The press was protected so that it could bare the secrets of government (expose deception in government) and *inform the people*."[13]

Though fallible then, the people are educable. Given new information, they will act as free men. They are *only* free when they are free to hear all sides of an argument, when they can voice their preferences, and when they can participate in the determination of their own fate by participating in the making of public policy. "The right to think, speak, and write freely without governmental censorship or interference is the most precious privilege of citizens vested with power to select policies and public officials," said Justice Black in 1968. "I view the guarantees of the First Amendment as the foundation upon which our governmental structure rests and without which it could not continue to endure as conceived and planned," wrote a younger Justice Black in 1941 (ending that thought with a footnote quoting Jefferson: "The basis of our government's being the opinion of the people, the very first object should be to keep that right").[14]

If change is to take place, and Black's vision of democracy was a dynamic, progressive one which embodied experimentation and change, even change in the basic Constitution itself, it must come from the people working through democratic procedures of representation. The Constitution is "the people's Constitution, and they were entitled to change it if they saw fit."[15] What especially rankled Justice Black was the naked presumptuousness of some judges who thought that they could amend the Constitution. "The people and their elected representatives, " Black wrote in a 1970 dissent, "not judges, are constitutionally vested with the power to amend the Constitution. Judges should not usurp that power in order to put over their own 'views.' "[16]

But Justice Black, just as vigorously as he defended the absoluteness of the First Amendment, vigorously rejected the notion that change should come from the barrel of a gun. Revolutionary lawlessness, violence, protests, demands were inconsistent with democratic processes.

> Our government envisions a system under which its policies are the result of reasoned decisions made by public officials chosen in the way the laws provide. These laws do not provide that elected officials...will act in response to peremptory demands of the leaders of tramping, shouting groups controlled by men who, among their virtues, have the ordinary amount of competing ambitions common to mankind...Government by clamorous and demanding groups is very far removed from government by the people's choice at the ballot box, i.e., a government of laws.[17]

As another of his former law clerks put it: "The one thing that Black always felt was that the end never justifies the means. Whatever the expediency of the moment it could not justify changing the system."[18] Violent revolutionary change in quest of illusory Panaceas was futile. Black put little stock in quick cure-alls. Evolutionary change, "a little freedom here, a greater degree of equality there," was the only way a democracy could advance.[19] (Anthony Lewis argues that Black, "the last of the agrarian radicals," had a Jeffersonian antagonism to cities. "Black thought the urbanization of America was changing its people's character for the worse, helping to cause lawlessness and violence that he deplored."[20]

So the "people," according to Justice Black, in a democracy, were its kernel of strength or, alternatively, its Achilles heel. But, "as a child of the Eighteenth Century Enlightenment and its Twentieth Century Champion,"[21] he always retained his faith in the strength of the people. He placed the burden of freedom on the people themselves; and he was optimistic enough to believe that the people, with full freedom to acquire information, debate, and peacefully petition for a redress of grievances, would, for the most part (there would always be error and mistakes), act fairly and wisely.

The Constitutional Pattern of Government

Justice Black had a "true passion for the Constitution," a passion that underscored his belief in a society based on the Rule of Law, binding on all men, regardless of status and power.[21] Agreeing with Lord Acton, Black feared power for "power corrupts" and judges, as well as legislators and executives, "have not been immune to the seductive influences of power."[22] The Constitution, however, a document written to limit power, is a *positive,* concrete instrument that "*clearly* marks the boundaries of governmental power" and provides the people with positive guarantees against governmental excesses: "The people put their trust, not in natural law but in positive constitutions, positive guarantees and a government that would stand responsible to the people."[23]

The Bill of Rights is the primary restraint on the government. In a powerful dissent in *Adamson v California,* Justice Black said:[24]

> I cannot consider the Bill of Rights to be an outworn eighteenth century strait jacket....Its provisions may be thought outdated abstractions by some. And it is true that they were designed to meet ancient evils. But they are the same kind of human evils that have emerged from century to century wherever excessive power is sought by the few at the expense of the many.

It demarcates, in Jefferson's words, (1) certain "rights" unceded by the people to the government, and (2) "fences against wrongs."[25] The former are absolute bars against governmental interference, i.e., freedom of religion, speech, press, and assembly. As Black said: "We have certain provisions in the Constitution which say 'Thou shalt not.' They do not say, 'You can go ahead and do this unless it is offensive to the universal sense of decency.' They do not say that....If they did, they would say virtually nothing. There would be no definite, binding place, no specific prohibition, if that were all it said."[26] The latter, the "fences against wrong," are restraints against unreasonable governmental actions, not absolute as the First Amendment is absolute ("Congress shall make no law" means, simply, that "Congress shall make no law."[27]), and these are found in the Fourth Amendment prohibition against "unreasonable searches and seizures, etc." They are bound together, for without the procedural fences against governmental wrongs, the substantive liberties of the First Amendment are placed in jeopardy.[28]

But, if the Constitution acts to keep the government from becoming punitive, for Black it also endows governments, both state and national, with certain almost unlimited powers with respect to social and economic policy-making.

> States have power to legislate against what are found to be injurious practices in their internal commercial and business affairs, so long as the laws do not run afoul of some specific constitutional prohibition, or of some valid federal law.[29]

The legislators, representatives of the people, and legislatures, as organs through which the will of the people is given substance, are the "transmission belts" for the people's will and through these vehicles the people can move toward the good life. And so, unless the governors run afoul of a *specific* constitutional prohibition, they have freedom to act in controlling the economy. In sum, "Black's basic principles," according to one observer, are "Jacksonian distrust of entrenched privilege and corporate greed; a firm belief in the prerogatives of legislatures as the representative organs in a democracy, and an aversion to judicial encroachment upon spheres of administrative and legislative action."[30]

Hugo Black believed very strongly "that the very government which must be made strong to deal with economic questions must be kept too weak to curb free expression."[31] And this must rank as one of the most difficult problems that Justice Black ever had to face in his long tenure as Associate Justice of the Supreme Court. In answering "this greatest of political issues,"[32] Black's thoughts on the role and function of the judges in a democracy need to be separately examined.

The Judges

Justice Black was fond of quoting Edmond Cahn's "quaint" statement: "A judge untethered by the text is a dangerous instrument."[33] For Black, the Constitution was the text and the judges were bound by their oath of office to decide cases according to the Constitution; above all, "to support the Constitution as it is, not as they think it should be. I cannot subscribe to the doctrine that consistent with that oath the judge can arrogate to himself a power to 'adapt the Constitution to new times.'"[34]

Given Black's thoughts about the governors, that is, that they must be absolutely without power in some areas and most powerful in others, judges had a very basic and valuable service or function to perform in a democracy: to maintain and protect the substance of the constitutional structure. "Even though I like my privacy as well as the next person," said Justice Black before a Columbia University audience, "I am nevertheless compelled to admit that the states have a right to invade it unless prohibited by some specific constitutional provision."[35] The judicial function was, in a real sense, a dual one, a "thou shalt not" and a "thou shall." First, maintaining the constitutional pattern meant that courts *must not* judge the "wisdom," "fairness," or "reasonableness" of economic and social legislative initiatives, this function being the constitutional prerogative of the state and national legislatures. Second, maintaining the constitutional pattern emphatically meant that courts *must not* back away from affirmatively protecting "federally protected rights" for, when such basic rights are encroached by the governors, the courts *must* "provide a remedy to rectify the wrong done."[36]

Regarding the negative function, that is, maximum judicial self-restraint as a function of the Court in economic and social matters, Hugo Black recalled that "my two law school professors taught us that legislators not judges should make the laws."[37] From the very first days on the Court to the last, Hugo Black adhered to that maxim of self-restraint—fighting advocates, in a life-long struggle, of the "substantive due process" philosophy who believed that a court could nullify legislation it felt to be contrary to self-created "evanescent" standards.[38] "I deeply fear for our constitutional system," Black wrote, "when life appointed judges can strike down a law passed by Congress or a state legislature with no more justification than that the judges believe the law is 'unreasonable.'"[39]

So insistent and consistent was Justice Black's commitment to this maxim that two of his colleagues, though at odds with each other philosophically, could fundamentally agree with each other regarding Black and his reputation as a "judicial activist." William O. Douglas, Jr. said that after a careful analysis of Black's opinions, one will "find plenty to disprove the charge that he is an 'activist' and a devotee of judicial power."[40] And Justice John M. Harlan, Jr. said of his colleague Black that "he rejects the open-ended notion that the Court sits to do good in every circumstance where good is needed and insists that we federal judges are contained by the terms of the Constitution, no less than all branches of governmental authority....No justice," concluded Harlan, "has worn his judicial robes with a keener sense of the limitations that go with them."[41]

With respect then to legislative action in the general economic and social arena, Black's clarion call was: leave basic policy changes to the people and the democratic processes. If the people don't like some regulatory legislation, if they think it is wrong, then let them change it! But not the judges! In response to arguments that the Courts could reach a faster and more desirable solution to problems than either legislators or executives, Black simply said: "I have known a different Court from the one today."[42]

The written constitutional pattern prohibits judges from saying: "Government, you can still do this unless it is so bad that it shocks the conscience of the judges."[43] This feeling was explicated in its pure form when (in an opinion that was a personal triumph for Justice Black's views in this constitutional controversy and which was a unanimous decision of the Court) Black wrote:

> Legislative bodies have broad scope to experiment with economic problems. and this Court does not sit to subject the state to intolerable supervision....We refuse to sit as a superlegislature to

> weigh the wisdom of legislation....Whether the legislature takes for its textbook Adam Smith, Herbert Spencer, Lord Keynes or some other is no concern of ours.[44]

If "strict construction" of the constitution barred judicial evaluations of the wisdom of economic and social legislation, then the same "strict construction" of the Constitution also meant, to Justice Black; that the courts had a vital positive function to perform: the defense of the Bill of Rights against legislative, executive, and bureaucratic encroachment by the Court "strictly" interpreting the *absolutes* in the Constitution:

> Under our constitutional system, Courts stand against any winds that blow as havens of refuge for those who might otherwise suffer because they are helpless, weak, outnumbered, or because they are non-conforming victims of prejudice and public excitement.[45]

Just as he decried judicial *intervention* in regulatory issues, Black decried judicial *abstention* in political and civil liberties issues. Just as he rejected judically created standards, "incongruous excrescences," employed to strike down economic legislation, Black rejected the employment by some judges of nebulous standards such as "clear and present danger," "grave and probable danger," and "balancing" to validate legislative and/or executive actions that wronged citizens. The command to the judges, he reiterated, was to decide politically difficult and uncomfortable constitutional cases according to what the Constitution said. "The public welfare," he wrote, "*demands* that constitutional cases *must* be decided according to the terms of the Constitution itself."[46]

For many years, too many for Black, this position was a lonely one on the Court for Black. But he never gave up his vision that the tide would turn. As he said, in his dissent in *Dennis v United States*: "Public opinion being what it now is, few will protest the conviction of these Communist petitioners. There is hope, however, that in calmer times, when present pressures, passions, and fears subside, this or some later Court will restore the First Amendment liberties to the high preferred place where they belong in a free society."[47] Justice Black consistently maintained that there was absolutely no way a judge could evade his responsibility to the simple words of the Constitution, regardless of what Presidents, legislatures, or Solicitor Generals argued to justify their usurpation of unceded rights of the people or their climbing over constitutionally created "fences against wrongs." In his very last opinion, Justice Black clearly expressed himself on this issue:

> The Government argues in its brief that in spite of the First Amendment, 'the authority of the Executive Department to protect the nation against publicaton of information whose disclosure would endanger the national security stems from two interrelated sources: the constitutional power of the President over the conduct of foreign affairs and his authority as Commander-in-Chief.'...The Government makes the bold and dangerously far-reaching contention that the courts should take it upon themselves to 'make' a law abridging freedom of the press in the name of equity, presidential power, and national security, even when the representatives of the people in Congress have adhered to the command of the First Amendment and refused to make such a law....No one can read the history (of the First Amendment's adoption) without being convinced beyond any doubt that it was injunctions like those sought here that Madison and his collaborators intended to outlaw in this Nation for all time.[48]

For Justice Black then, the essential, positive function of the courts was to declare null and void any governmental action that deprived a person of basic, clearly defined constitutional rights.

The "Rule of Law" and the Chief Enemy of Democracy

Justice Black's views of the judges and the constitutional pattern tends to clarify his notion of the "Rule of Law." For Black, the Rule of Law signified a government of exact, precise laws enacted under the authority of the written Constitution, and in accordance with the democratic and electoral processes prescribed in that basic, fundamental Law.

Repelled by the discretion of judges, by the growth of lawlessness and revolutionary activity in America, Black sought clarity, simplicity, and predictability in the law: "If the time has come when pupils of state-supported schools, kindergartens, grammar schools or high schools, can defy and flout orders of school officials to keep their minds on their own school work, it is the beginning of a new revolutionary era of permissiveness in this country fostered by the judiciary."[49] "This search for simple doctrine," said A. E. Dick Howard, a former law clerk of the Justice, "is a reflection of Black's dedication to the 'Rule of Law.'"[50] The Rule of Law, for Black, was equated with clear, uncluttered laws which are the consequence of the democratic processes. Opposing the Rule of Law was discretionary law-making by judges rewriting the Constitution and violent law-making by lawless men and women (and children)—both of these actions being violative of the Constitution and injurious to the peace and order of the community.

Certainly, then, judge-made law, conflicting with the idea of the Rule of Law and which was an "encrustation on the Constitution,"[51] and violent actions were threats to the democratic vision of Justice Black. But, while dangerous tendencies in themselves, they were symptoms and consequences of an even more dangerous threat to the democratic system. This prime threat, to Black, was a people unequipped to function as governors. While governmental encroachments, judicial discretion, and violence were evils, the real danger was impatience with the Rules of Law, an unwillingness to learn, conformity, superstition, "and utter, benighted ignorance."[52] Black wrote, in 1946, that "the public has an...

interest in the functioning of the community in such manner that the channels of communication remain free....To act as good citizens they must be informed. In order to enable them to be properly informed their information must be uncensored."[53] Black believed that, while the danger always existed that the system would fall, the people would overcome superstition and ignorance if given information. That, at least, was his hope and his vision.

The Vessel for Justice Black's Vision: His Opinions

Each judge has a distinctive "style." For Justice Black, quite consistent with his view of the nature and form of the Rule of Law, the style and object was simplicity. He had, in the words of a former law clerk, "a fundamental faith in clarity of communications that shunned complicated opinions and carefully qualified judicial reasoning so that 'my uncle on the farm behind the plowhorse' could understand every opinion we worked on."[54] Black believed that almost every legal, constitutional issue could be reduced to a "simple straight-forward question and subjected to common sense analysis."[55] Still another observer recalled that

> Black disliked the pretentious word where a simple word will do. His opinions are notably—and deliberately—free of Latin tags, those badges of erudition of which lawyers are so proud. He has been known to admonish a law clerk, in his own writing, 'to use, not the language of Oxford, but the language of your country forebears.'[56]

And this style had a logic to it. "The writing of simple opinions in clear language is a direct function of the Justice's belief that the law and its ways ought to be intelligible to the citizenry of Clay County, Alabama as to the law faculty of a great University."[57] It was Black's way of continuing the vitally important educational process by which the people overcome ignorance and mental sloth. He eschewed fancy words for plain, old-fashioned ones. Black, said a law clerk, "never lost sight of the fact that the work of the Court was addressed to the country as a whole rather than to the lawyers, the government, or the court watchers."[58] As Paul Freund said: "There is a touch of Jeremy Bentham in Justice Black, a Bentham with an unmistakenly American accent. The intense energies of both were engaged by zeal to reform the law, to cleanse away its excrescences, to look upon law as a clean instrument of popular will, not as the patina of judges' gloss."[59] In their own way, Justice Black's opinions have become part of the stream of communication by which the people become informed. As Associate Justice of the Supreme Court, he became a teacher.

In many hundreds of opinions written over thirty-four years, Justice Black had clearly, tenaciously, doggedly expressed a basic theme with certain basic variations. The theme, the vision of democracy and the constitutional pattern which gave it existence. Regarding the variations of this theme, Black:

> clearly rejected judicial discretion, via "natural law" interpretations of Due Process and Equal Protection; clearly affirmed the prerogatives of the governors to legislate for the "public welfare," i.e., freedom to regulate all aspects of the economy;
> clearly indicated that the government, while Supreme in some areas, was greatly and absolutely proscribed from interfering with the citizen's right to enjoy the freedoms of the Bill of Rights;
> showed an intense devotion to the ideal of democracy and to the Rule of Law;
> never lost faith in the people nor ever lost his passion for the Constitution.

A former law clerk of Justice Black's, who worked for the Justice in the early sixties, wrote that the characteristics that impressed him most about Black were: [Black's] "intellectual honesty, his devotion to the Constitution, his vision of the country and of the role that the Court and the Constitution played in the life of the country, and his strong belief in the good sense of the people of the country."[60]

The rest of this volume will focus on Black's essential views in order to spell out clearly his commitment to Democracy. The cases selected in the four areas–economy, the society, procedural due process, and first amendment freedoms–are representative of Justice Black's views. Though the chapters devoted to these four substantive areas do not offer a complete catalogue of his opinions in those areas, they do offer an accurate view of Black's views on Freedom. (Indeed, a volume is in preparation dealing with the subject of Justice Black and the Negro Rights movement.) It was deemed the better part of valor to examine carefully the close to one thousand opinions written by Black in thirty-four years and select those that most adequately reflect his basic views. To do anything else would be, in Hugo Black's own words in a letter to the author (May 21, 1966), "too big a job."

2

Black's Assault on Substantive Due Process: Regulating the Economy

Justice Black's Absolute Rejection of the Substantive Due Process Concoction

The Judicially Created "Metaphysical Wilderness" Called Substantive Due Process

An acute observer of the Supreme Court's activities commented, after Hugo Black's first term on the Bench, that "laymen as well as judges are beginning to realize that Black's solitary dissents, instead of revealing a perverse temperament and a lack of 'legal craftsmanship,' may well guide the Court out of the *metaphysical wilderness* into which it has wandered."[1] Like the biblical children of Israel, the Court had been wandering around—for over fifty years—in the metaphysical wilderness it created called substantive due process. Since the 1880s, the Court had employed this judicially created doctrine, whereby the judges would review the "reasonableness" of state and federal economic and social legislation by striking a balance between the public good and the private rights of property and economic liberty, to invalidate a wide range of legislation passed by state and national representatives that attempted to control and regulate the economy of the society.

Put simply, substantive due process was a doctrine that authorized courts to hold laws unconstitutional when "*they believe* the legislature has acted unwisely."[2] The legislation was deemed to be unreasonable if it was "incompatible with some particular economic or social philosophy" possessed by and protected by the judges.[3] From a procedural protection that guaranteed an accused defendant the "lawful judgment of his peers by the law of the land,"[4] the due process clause of the Fifth and Fourteenth Amendment took on a "substantive" meaning after the Civil War.

In the beginning, this "substantive" view of Due Process was held by a small minority. It was first enunciated in the *Slaughterhouse Cases* of 1873 where a majority of the justices of the Supreme Court held that Louisiana could enact legislation regarding the slaughtering of cattle, for the public health and safety, even though, in so doing, it limited the prerogatives of out-of-state butchers.[5] Justice Bradley, dissenting, argued that the Due Process clause imposed substantive limits on state economic regulation legislation. "In my view," he said, "a law which prohibits a large class of citizens from adopting a lawful employment, or from following a lawful employment previously adopted, does deprive them of liberty as well as property, without due process of law. Their right of choice is a portion of their liberty; their occupation is their property."

By the end of the next decade, the Bradley dissent became the perspective of the Supreme Court. In 1886, the Court held that corporations were "persons" within the meaning of the Due Process clause[6] and, the following year, in the case of *Mugler v. Kansas,* the Supreme Court stated that it was prepared to examine the substantive reasonableness of state legislation. Sustaining a law passed by the Kansas legislature prohibiting intoxicating beverages, the Court said, however, that

> not every statute enacted ostensibly for the promotion of public morals, the public health, or the public safety would be accepted as a legitimate exertion of the police power of the state. The courts would not be misled by mere pretenses; they were

obligated to look at the substance of things.[7]

In *Mugler*, then, the majority was saying that if a purported exercise of the state's police powers "has no real or substantial relation to those objects, or is a palpable invasion of rights secured by the fundamental law, it is the duty of the Courts to so adjudge."[8] This left the judges of the Supreme Court free to decide consitutional questions not according to what the Constitution said but on the basis of their own policy judgments. If, in the eyes of the justices of the Court (and in their hearts and minds), a regulatory device established by the legislature was "fair," "reasonable," or "inoffensive," it would be legitimized–if it was "unreasonable," then it was the "duty" of the Court to nullify the law. This new judicial creation, called by Black the "Allgeyer-Lochner-Adair-Coppage constitutional doctrine,"[9] was firmly embedded in the Court's laissez-faire majority's arsenal of weapons to be used to combat legislative encroachment of vested economic rights by the turn of the century.

Allgeyer v. Louisiana, an 1897 case, was the beginning of an epoch in the history of the Supreme Court whereby the judges struck down, as unconstitutional violations of the Due Process clause, state legislation that attempted to regulate child labor, mine safety, health standards in industry, etc. (*Mugler* is distinguishable from the cases that followed because the Court had *validated* the legislation.) A Louisiana Statute prohibited persons from doing business in insurance for any company which had not complied in all respects with Louisiana law. Allgeyer had been convicted for violating the law; he appealed to the Court and it reversed the judgment based on the fact that the Louisiana law was an unconstitutional infringement of Allgeyer's liberty without due process of law. Rufus Peckham, recently appointed New Yorker to the Bench, wrote the opinion:

Liberty is deemed to embrace the right of the citizen to be free in

> the enjoyment of all his faculties; to be free to use them in all lawful ways; to live and work where he will; to earn his livlihood by any lawful calling; to pursue any livlihood or avocation and for that purpose to enter into all contracts which may be proper, necessary, and essential to his carrying out to a successful conclusion the purposes above mentioned....When we speak of the liberty of contract for insurance we hold that it was a proper act, one which the defendent's were at liberty to perform and which the state legislature's had no right to prevent, at least with reference to the Federal constitution.[10]

In 1905, the Supreme Court handed down the *Lochner v New York* decision. Written by Justice Peckham, the Court invalidated a New York State statute that prohibited employment in bakeries for more than sixty hours per week or more than ten hours per day. The statute, wrote Peckham, interfered with the right of contract between employer and employee and "there is no reasonable ground for interfering with the liberty of persons or the right of free contract, by determining the hours of labor in the occupation of a baker." Dissenting, Justice Oliver W. Holmes, Jr., said simply and profoundly: "The Fourteenth Amendment does not enact Mr. Herbert Spencer's *Social Statics.*"

> A constitution is not intended to embody a particular economic theory, whether of paternalism and the organic relation of the citizen to the state or of laissez-faire. It is made for people of fundamentally differing views and the accident of our finding certain opinions natural and familiar or novel and even shocking ought not to conclude our judgment upon the question whether statutes embodying them conflict with the Constitution of the United States.[11]

Two other cases, *Adair v United States* and *Coppage v Kansas,* round out the form and substance of the constitutional doctrine so emphatically despised by Hugo Black. Both dealt with the "yellow dog" contract phenomenon, i.e., an arrangement whereby the employer hires employees on the condition that they do not join a Union; both were attempts by the national and a state legislature to protect the workers right to organize Unions. Both were held, by the Supreme Court, to be unconstitutional–violative of the Due Process Clauses in the Fifth and Fourteenth Amendments.[12] And so, from the 1890s to the 1930s, while there were statutes that were upheld as "reasonable" legislative initiatives in regulating economic activities,[13] the critical fact was that the Court was subjecting *all* of these statutes to the test of reasonableness; the Court was employing its own values and policy preferences in determining the validity of legislation passed by state and national legislators.

Hugo Black's Proposal for a Radical Change

Hugo Black grew up during the high tide of the Populist movement in Alabama and the country and, while he never joined or worked for the Populist Party, Black readily adapted certain elements of the Populist message. Particularly relevent to Black was the economic philosophy of Populism–its egalitarian economic ideas emphasizing rate regulation and anti-monopoly legislation by the state to protect the people.[14] According to those who knew Black, he "never lost contact with his relatively humble origins in Alabama; he cared as a lawyer, as a Senator, as a Justice about the common people and their problems."[15]

Running for the United States Senate in 1926 (an election he won), Black ran as the "Poor Man's Candidate." His campaign slogan: "I am not now, and have never been, a railroad, a power company, or a corporation lawyer."[16] Elected to the Senate, he was one of the sponsors of the Fair Labor Standards Act, one of the staunch supporters of Roosevelt's New Deal, and an acid Senate Investigator of Merchant Marine and Airline subsidies, and the Public Utility lobbying practices and influence-peddling in Washington,

D. C.[17]

One basic goal of Senator (and later as Justice) Black was to *absolutely abolish* the "substantive due process" doctrine of the Court. In the Senate, in 1937 (he was an ardent supporter of Roosevelt's Court-Packing plan), he said:

> A bare majority of the members of the Supreme Court of the United States have been for a long number of years assuming the right on their part to determine the reasonableness of state and federal laws. The Constitution never gave that majority any such power....The Federal government has complete, unrestricted power to regulate interstate commerce...unless there is something in the Constitution itself which directly stands in the way of that regulation of interstate commerce.[18]

As a Senator, Black would have "packed the Court" with judges who agreed with him on this issue so that "concoction" would be overturned and buried. Black's proposal for radical change was simply judicial abstention—unless the economic or social legislation overtly conflicted with a specific prohibition in the Constitution itself. As he said many years later, "I cannot accept a Due Process Clause interpretation which permits life appointed judges to write their own economic and political views into our Constitution."[19]

The Court in the 1930s was, to Black, a defender of old, outworn ideas; it was acting to preserve and defend big business monopolies as against the efforts of labor and government to minimize the concentrated power of business and industry. Black had "deep convictions" about "entrenched privilege," about anti-trust legislation, the control of financial institutions, the intervention of the courts into labor disputes. Boiled down, these "fixed principles of political agitation"[20] held by Black were that the people should not be denied the opportunity to better themselves economically and socially and that the government has a right, consistent with the "General Welfare" and other police powers, to legislate so that the people could better themselves. This meant that the government had to set rates for public utilities that were fair to the people; that the government had to pass legislation that would protect labor in their disputes with management; that the government had to pass legislation that would break up monopoly—monopoly that was choking competition to death in America. As he said on the Senate floor in 1930:

> Monopoly should be discouraged....Chain groceries, chain dry goods stores, chain drugstores, chain clothing stores, here today and merge tomorrow, grow in size and power. Railroad mergers, giant power monopolies, bank mergers, steel mergers, all kinds of mergers, concentrate more and more power in the hands of the few. In the name of efficiency, monopoly is the order of the day....We are rapidly becoming a Nation of a few business masters and many clerks and servants. The local business man and merchant is passing, and his community loses his contribution to local affairs as an independent thinker and executive.[21]

Competition, "unfettered competition," "unrestrained interaction of competative forces,"[22] was the essence of the American economic system, thought Black. The Government was responsible for maintaining such a free system; the Court was not to interfere in this legislative task. As one Black biographer wrote, "not only Congress (and state legislatures) but most of the quasi-legislative agencies of the national government have found in him (Black) a defender of their actions."

State Regulation of the Economy

Hugo Black's "literalist" approach in *all* constitutional issues was "direct and untortured."[24] Regarding the Court's posture on economic and social legislation, Black drew no subtle distinctions: the Court had been wandering in the metaphysical wilderness of "substantive due process" and it had to be led out. (Hugo Black let it be known to the author that the very first book Black read, along with the Bible, was *The Wandering Jew*! Interview with Justice Hugo Black, in his Chambers, February 1969.) His attempt to lead the Court away from intrusions into the states' regulation of economic problems was a successful one as an examination of some of his opinions indicates.[25]

Hugo Black believed strongly that the states had the constitutional mandate to establish what they considered to be fair rates for public utility services to the people. In 1937, in the case of *McCart v Indianapolis Water Company*,[26] this issue came before the Supreme Court. The Public Service Commission of Indiana had established new water rates in 1932. The Indianapolis Water Company, alleging that these new rates were confiscatory, sued for a permanent injunction in the United States District Court. Properly hearing the case, the District Court judge dismissed the suit. The Company appealed to the Circuit Court of Appeals and that court saw confiscation and issued the injunction. The state then appealed to the United States Supreme Court and it, in turn, issued a short *per curiam* opinion sending the case back for a new trial. Hugo Black was the sole dissenter.

The rate-making issue, he said, was not one for judicial determination. According to a custom which "this Court declared had existed from time immemorial," state legislatures decided what maximum rates for public services should be. If there were abuses, "the people must resort to the polls, not the courts."[27]

> Where ever the question of utility valuation arises today, it is exceedingly difficult to discern the truth through the maze of formulas and the jungle of metaphysical concepts sometimes conceived and often fostered by the ingenuity of those who seek inflated valuations to support excessive rates....Completely lost in the confusion of language–too frequently invented for the purpose of confusion–commissions and courts passing on rates for public utilities are driven to listen to competing speculations, estimates, and guesses, all under the name of 'reproduction costs.'

Courts, Black was saying, should not get caught up in the confusion, intentionally created by the big corporation lawyers so that their clients could make even higher profits at the expense of the consumer, surrounding rate making. The legislators will act fairly; in any event the Constitution does not prohibit the state of Indiana "to deny the company six per cent income on a still higher valuation of a canal that never, at the outset, cost the company more than $50,000.... I believe the state of Indiana has the right to regulate the price of water in Indianapolis, free from interference by federal courts. I am of the opinion that federal courts have no jurisdiction to proceed in this cause."[28] From his first days on the high bench, Hugo Black was to constantly reiterate his (legislative) critique of substantive due process, a view rooted in his own past.

A few years later, in a Texas case dealing with the issue of regulation and interference by the federal courts in such state activities,[29] Hugo Black, writing for the Supreme Court majority, was able to take the *McCart* dissent and turn it into the law of the land. (This phenomenon, of seeing earlier dissents turn into majority views, was not an uncommon one for Justice Black.) The Texas Railroad Commission's responsibility was to conserve the resources, revenues, and to monitor the impact of industry on the whole economy of the state. The Commission had issued an order allowing Burford, a small businessman-oil speculator, to drill four oil wells on a small plot of land in the East Texas oil field. The Sun Oil Company attacked the validity of the order and, instead of bringing suit in state court where it might be defeated, asked the Federal District Court to invalidate the order. The District Court Judges, using discretion, refused to hear the complaint. On direct appeal to the Supreme Court (it was a special three-judge District Court panel), the High Court in an opinion written by Hugo Black affirmed the District Court decision.

He reiterated his *McCart* view that federal courts have no constitutional right to interfere with state regulatory activities unless it is alleged that some specific provision of the federal Constitution is violated. "As a practical matter," Black wrote, "the federal courts can make small contribution to the well-organized system of regulation and review which the Texas statutes provide. Texas courts can give fully as great relief, including temporary restraining orders, as the federal courts. Delay, misunderstanding of local law and needless federal conflict with the state policy, are the inevitable product of this double system of review."[30] "Equitable discretion," he concluded, "should be exercised by the federal courts because these questions of regulation of the industry by the State administrative agency *so clearly* involves basic problems of *Texas* policy."[31] To the point, then, Black's opinion affirmed the "hands off" philosophy he had held for many years.

Still another controversial economic issue that developed in the depression-ridden decade of the thirties was that of the states securing additional revenues for public services through taxation of corporations. In an early opinion, Black came to grips with just one aspect of the larger issue. California had passed a tax of 2.6 percent on gross premiums received on business done in the state by out-of-state corporations. It was a tax for the privilege of doing business in California and Connecticut General Life Insurance Company argued that such a tax violated the "Due Process" Clause of the Fourteenth Amendment. The Supreme Court, in an opinion written by Chief Justice Harlan Stone, concluded that that tax was void because California did not have the constitutional power to tax the property and activities of a foreign corporation. "A corporation which is allowed to come into a state and there carry on its business may claim as an individual may claim, the protection of the Fourteenth Amendment against a subsequent application to it of state law....The Due Process clause denies to the state power to tax or regulate the corporation's property and activities elsewhere."[32] Black vehemently dissented from the majority opinion.

First of all, he argued that if, as the Court had said in the past, "California has the lawful constitutional right to impose conditions on foreign corporations so as to protect domestic corporations, its own elected legislative representatives should be the judges of what is reasonable and proper in a democracy."[33] But, beyond that reaffirmation of the power of the states to deal with economic problems, Black took issue with the continued judicial remodeling of the constitutional protections. "I do not believe the word 'person' in the Fourteenth Amendment includes corporations," Black argued. "Neither the history nor the language of the Amendment justifies the belief that corporations are included within its protection....The history of the Amendment proves that the people were told that its purpose was to protect weak and helpless human beings and were not told that it was intended to remove corporations from the control of state governments."[34]

Warming to his attack on the behavior of the Court majority, Black went on to say:

> If the people of this nation wish to deprive the states of their sovereign rights to determine what is a fair and just tax upon a corporation's doing a purely local business within their own state boundaries, there is a way provided by the Constitution to accomplish this purpose. That way does not lie along the course of judicial amendment to that fundamental charter. An Amendment having that purpose could be submitted by Congress as provided by the Constitution. I do not believe that the Fourteenth Amendment had that purpose, nor that the people believed it had that purpose, nor that it should be construed as having that purpose.[35]

In his early years on the Court, Hugo Black was to dissent

again and again whenever the Court majority invalidated a state tax program. In 1938, he dissented in *Quin, White and Prince, Inc. v Henneford.* Washington state had a tax which brought into its coffers one half percent of the gross receipts of taxpayers doing business out of state. Quin and others were in the business of marketing fruit in Washington and then shipping the produce from Washington to other states and foreign countries. They argued that the tax was an unfair burden on "interstate commerce" and, in an opinion written by the Chief Justice (Stone), the Supreme Court agreed and voided the tax law.

In his dissent, Justice Black pointed out that this issue (whether there was a burden on interstate commerce) was a complex one; "only a comprehensive survey and investigation of the entire national economy–which alone Congress has power and facilities to make–can indicate the need for, as well as justify, restricting the taxing power of the state....No court can make such a broad and deliberate investigation."[36]

While it is essential that the state of Washington not violate the Commerce clause,

> it is of equal import that the judicial department of our government scrupulously observe the constitutional limitations & that Congress alone should adopt a broad policy of regulation–if otherwise valid state laws combine to hamper the free flow of commerce.[37]

Even if the judges believe that Congress has not acted vigorously, and even if their beliefs are correct, this, Black concluded, "is an inadequate reason for the judicial branch–without constitutional power–to attempt to perform the duty constitutionally reposed in Congress."[38]

Black also dissented in the 1940 case of *Wood v Lovett.*[39] The state of Arkansas, faced with the fact that twenty-five percent of the real property in the state was tax delinquent, passed legislation in 1935 allowing the state to sell real or personal property for non-payment of taxes. These proceedings, according to the 1935 law, could not be set aside by any proceedings at law or equity because of irregularity, omission, or mistakes: once seized for non-payment and sold, that was it! In 1936, the Arkansas Commissioner of State Lands sold lands held by Lovett since 1932, but seized by the state for non-payment of taxes, to Wood. A year later, 1937, the Arkansas legislature repealed the 1935 Statute. In 1939, Lovett brought suit in state court against Wood in an attempt to reacquire his lands. Lovett alleged (and the allegation was accepted as true by Wood's lawyers in the state trial) that there were irregularities in the proceedings which led to his losing his lands—but which were ignored due to the express command in the 1935 statute. The Arkansas courts ruled in Lovett's favor and Wood, who stood to lose the property he had purchased from the state at bargain rates, appealed to the Supreme Court of the United States. His argument: the 1937 statute violated the Constitution because it impaired the obligation of his contract with the state (Article I, Section 10- the "Contract" Clause). In a brief opinion, the Supreme Court majority accepted the contention that the 1937 Arkansas statute ran afoul of the "contract" clause and declared that Act unconstitutional. Wood retained the property.

Black was the dissenter. The problem, non-payment of taxes, was a nationwide one, he argued. The 1937 Statute declared unconstitutional was one of many actions adopted by the states "in an effort to meet the baffling social and economic problems growing out of a nationwide depression."[40] It was an attempt by Arkansas, in 1935, to recoup the lost revenues that led to the dilemma for Lovett. The legislators in 1935 "were persuaded of the wisdom of such a step."[41] It was clear to Black that the repealing legislation came about because "legislators became convinced that the law had worked directly contrary to the state's policy of obtaining benefits believed to flow from continuity of possession by home owners and farmers, that it had accomplished inequitable results and it had thereby operated injuriously to the interests of the state and that sound policy dictates its repeal."[42]

Arkansas legislators, said the Justice from Clay County, Alabama, were trying to seek a rational and fair way out of just one of the crises created by the depression. This was not only within the state's power to do so, "it was also their *imperative duty.*

> Without attempting to judge the wisdom or inequities of either act, it is easy to see that both represented attempts, rational and understandable attempts, to achieve such a solution. To hold that the Contract clause of the Federal Constitution is a barrier to the 1937 attempt to restore to the distressed landowner the remedy partly taken away by the 1935 Act is, in my view, wholly inconsistent with the spirit and the language of *that* Constitution.[43]

Speaking here was the "Candidate of the Poor Man," for Justice Black, perhaps emphathizing more than his colleagues, went to the heart of the matter. What he saw was land speculators, buying land up for sale due to the poverty of good farm people, subtly using constitutional phrases—successfully as it turned out, to thwart the attempts by the representatives of the people, the Arkansas legislators, to rectify a series of misfortunes due to a bad law. The people, through the polls and through the democratic process, have the right to get rid of bad laws by passing statutes such as the one Arkansas passed in 1937. And the courts, non-elected federal organs, ought not to interfere in these democratic activities.

There were two cases that illustrate the nagging fear that Black held regarding judicial policy-making in this area of taxation. Like the *Quin* case, both dealt with the question of whether or not the tax was an undue burden on interstate commerce; unlike *Quin*, however, the Court majority ruled that there was no undue burden shown. Black concurred in both opinions because he felt that the Court should not be judging–even if it led to acceptance–state economic, and social (see his *Southern Pacific v Arizona* dissent in the next section) legislation. In one case, Minnesota used a General Minnesota Personal Property Tax to tax Northwest Airlines, which had its principle business offices located in that state.[44] The Airline argued that this tax violated the Due Process clause and was an undue burden on interstate commerce in violation of the Commerce clause. Justice Frankfurter, for the majority of the Supreme Court, said that the tax was a reasonable exercise of the state's taxing powers and not in violation with the Constitution. Concurring, Black simply said: "These state taxation problems, it seems to me, call for congressional investigation, consideration and action. The Constitution gave that branch of government the power to regulate commerce...and until it acts I think we should enter the field with extreme caution."[45]

Two years later, Black was not so cautious with his words. The state of Washington had ordered International Shoe Corporation, a corporation chartered in the state of Delaware, to pay a specified amount of the wages paid its employees within the state into the state Unemployment Compensation Fund. International argued that this was an undue burden on interstate commerce and challenged the program in the Court. Chief Justice Stone wrote the opinion for the Court majority upholding the legislation as reasonable. Black concurred, but with a biting lecture on judicial restraint directed to his brethren:

> There is a strong emotional appeal in the words 'fair play,' 'justice,' and 'reasonableness.' But they were not chosen by those who wrote the original Constitution or the Fourteenth Amendment as a measuring rod for this Court to use in invalidating State or federal laws. No one, not even those who most feared a

> democratic government, ever formally proposed that Courts should be given power to invalidate legislation under any such elastic standards....The application of the 'natural law' concept makes judges the supreme arbiters of the country's laws and practices....This result, I believe, alters the form of government our constitution provides. I cannot agree.[46]

But Justice Black was to have the last word in the area of taxation of private corporations by states. Section 10 of the Reconstruction Finance Corporation Act, had forbidden states to tax the personal property of the RFC or its subsidiaries. It did provide, however, for taxation of real property subject to state taxation just as other real property was taxed. The case arose in the courts because an RFC subsidiary, the Defense Plant Corporation, acquired land in Beaver County, Pennsylvania, built a plant on the property, and then leased the facility to the Curtiss-Wright Corporation for the manufacturing of war equipment. Beaver County taxed the machinery in the plant and the Supreme Court of Pennsylvania held that the machinery was real property under a long-established rule in Pennsylvania applying to all essential machinery of a manufacturing plant. It said that the tax was not discriminatory; rather, it was an even-handed application of a general tax principle in the state. The Reconstruction Finance Corporation appealed the State Court decision to the Supreme Court and, in an opinion written for a unanimous Court, Justice Hugo Black affirmed the decision of the state Supreme Court.

The key, for Black, was fair employment of the real property principle:

> We think the congressional purpose can best be accomplished by application of settled state rules as to what constitutes real property, so long as it is plain, as it is here, that the state rules do not affect a discrimination against the government, or patently run counter to the Act. Concepts of real property are deeply rooted in state traditions, customs, habits, and laws. Local tax

> administration is geared to these concepts. (To force the state to change long-standing practices) would create the kind of confusion and resultant hampering of local tax machinery which we are certain Congress did not intend.[47]

Here again, Justice (late Senator) Black was reaffirming the primacy of the Congress, as well as the State and local legislators, in this area of policy making. Over and over again, Black would use his years of experience as a legislator to determine the "intent" of other legislators but in a manner that almost never–in economic and social policy areas–*narrowed* their powers to control and regulate.

Turning from rate-making and taxing powers of the states to the general regulatory powers of the state, one finds Black's opinions following the same pattern. A solitary dissenter in the early years, Black became the spokesman for the Court, the spokesman for judicial deference to legislative judgments, in the later years. His dissents, clear and simple, became the light out of the wilderness for the Court.

An early case, *Polk Company v Glover,* 1938, illustrates the general pattern of judicial response and action at that time. A Florida statute required that all containers of canned citrus fruit bear a label naming the state or county where produced and, if produced in Florida, the name "Florida" was to appear on the "substance" of each container. Canners protested and took their case into the federal courts. They argued that such legislation violated both the Due Process and the Commerce clauses of the Constitution. The three judge district court placed a temporary restraining order on the enforcement of the statute, pending appeal. The majority of the Supreme Court sent the case back to the District Court for a discussion of the merits of the Florida statute. Justice Black dissented.

He maintained that state laws were continuously subjected to attack by "those who do not wish to obey them. Accordingly, it becomes increasingly important to protect state governments from needless expensive burdens and suspensions of their laws incident to federal court injunctions issued on allegations that show no right to relief." The statute was a legislative attempt to eliminate fraud and that enforcement of the statute was well within the power of the legislative branch of government.

> Legislators under our system determine the necessity for regulatory laws, considering both the evils and benefits that may result....Their inquiries are not subject to the strict rules of evidence which have been found essential in proceedings before courts. Legislators may personally survey the field and obtain data and broad perspective which the necessary limitations of court litigation make impossible.[48]

If, on remand, the lower court sees the statute as a violation of the Constitution, then "the final determination of the wisdom and the choice of legislative policy has passed from the legislators—elected by and responsible to the people—to the courts."[49] Court policy, he was arguing, should be: utmost deference to legislative prerogatives.

Black again was the solitary dissenter in the *Southern Pacific Company v Arizona* case some years later. That state had passed legislation restricting the length of railroad cars entering Arizona to no more than fourteen passenger cars and no more than seventy freight cars. The Train Limit Law, passed at the turn of the century, was an attempt to provide safety standards by the state on traffic within its boundaries; an enactment under the "police powers" of the state. The Southern Pacific Company charged that this statute was an undue burden on interstate commerce and therefore unconstitutional. Chief Justice Stone, writing for the majority, held that the Arizona law did contravene the Constitution. When Congress does not act, he said, the Supreme Court of the United States "and not state legislatures is the final arbiter of competing national and state interests."[50] Black's dissent vigorously attacked the philosophical basis of the Stone opinion.

"The whole theory of our government, federal and state," he said, "is hostile to the idea that questions of legislative authority may depend upon opinions of judges as to the wisdom or want of wisdom in the enactment of laws under powers clearly conferred upon the legislature. What the Court decides today is that it is unwise governmental policy to regulate the length of trains."[51]

Congress alone has the power to deal with this issue of commerce. And Congress was well aware of the Arizona Train Limit law. And only Congress could act to reduce the impact of that state law. But, "even though Congress is perfectly content to leave the matter to the different state legislatures, this Court, on the ground of 'lack of uniformity,' will require it to make an express avowal of that fact before it will permit a state to guard against that admitted danger (to the public Safety)."[52]

> Representatives elected by the people to make their laws, rather than judges appointed to interpret those laws, can best determine the policies which govern the people. That at least is the basic principle on which our democratic society rests.

By the end of the forties, however, Justice Black's views on general regulatory powers of the states became the views of the majority of the Court. Except for *Morey v Doud,*[53] where the Court voided an Illinois law because it exempted American Express Company from the regulations in it covering currency exchange businesses (Black dissented because he felt the legislators had the right to exempt from the law's coverage known and solvent businesses from a statute passed to protect the public from fraudulent, fly-by-night companies), the Court has consistently refused to examine the reasonableness of economic legislation. Justice Black wrote the two watershed opinions for the Court, reflecting its changed attitude: *Lincoln Federal Labor Union v North-*

western Iron and Metal Company,(1949), and *Ferguson v Skrupa* (1962).

Lincoln Federal, similar to a case decided a year earlier by the Court, Black writing the opinion in that one also,[54] dealt with a Nebraska "Right to Work" Amendment to the Nebraska Constitution which stated that no person was to be denied an opportunity to work because he/she was not a member of a labor union. Black, as he did in the AFL case, argued that there was no denial of Free Speech and Association, nor was there a violation of Due Process and Contract clause provisions of the Federal Constitution. The decisive question, wrote Black, was: does the Due Process Clause "forbid a state to pass laws clearly designed to safeguard the opportunity of non-union members to get and hold jobs free from discrimination against them because they are non-union workers?"[55] It does not, he emphatically answered.

> This Court...has consciously returned closer and closer to the earlier constitutional principle that states have power to legislate against what are found to be injurious practices in their internal commercial and business affairs, so long as their laws do not run afoul of some specific constitutional prohibition, or of some valid federal law....Under this constitutional doctrine the Due Process clause is no longer to be so broadly construed that the Congress and the state legislature's are put in a strait jacket when they attempt to suppress business and industrial conditions which they regard as offensive to the public welfare.[56]

In 1962, in the *Ferguson* case, the Supreme Court finally arrived at the earlier constitutional principle alluded to by Black in *Lincoln*. The case involved a Kansas statute which made it a misdemeanor for a person to engage in the business of debt adjusting except as incident to the lawful practice of law. The statute was challenged by Skrupa, doing business as Credit Advisors, Inc., in the lower federal courts and a three-judge District Court invalidated the state law as violative of the Due Process Clause of the Fourteenth Amendment. The Supreme Court, in this watershed case, overturned the lower courts and effectively laid to rest the "Lochner" doctrine.

The District Court, said Black, used an outworn philosophy to invalidate the law. "Under our system of government created by our Constitution, it is up to the legislators, not the courts, to decide on the wisdom and utility of legislation."[57] There was a time, he said, when Due Process was used to strike down laws which the judges thought were unreasonable—"but this doctrine has long since been discarded."[58] Legislative bodies "have broad scope" to experiment with economic problems and "this Court does not sit to subject the state to intolerable supervision."[59] He concluded by saying that:

> We emphatically refuse to go back to the time when the courts used the Due Process Clause to strike down state laws regulatory of business and industrial conditions because they may be unwise, improvident or out of harmony with a particular school of thought. Nor are we able to or willing to draw lines by calling a law 'prohibitory,' or 'regulatory.' Whether the legislature takes for its textbook Adam Smith, Herbert Spencer, or Lord Keynes, or some other *is no concern of ours.*[60]

And so, in the area of state regulation of economic and industrial relations, Black's views ultimately became the views of the entire Court.

Federal Powers to Control National Economic Problems

Democracy meant that the state governments had adequate powers to deal with their problems and, according to Black, where the courts would not act as "big brothers" telling the states what was good for them.[61] Regarding national problems, Black's approach, as already seen the state cases, was fundamentally a congressional approach: "He (Black) is Congress' man. Congress has all the power it needs for any national purpose."[62] Hugo Black's great concern, as Senator and as Justice, was monopoly and monopolistic practices and he had no qualms about "willingly go(ing) as far as (a) constitutional provision can be taken in construing it"[63] if it meant that Congress could contain and minimize the evil impact of oligopolic industrial practices. His record as Justice of the Supreme Court attests to his vigor in the defense of his view of democracy:

> Since Black's appointment some thirty years ago, there have been something over 200 cases decided by the Court involving antitrust and related questions. Black has written opinions in almost fifty of these cases; of these, thirty opinions were written for a majority of the Court, less than half that number were dissents; the rest were concurring opinions. In these 200-odd cases, Black voted against the application of the antitrust laws only about 20 times.[64]

For Justice Black, "it was vital that there should be no power vacuum in which business can operate, free of any accountability to the public,"[65] State legislatures could not effectively restrain and control national and international businesses and industry; it was Congress' job to police these activities. And, in the Commerce Clause especially, the Constitution granted Congress the necessary power to combat privilege and monopoly. If, as will be seen in Chapters Four and Five, the Constitution prohibited government from acting *punitively* with respect to political freedoms, certainly, Black maintained, that same Fundamental Law empowered the Congress to act *positively* with respect to controlling big business and industry.[66]

Congress, according to Justice Black, did act effectively in meeting the challenge of big business by employing the Commerce power to create Anti-trust legislation, in particular the Sherman Anti-trust Act. With Black sitting on the Court, and writing some of the watershed opinions in this area, anti-trust application was extended to cover insurance,[67] liquor,[68] newspapers,[69] foreign commerce,[70] automobile price-fixing,[71] stock exchange activities,[72] clothing retailers,[73] and mergers.[74] A quartet of cases in the area of anti-trust presents a lucid picture of Black's thoughts.

The Fashion Originators Guild of America was a group of manufacturers of women's garments and textiles that organized to control outlets, and boycott those stores that refused to follow the Guild's guidelines. The Securities and Exchange Commission charged the group with committing practices that constituted unfair methods of competition tending to monopoly and issued a "cease and desist" order in violation of the Sherman and Clayton Anti-trust Acts. The order was affirmed by the Court of Appeals and the Guild appealed to the Supreme Court. The Supreme Court, in an opinion written by Hugo Black, affirmed the decision of the Court of Appeals. In this first of many opinions dealing with anti-trust, Black condemned group boycotts by apparel manufacturers. The Guild, he said, was

> in reality an extra-governmental agency, which prescribes rules for the regulation and restraint of interstate commerce, and provides extra-judicial tribunals for determination and punishment of violation and thus trenches upon the power of the national legislature and violates the statute."[75]

The Guild's activities were found to be a clear violation of the antitrust laws and they could not continue in force: the "cease and desist" order was upheld as a legitimate exercise of an agency of the national government.

In another major antitrust case a few years later, *United States v. Southeastern Underwriter's Association,* the question of whether insurance companies, conducting a substantial part of business across state lines, engaged in interstate commerce and therefore become subject to Sherman Anti-Trust Act provisions came to the Court. The government contended that Southeastern had conspired to restrain interstate commerce and trade by fixing and maintaining arbitrary and non-competative premium rates. The lower Court held that the Act did not apply to insurance. Justice Black, for the Court, disagreed.

He maintained that Congress did not intend that the business of insurance be exempt from the operation of the Sherman Act.

> The Commerce power granted Congress is a broad positive power. It is the power to legislate concerning transactions which reach across state lines, affecting the people of more states than one....Our basic responsibility in interpreting the Commerce clause is to make certain that the power to govern intercourse among the states remains where the constitution placed it. That power...is vested in the Congress, available to be exercised for the national welfare as Congress shall deem necessary. No commercial enterprise of any kind which conducts its activities across state lines has been held to be wholly beyond the regulatory power of Congress under the Commerce clause. We cannot make an exception of the business of insurance.[76]

A year later Justice Black wrote the opinion for the Court in a case that extended anti-trust controls into the area of newspapers. The Associated Press, the government contended in its case, violated the Sherman Anti-trust Act because it blocked the dissemination of news stories to non-members of the Association. The injunction it sought was granted by the three-judge District Court and the AP appealed the decision. The Supreme Court held that news was interstate commerce and fell under the control of the Sherman Act.

Trade restraint was obvious when one examined the by-laws of the Association, Black wrote. Their "net effect" is to make it impossible for new papers to enter most cities in America because it was blocked from getting the news. "Trade restraints of this character, aimed at the destruction of competition, tend to block the initiative, which brings newcomers into the business and to frustrate the free enterprise system which it was the purpose of the Sherman Act to protect....Trade in news carried on among the states is interstate commerce."[77]

Addressing himself to the argument made by AP that the injunction violated their member's freedom of press, Black vehemently rejected that contention:

> Surely a command (First Amendment's Freedom of Press) that the government itself shall not impede the free flow of ideas does not afford non-governmental combinations a refuge if they impose restraints upon that constitutionally guaranteed freedom. Freedom to publish means freedom for all and not for some. Freedom to publish is guaranteed by the Constitution, but freedom to combine to keep others from publishing is not. Freedom of the press from governmental interference under the First Amendment does not sanction repression of that freedom by private interests. The First Amendment affords not the slightest support for the contention that a combination to restrain trade in news and views has any constitutional immunity.[78]

In a case thought by many to be his clearest statement of the nature of anti-trust legislation, the *Northern Pacific Railroad Company v United States,* 1957, Justice Black dealt with the practice of "preferential routing" agreements by which lessees of railroad property had to agree to ship on that railroad line all their goods and produce. The District Court judge issued an order, at the request of the government, enjoining the railroad from enforcing such routing agreements because such agreements were unlawful restraints of trade in violation of the Sherman Act.

In upholding the judgment of the District Court, Black wrote that:

> The Sherman Act was designed to be a comprehensive charter of economic liberty aimed at preserving free and unfettered competition as a rule of trade. It rests on the premise that the unrestrained interaction of competative forces will yield the best

> allocation of our economic resources, the lowest prices, the highest quality and the greatest material progress, while at the same time providing an environment conducive to the preservation of our democratic political and social institutions. But even were that a premise open to question, the policy unequivocally laid down by the Act is competition.[79]

Competition was the essence of the American system: anything that blocked this competition had to be removed by government. This was the message of Hugo Black with respect to the dangers of big business and industry. Let the little man breathe; let him be able to engage, vigorously, in competition with others and all will benefit.

While there are certain limits to antitrust activity, these are narrowly drawn ones that bar, for example, the Sherman Act from being used to limit railroad companies from financing a publicity campaign in favor of state legislation restricting the trucking industry.[80] Black's great concern for personal rights led him to dissent in cases where antitrust actions led to infringement of personal or political freedom. For example, in *United States v Weldon,* Black and Douglas dissented from the Court's ruling that an antitrust immunity statute did not apply to a hearing before a congressional investigating committee.[81] He said, in dissent: "Important as I believe the antitrust laws to be, I believe it is more important still that there should be no room for anyone to doubt that when the government makes a promise, it keeps it."[82]

What if there were deficiencies, gaps, in federal legislation that was passed to regulate and control big business? Black, in an opinion written for the Court in 1941, dealt with this problem head-on and in a manner that was totally consistent with the theory of government and democracy that has been presented thus far.[83] Bethlehem Steel Corporation had entered into a series of contracts with the government during the First World War to construct naval vessels for the war effort. (Actually it was a subsidiary that signed the contracts,

Bethlehem Shipbuilding Corporation). Profits reaped by the Shipbuilding Corporation *alone,* not counting the fact that that corporation purchased its steel from Bethlehem Steel Corporation, amounted to over twenty-four million dollars! The United States government argued that there was fraud involved in the manufacture of the vessels and the "bonus" clause of the contracts should have been severed and money returned to the government.

Black, in ruling against the government's arguments that fraud and excess profits existed, said that Bethlehem Steel had a right to the profits because Congress did not adequately cover the complexities and nuances of wartime production activities—and *only* Congress could rectify the situation:

> The problem of war profits is not new....To meet this recurrent evil, Congress has at times taken various measures—price fixing limits on profits, taxation on high profits. But if the executive is in need of additional laws by which to protect the nation against war profiteering, the Constitution has given power to Congress, not to this Court, to make them.[84]

Regarding the issue of Federal rate-making by such quasi-legislative/executive agencies such as the Interstate Commerce Commission or the Federal Power Commission, Black was of the same mind and view he held and expressed in the state rate-making cases mentioned earlier: he did not think "it is permissible for the Courts to concern themselves with any issues as to the economic merits of a rate base....It is not the Function of the Courts to prescribe what formula should be used."[85] The case involved provisions of the Natural Gas Act of 1938 regulating the price of natural gas originating in one state and transported to another. The gas company argued that the price set was done so in violation of the Due Process and Commerce Clauses of the Constitution. Chief Justice Stone, again (as in other cases writing for the majority in this constitutional area) judged the reasonableness of the regulatory legislation and adjudged it to be reasonable.

Black concurred because he, along with Murphy and Douglas, could not accept the fact that the Court was judging the reasonableness of the legislation–something the Court had no right in doing. "We must record our disagreement from an opinion which, although upholding an action of the Commission on these particular facts, nevertheless gives renewed vitality to a 'constitutional' doctrine ("Lochner") which we are convinced has no support in the Constitution."[86]

If Black eschewed judicial examination of the economic merits of a rate base created by an agency of the Federal government, he did at times call for judicial activity in the area of rate-making if the agency went beyond the powers given· to it by Congress in the enabling legislation. For example, in *Interstate Commerce Commission v Inland Waterways,*[87] Black dissented from the Supreme Court holding that an ICC order was valid.

A three judge District Court enjoined the enforcement of an ICC order that compelled farmers to use higher-priced rail facilities instead of low-priced barge transportation to ship their grain to the east coast from Chicago. The railroad charged higher transshipment rates to farmers whose corn and grain came to Chicago by barge than to those farmers who shipped their grain by rail to Chicago. (There was an eight cent disadvantage, per bushel, for farmers who shipped via barge to Chicago according to the ICC order that had been challenged by Inland, a barge company.) The Supreme Court reversed the District Court judgment and upheld the validity of the ICC order.

Black dissented because he felt the ICC order violated a specific section of the Interstate Commerce Act. "Congress has made the policy judgment," he said, "and has flatly forbidden the Commission to do what it has done (and which the Court has approved).[88] Section 2 of the Act, he pointed out, prohibits a carrier from demanding a charge higher or lower than is charged by any other person for doing for him "a like and contemporaneous service in the transportation of a like kind of traffic under substantially similar circumstances and conditions."[89] Black argued that the ICC order also violated Section 3(4) of the Act which forbids carriers from discriminating in their rates, fares, and charges between connecting lines."[90] The tariff was an unjust discrimination within the meaning of the Act, and should be struck down as an unconstitutional usurpation of power: "The day for action by this Court is *now,*" Black concluded.[91] While Black deferred to legislative initiatives, he absolutely refused to accept situations where the Congress or agencies created by the national legislature acted in such a manner as to conflict with the Constitution or with validly enacted laws. The ICC had acted in a manner inconsistent with the Act: the duty of the Court was to declare this clear-cut, obvious action null and void!

Labor relations issues are a final example of Hugo Black's critique of big business and court intervention in economic activities. In an early opinion, written for a unanimous Court, Black expressed, in clear concise terms, the function of the courts in this area. The National Labor Relations Board had issued a ruling voiding a steamship company's dismissal of "tenured" crew members and officers due to their unionizing activities. The Court of Appeals refused to enforce the NLRB order and the agency appealed to the Supreme Court. Black said the ruling must be enforced: "In that Act Congress provided, the findings of the Board as to the facts, if supported by evidence, shall be conclusive. It is of paramount importance that courts not encroach upon this exclusive power of the Board if effect is to be given the intention of Congress to apply an orderly, informed, and specialized procedure to the complex administrative problems arising in the solution of industrial disputes."[92] The Board had the expertise, the time, and, above all, the power to issue definitive rulings, Black maintained. It was created to serve a particular purpose. Courts must not intervene unless the Action of the Board violates the Act's provisions that established it.

> Congress has left questions of law which arise before the Board—but not more—ultimately to the traditional review of the judiciary. (As it did in setting up other administrative bodies.) Not by accident, but in line with a general policy, Congress has deemed it wise to entrust the finding of facts to these specialized agencies.[93]

In setting labor policy, the Congress has complete authority to do away with any and all former man-made standards, Justice Black argued. For example, a case came to the Court dealing with a Congressional Amendment to the Federal Employees Liability Act. The amendment removed from labor law the doctrine of "assumption of risk" and replaced it with (from the standpoint of the injured employee a marked improvement) the "comparative negligence" standard (this standard permitted a jury, so instructed by the judge, to compare the negligence of the employee and the employer in determining liability). A lower court directed a judgment against the worker's executor [The worker fell to his death] because the worker had assumed the risks of his profession and therefore there was no duty owed him by his employer, the Atlantic Coast Line Railroad. The Court was employing the old, repealed, standard of "assumed risk" and, therefore, the Tiller (executor) lawyers appealed the decision before the Supreme Court. Black wrote the opinion for the Court; he overturned the directed ruling of the lower court against the dead worker and sent the case back for trial consistent with the new standards developed by the Congress in 1939:

> We hold that every vestige of the doctrine of assumption of risk was obliterated from the law by the 1939 Amendment and that

> Congress, by abolishing the defense of assumption of risk in that statute, did mean to not leave open the identical defense for the master by changing its name to 'non-negligence.'[94]

Remanding the case back to the trial court, Black wrote that: "where the facts are in dispute and the evidence in relation to them is that from which fair-minded men may draw different inferences, the case should go to the jury."[95]

Yet, if Black believed that the action of the National Labor Relations Board in a particular case contradicted a *specific* provision of the congressional legislation empowering the Board to act, there were limits to be drawn. In a 1966 opinion, Black dissented from a Court decision that upheld an NLRB order.[96] Lawful strikes had been called at two Allis-Chalmers plants in accordance with authorized union procedures. Some union members had crossed picket lines and worked during the strike. After settlement of the dispute, the Union fined these members in amounts ranging from $20 to $100. The company, in turn, filed unfair labor practice charges against the Union locals. The Board ruled that the union conduct, even if considered restraint, came within the provisions of Section 8 of the Act which allowed, gave, labor unions the right "to prescribe its own rules with respect to acquisition and retention of members." The Court of Appeals reversed the decision of the Board, stating that the locals committed an unfair labor practice by restraining and coercing members in their Section 7 rights, i.e., the right of a union member to "refrain from concerted activities of the union." On appeal, the Supreme Court reversed the Court of Appeals and upheld the ruling of the Board. Congress, the opinion stated, did not intend to propose those types of limits on the internal affairs of Unions. Justice Black dissented.

A policy judgment held by members of the majority was the real reason for the Court's decision, Black wrote. The judgment? "Unions, especially weak ones, need the power to impose fines on strikebreakers and to enforce these fines in court."[97] But this policy judgment, itself an improper posture for the Court to take, was at odds with the Congressional intent:

> Although the entire mood of Congress in 1947 (the year the amendments were passed) was to curtail the power of Unions, as it had previously curtailed the power of employers in order to equalize the power of the two, the Court is unwilling to believe that Congress intended to impair the usefulness of labor's cherished strike weapon. I cannot agree with this conclusion or subscribe to the Court's unarticulated premise that the Court has power to add a new weapon to the union's arsenal (economic) whenever the Court believes that the union needs that weapon. That is a job for Congress, not this Court.[98]

In one of his last opinions written on this issue, *Boys Markets, Inc., v. Retail Clerks Union, Local 770,* Black reaffirmed his commitment to the supremacy of legislative power and to the narrow role of the federal courts. It was, as was so many of his important decisions, a dissenting voice.[99] The Supreme Court majority had overturned an interpretation of the Norris-LaGuardia Act of 1932 whereby courts had been barred from enjoining a strike in breach of a no-strike clause in a collective bargaining agreement. In *Boys* the Court held that the grievance was subject to arbitration and an injunction could be issued while the matter was being arbitrated.

Black maintained that the Court majority did not show deference "to the primary responsibility of the legislature in the making of laws....The Court undertakes the task of interpretation, not because the Court has any special ability to fathom the intent of Congress, but rather because interpretation is unavoidable in the decision of the case before it."[100] And, in a manner as biting as any decision Black ever wrote, he said:

> Altering the important provisions of a statute is a legislative function....It is the Congress, not this Court, that responds to the

> pressures of political groups, pressures entirely proper in a free society. It is Congress, not this Court, that has the capacity to investigate the divergent considerations involved in the management of a complex national labor policy. And it is Congress, not this Court, that is elected by the people. This Court should, therefore, interject itself as little as possible into the law-making and law-changing process.[101]

Recapitulation

Hugo Black, in dealing with economic constitutional issues (and, as will be shown, social, procedural, and political issues as well) was a true "literalist." If the state regulation did not conflict with a specific constitutional prohibition, then the state regulation was valid. The law may very well be stupid, it may very well run counter to the philosophic disposition of the judges, but if it did not conflict with the Constitution, it was, in all its glorious mediocrity, a legitimate expression of the people's will.

The only time Black voted against such economic measures passed by state or the Federal legislature was when the statute in question conflicted with the Constitution or, in the case of Federal quasi-legislative agencies, when the action clearly came into conflict with the enabling legislation. Otherwise, the legislative initiative in regulating the economy must not be judged substantively by the judges. "It is my obligation as a judge," Black said in an interview in 1968, "to take this Constitution literally." "I follow the Constitution and the laws," said Black, "before I follow my feelings of what is right or fair."[102] This attitude was a deeply embedded one; an attitude that Black simply refused to modify during all his years in public office. As a law clerk of Black's put it recently: "Justice Black tenaciously (even obstinately) held his ground and would not compromise his principles."[103] Still another of his clerks said simply: "He never signed an opinion he did not believe in....Further, he recanted very little."[104]

In the area of economic regulation, the legislators—representing the people far, far better than nine men could ever do—had the last word. This was a principle Black developed as a young campaigner in Alabama, "The People's Candidate," and this was a principle that Black kept and revered until his death.

3

Black's Assault on Substantive Due Process: Regulating Social Relations

Late Associate Justice John M. Harlan, Jr., whose perception of the meaning of Due Process of Law differed radically from Black's, quite often voted with Black not to overturn state legislation regulating economic and social relations (Harlan's belief in a strong Federalism, coupled with a skeptical view of the ability of the Courts to preserve a free society, led him to the position he took in these eco-social issues.[1]) As will be seen in Chapter Four, Justice Harlan (and Justice Felix Frankfurter) believed in sustaining state criminal proceedings if they satisfy a test of "fundamental fairness." Justice Black, of course, rejected–out of hand, absolutely–this "Natural Law" standard. While they differed on the meaning of Due Process, both Black and Harlan were warm friends. Harlan once said of his colleague from Alabama: "Black considers himself to be a judge of cases, not of 'causes,' and unhesitatingly sets himself against federal judicial intervention whenever he is unable to find in the Constitution or valid legislative authority the basis for such action."[2] That this estimate of Justice Black is valid has, by this time, already been seen in his economic issues opinions. Its accuracy is seen even more vividly by examining Black's opinions in issues dealing with birth control, divorce, illegitimate children, public housing, and other social (and quite emotional) issues. If Black refused to impart a particular economic philosophy into Due Process, he certainly was not about to take up a "cause" such as "free love" and give it a cloak of constitutionality.

Black often said that he "liked his privacy as well as the next person," but that the state could "invade it" unless prohibited by the Constitution.[3] As will be seen in subsequent chapters, this meant that the state could not interfere with a person's First Amendment rights absolutely and it also meant that a state had to try a person according to the "laws of the land." But what about a state law that, reflecting community standards of morality and passed in accordance with democratic processes and procedures, prohibited interested citizens from receiving birth control information? Or what was the constitutional standing of an amendment passed by the people that restricted open housing? Could a trespass law by enforced against Black protesters—albeit peaceful protesters? These are but a few of the many socially oriented constitutional issues that came to the Court while Justice Black was sitting. His response to these and other questions, paralleling his response to economic constitutional questions, was clear: the Constitution was not to be used as a device to legitimize particular social causes; if that document did not prohibit state action clearly and specifically, then, even though judges may dislike the law (and Black did say that, personally, some of these laws that he would have legitimized by abstention were obnoxious, stupid, and/or shocking),[4] that state action was constitutional.

General Social Legislation Issues

In one of Black's very first cases as a Justice of the Supreme Court, such a social issue arose from the Indiana State courts. The Indiana legislature, in 1927, had passed a Teacher Tenure Act which provided tenure for teachers who served under contract for five or more successive years. The contract then became an indefinite one until succeeded by a new one signed by both the teacher and the state authorities. In 1933 an Act was passed amending the 1927 Act insofar as township teachers were concerned and permitted the school authorities to terminate employment of such teachers without regard to the limits and the conditions of the 1927 law. Faced with economic difficulties brought on by the depression, Indiana legislators believed that, through termination and consolidation of rural school districts, the state could save money. The repealing Act was challenged by those teachers adversely affected by it and they succeeded in having the 1933 Act nullified by the lower courts. The State brought the case to the Supreme Court and, in an opinion written by Justice Roberts, the High Court upheld the actions of the lower courts, stating that, under the 1927 Act, the right of permanent teachers to continuous employment upon an indefinite contract was a contractual relationship between the teacher and the state, and the obligation of such a contract was unconstitutionally impaired by the 1933 Repealing Act.

Justice Black dissented from the majority opinion. Article 8 of the Indiana Constitution gave the Indiana General Assembly the duty "to provide by law for a general and uniform system of common schools." In carrying out its constitutional mandate, Black argued, the legislators have "found it necessary—as have other states—to alter legislative policy from time to time....The right of teachers to serve until removed for cause was not given by contract, but by statute...by grant of a repealable statute."[5] The power over schools is a legislative power. If the legislature is not satisfied with one plan, "it is not precluded from trying another...for mistakes and abuses it is answerable to the people, but not to the Court."

> I believe the people of Indiana, if they prefer, have the right under the Federal Constitution, to entrust this important public policy to their elected representatives rather than to the Courts.

> Democracy permits the people to rule. I cannot agree that the constitutional prohibition against impairment of contracts was intended to—or does—transfer in part the determination of the educational policy of Indiana from the legislature of that state to this Court.[6]

Another controversial public policy of the states, with racial overtones, came to the attention of the Court in its 1965 term. This was the case challenging the validity of the state poll tax of Virginia. Justice William O. Douglas, writing for the majority, said that conditioning the right to vote on the payment of a fee or a tax violated the Fourteenth Amendment. "We conclude that a State violates the Equal Protection Clause of the Fourteenth Amendment whenever it makes the affluence of the voter or payment of any fee an electoral standard."[7]

Black dissented. "Although I join the Court in disliking the poll tax, this is not in my judgment a justifiable reason for holding this poll tax unconstitutional. Such a holding on my part would, in my judgment, be an exercise of power which the Constitution does not confer upon me."[8] The Court, he maintained, was using the "old 'natural-law-due-process' formula to justify striking down state laws," but it "cannot use the Clause as though it were a blank check to alter the meaning of the Constitution as written so as to add to it substantive constitutional changes which a majority of the Court at any given time believes are needed to meet present-day problems."[9] For the Court to claim that the law was unreasonable and invidious "amounts, in my judgment, to an exercise of power the Constitution makers refused to give to the judicial branch of government."

The law, he said, was not invidious—it did not specifically come into conflict with the Constitution. As a matter of fact, said Black in obiter dicta, "state poll taxes can reasonably be found to rest on a number of state policies, including: (1) desire to collect revenue, and (2) its belief that voters who pay a poll tax will be interested in furthering the state's welfare when they vote."[10] But all this is besides the point, he concluded. Or at least it should be when the Supreme Court hears the issue.

> I only conclude that the primary, controlling, predominant if not the exclusive reason for declaring the Virginia law unconstitutional is the Court's deep-seated hostility and antagonism which I share to making a payment of a tax a prerequisite to voting.... When a 'political theory' embodied in our Constitution becomes outdated, it seems to me that a majority of the nine members of this Court are not only without constitutional power but are far less qualified to choose a new political constitutional theory than the people of this country proceeding in the manner provided by Article V.[11]

This *Harper* dissent vividly depicts the self-abnegation belief of Justice Black: the poll tax shocked him, yet, if it was to be changed, the people had to make the change through the normal channels of accommodation—the legislative assembly.

Dissenting in a case dealing with the issue of divorce, Black continued to argue against judicial involvement in essentially legislative matters. A man and a woman, living in North Carolina, left their respective spouses, went to Nevada, got divorces, remarried, and returned to North Carolina. There they were arrested and convicted for "bigamous cohabitation." The state courts upheld the conviction and they appealed to the Supreme Court for relief. Justice Frankfurter, writing for the Court, held that the judgments of conviction were not invalid as denying the Nevada divorce decrees the "full faith and credit" required by Article IV.

Black angrily attacked "this latest expansion of federal power and constant diminution of state power over marriages...which the Court derives from adding new content to the Due Process Clause. The elasticity of that clause necessary to justify this holding, is found, I suppose, in the notion that it was intended to give this Court unlimited authority to supervise all assertions of state and federal power to see that they comport with our ideas of what are 'civilized standards of law.'"[12] Due process of law, Black asserted, is not "a blank sheet of paper provided for Courts to make changes in the Constitution and the Bill of Rights."[13] The power over divorces rests in the states; the Constitution calls for "full faith and credit" as a by-word for interstate relations. North Carolina violated the Constitution, therefore the conviction should be reversed. Simple and clear logic accompanied by judicial abstention, unless a specific constitutional provision had been violated or ignored, was the essence of the Black response to this issue.

In the recent "birth control" case,[14] Black really condemned judicial malfeasance. The Executive Director of the Planned Parenthood League of Connecticut was convicted as an accessory for giving married persons information and medical advice on how to prevent conception. (A Connecticut statute had made it a crime for any person to use any drug or article to prevent conception.) Justice Douglas, speaking for the Court, held that the Connecticut statute violated the right of marital privacy which "is within the penumbra of the specific guarantees of the Bill of Rights... formed by emanations from this guarantee that helps give it life and substance."[15] Justice Goldberg, in a case that saw many points of view presented in six different opinions, concurred. He argued that the Ninth Amendment to the Constitution "shows a belief of the Constitution's authors that fundamental rights exist (such as the right of marital privacy) that are not expressly enumerated in the first eight Amendments and an intent that the list of rights included there not be deemed exhaustive."[16] In determining these fundamental rights judges will not use their "personal and private notions. Rather, they must look to the traditions and collective conscience of the people to determine whether a principle is so rooted there as to be ranked as fundamental."[17]

Justice Byron White concurred. So did Justice Harlan. He disagreed with both the Douglas view and with the Black dissenting view. "The proper constitutional inquiry in this case," he wrote, "is whether the Connecticut statute infringes the Due Process Clause of the Fourteenth Amendment because the enactment violates basic values 'implicit in the concept of ordered liberty.'"[18] Believing that the Connecticut statute did violate that substantive formula (announced in *Palko v Connecticut,* a 1937 case which will be discussed in Chapter Four), Harlan voted to throw out the conviction.

Black (and Stewart) dissented. "I personally feel that this law is every bit as offensive to me as it is to my brethren. I subscribe to every one of their graphic and eloquent strictures—except their conclusion that the evil qualities they see in the law make it unconstitutional."[19] The Douglas, Goldberg, and Harlan opinions, Black maintained, used formulas based on "Natural Law" and, if they are to prevail, "they require judges to determine what is or is not constitutional on the basis of their own appraisal of what laws are unwise or unnecessary. The power to make such decisions is of course that of a legislative body."[20] Directing a barb at Justice Goldberg, Black stated that "the scientific miracles of this age have not yet produced a gadget which the Court can use to determine what traditions are 'rooted in the collective conscience of the people.'"[21]

> My point is that there is no provision of the Constitution which either expressly or implicitly vests power in this Court to sit as a supervisory body of acts of duly constituted legislative bodies and set aside their laws because of the Court's belief that the legislative policies adopted are unreasonable, unwise, arbitrary, capricious, or irrational.[22]

The Court, in 1967, found itself involved in yet another controversial social policy: the manner in which illegitimate children were dealt with in various laws dealing with inheritance, legal status, etc. *Levy v Louisiana* was the case that led to the initial intervention on the part of the Court dealing with rights of illegitimate children. The appellant brought an action to the Louisiana courts, on behalf of five illegitimate offspring of Mrs. Levy (who nurtured them, took them to Sunday School, acted in all ways, except legally, as the children's mother) for the wrongful death of their mother. The Louisiana trial court dismissed the suit (affirmed by the Louisiana Court of Appeal) because "surviving child" under the Wrongful Death Act did not include "illegitimate child," denial of whose right of recovery for the wrongful death of his natural-but-not-legal mother was "based on morals and general welfare because it discourages bringing children into the world out of wedlock." Justice Douglas, speaking for the Court majority, overturned the law because the question of legitimacy or illegitimacy had no relation to the nature of the wrong allegedly inflicted on the mother.[23]

Justice Black joined Justice Harlan in dissenting from the opinion of the Court. Harlan pointed out that Louisiana created both rights, that is, the legally cognizable interest in the wrongful death of another, and the inherent personal right of another to recover for tortuous injuries to the body. "The question," Harlan raised, "is whether the way in which Louisiana has defined the classes of persons who may recover is constitutionally permissible."[24] Harlan and Black maintained that the classification was one that Louisiana legislators had the right to draw and that it was not an unconstitutional violation of the Constitution's Fourteenth Amendment. "The whole scheme of the Louisiana Wrongful Death Statute, which is similar to that of most other states, makes everything the Court says about affection and nurture and dependence altogether irrelevant. The only question in any case is whether the plaintiff falls within the classes of persons to whom the State has accorded the right of action for the death of another."[25] (Black did not have to write a separate dissenting opinion because the Harlan view, not incorporating any fundamental fairness" formula, perfectly paralleled Justice Black's views regarding the prerogatives of state legislators.)

Three years later, during the 1970 term, Justice Black (Justice Harlan joining him) wrote the *majority* opinion for the Supreme Court validating a Louisiana law dealing with the status of illegitimate children. Before he died, Ezra Vincent acknowledged that Rita Vincent was his illegitimate child. This did not, under Louisiana law however, give the child a legal right to share equally with legitimate offspring and relatives in his estate—although it did give the child the right to claim support for upbringing. Lou Bertha Labine, the girl's mother, challenged the Louisiana law, arguing that it was violative of both the Due Process and the Equal Protection Clauses of the Fourteenth Amendment.

Expressing this time the view of the Court majority, Justice Black expounded on his view of the judicial function.

> The people of Louisiana, through their legislature, have carefully regulated many of the property rights incident to family life.... Many will think that it is unfortunate that these rules are so rigid. Others will think differently. But the choices reflected by the Intestate Succession Statute are choices which it is within the power of the state to make. The federal constitution does not give this Court the power to overturn the State's choice under the guise of constitutional interpretation because the justices of this Court believe that they can provide better rules.[26]

States have the constitutional power to make such rules, rigid rules. "Absent a specific constitutional guarantee, it is for the legislature, not life-tenured judges of this Court, to select from among possible laws. We cannot say that Louisiana's policy provides a perfect or even a desirable solution or the one we would have provided for the problem....Neither can we say that Louisiana does not have the power to make such laws."[27] The Court, Black said, "concludes that in the circumstances presented in this case, there is nothing in the vague generalities of Equal Protection and Due Process Clauses which empowers this Court to nullify the deliberate choices of the elected representatives of the people of Louisiana."[28]

At about the time the question of the status of illegitimate children came to the Court, another equally controversial social issue arrived: the issue of open housing. And, as in the Louisiana cases, it was Justice Harlan, joined by Black, who wrote the initial dissenting opinion to be followed, in 1970, by Justice Black writing an opinion for the majority of the Court rejecting the earlier Court view. Of course one was aware of the changing composition of the Court—the Nixon appointees—a factor that greatly accounted for the elevation of the Black-Harlan dissenting opinion into the voice of the majority of the Court. Black was aware of this fact of life; he was on the Court long enough to see many changes in Court personnel and policy. That was why he did not want to see judges involving themselves in economic-social legislative evaluations. If judges were allowed to rule on the reasonableness of policy, then Eisenhower judges would do this, Kennedy judges, that, Johnson judges the other thing, and Nixon judges—who knew?

Between 1959 and 1963, the California legislature passed a series of statutes regulating racial discrimination in housing. In 1964, as the result of the conclusion of an initiative and referendum action by California citizens, Proposition 14 became Article 1, Section 26 of the California Constitution. This Amendment prohibited the state from interfering with the right of a landowner to sell or lease or not to sell or lease his land to whoever, at his absolute discretion, he chooses. California's Supreme Court declared the law to be in violation of the Equal Protection Clause of the Federal Constitution and nullified it. Reitman, the property owner unwilling to sell to Mulkey, a black citizen of California, appealed the decision to the Supreme Court of the United States. Justice White, writing for the Court, upheld the decision of the California Supreme Court because the enforcement of the Amendment would involve the state in an invidious, discriminatory "state action" prohibited by the Fourteenth Amendment.

Harlan, joined by Black, dissented. "The Fourteenth Amendment does not compel a state to put or keep any particular law about race on its books. It only forbids a state to pass or keep in effect laws discriminating on account of race. Califorñia has not done this."[29] The law, he said, was permissive and not coercive and "it has been adopted in this most democratic manner. (It) should not be struck down by the judiciary without pervasive evidence of an invidious purpose or effect."[30]

> The electorate itself overwhelmingly wished to overrule and check its own legislature on the matter left open by the Federal Constitution. By refusing to accept the decision of the people of California and by contriving a new and ill-defined constitutional concept to allow federal judicial interference, I think the Court has taken to itself powers and responsibilities left elsewhere by the Constitution.[31]

Two years later Justice Black wrote the dissenting opinion in a case that came from Ohio, also dealing with the open housing issue.[32] The Akron City Council enacted a fair housing ordinance. It established a Commission on Equal Opportunity in Housing to enforce anti-discrimination sections through conciliation, persuasion and, if necessary, judicially enforcible orders. A repealing ordinance was proposed, placed on the ballot by petition, and passed which provided that any ordinance, including those in effect at the time of the passage of the Amendment, that regulated the use, sale, tranfer, leasing, financing of real property on the basis of race, color, religion, national origin, and ancestry must first be approved by a majority of voters before becoming operative. The Ohio trial court denied Hunter's housing discrimination complaint, holding that the Fair Housing Ordinance had been rendered ineffective by the Charter Amendment. The Ohio Supreme Court affirmed the judgment of the trial court and the case came before the Supreme Court of the United States.

Justice White, who wrote the opinion in the *Reitman* case, expressed the judgment of the Court majority. Holding that because the Amendment contains a specifically and explicitly racial classification, thereby placing a special burden on racial minorities within the governmental process by making it more difficult for them to secure legislation on their behalf, and because Akron had not justified its discrimination against minorities, there was a violation of the Fourteenth Amendment's protections.

Black dissented. "There is no constitutional provision anywhere which bars any state from repealing any law on any subject at any time it pleases."[33] The Court majority, because its conscience was shocked, because its sense of fairness has been offended, had barred the state from repealing laws the Court felt should be retained. "I think the Court needs to control itself," he said simply and to remember that government in America is "of the people, by the people, and for the people."

> There may have been other state laws held unconstitutional in the past on grounds that are equally as fallacious and undemocratic as those the Court relies on today, but if so I do not recall such cases at the moment.[34]

But Black was to have the last word on this issue and it was spoken for the majority of the Court in the case of *James v Valtierra,* in 1970.[35] The appellees were eligible for low-cost housing and they challenged the requirement in Article 34 of the California Constitution which stipulated that no low-cost housing project could be developed, constructed, or acquired without the consent of a majority of those voting at a community election. There had to be a mandatory referendum before the state would acquire or develop public housing. A three judge District Court enjoined the enforcement of the referendum provision on the grounds that it violated the Fourteenth Amendment. The Supreme Court overruled the lower court judgment.

Black, writing for the majority, said that the provision described in Article 34 "demonstrates devotion to democracy, not to bias, discrimination, or prejudice."[36]

> The people of California have also decided by their own vote to require referendum approval of low-rent public housing projects. This procedure assures that all the people of a community will have a voice in a decision which may lead to large expenditures of local governmental funds for increased public services and to lower tax revenues. It gives them a voice in decisions that will affect the future development of their own community. This procedure for democratic decision-making does not violate the constitutional command that no state shall deny to any person the "equal protection of the laws."[37]

In *James v Valtierra* and in earlier cases, Black continued to grapple with the problem of Supreme Court justices using flexible, substantive formulas (which were affixed to Due Process and, to a limited extent, to Equal Protection) by which they evaluated the "fundamental fairness," "reasonableness," or "invidiousness" of state legislation in the area of social relations. As seen and will be seen in the remaining portions of this Chapter, he was less successful with respect to limiting judicial intervention in social actions of states than he was in getting the Court to restrain itself with respect to economic initiatives.[38]

Constitutional Differences between Civil and Criminal Cases

In Black's last years on the Court, a novel procedural question associated with these social conflicts appeared.

Essentially, it was whether or not, in civil matters–divorce procedures, garnishment of wages, administrative investigations of welfare clients–government need be "hampered or handicapped by strict and rigid due process rules the Constitution has provided to protect people charged with crime."[39]

A Wisconsin garnishment procedure case was one of the first such type of litigation that raised the question.[40] (Under the Wisconsin law, a court clerk issued a summons at the request of the creditor's lawyer. The lawyer, serving the garnishee [the employer] the summons, set in motion machinery whereby the wages of the employee [half of weekly wages are given the worker for subsistance] were frozen. The creditor had ten days in which to serve the summons on the debtor *after* service on the garnishee. The wages could be unfrozen if the wage earner won on the merits of the suit on the debt.) Sniadach's wages were frozen because he allegedly owed money to the Family Finance Corporation (over $400). He moved, in the state courts, that the proceedings be dismissed for failure to meet the Fourteenth Amendment's procedural due process requirements. The Wisconsin courts upheld the garnishment process and Sniadach went to the Supreme Court for equity. The Supreme Court obliged for, in a decision written by Douglas, the majority argued that that Wisconsin procedure was an obvious taking of property without notice and prior hearing. As such it does violate fundamental principles of due process.

> The question is not whether the Wisconsin law is a wise law or an unwise law. Our concern is not what philosophy Wisconsin should or should not embrace. We do not sit as a super-legislative body....The sole question is whether there has been a taking of property without due process of law![41]

As indicated, the answer was yes. The garnishment of wages procedure "is a most inhuman doctrine," Douglas concluded.[42]

Justice Black dissented. The Court decided that the procedure was unconstitutional because it was a "bad" state policy and that type of judgment, Black said once again, was one the Court did not have the power to make.

> The emotional rhetoric might be very appropriate for Congressmen to make against some phases of the garnishment laws....But, made in a Court opinion, holding Wisconsin's law unconstitutional, they amount to what, I believe, to be a plain, judicial usurpation of state legislative power to decide what the state's laws shall be. The Wisconsin law is simply nullified as though the Court had been granted a super-legislative power to step in and frustrate policies of states adopted by their own elected legislators. The Court thus steps back into the due process philosophy which brought on President Roosevelt's Court fight.[43]

In an *Addendum* to his dissent, Black directed his attack at the Harlan "fundamental fairness-Anglo-American legal heritage" formula for determining whether or not due process had been violated. (Chapter Four, which deals specifically with the subject of procedural due process, will develop this Frankfurter/Harlan vs Black theoretical dispute fully.) Black argued that all tests, whether Harlan's, or Goldberg's "notions of justice of the English-Speaking peoples," or Frankfurter's "shock-the-conscience" test, "represent nothing more or less than an implicit adoption of a Natural Law concept under which our system leaves to judges alone the power to decide what the Natural Law means. These tests leave them wholly free to decide what *they* are convinced is right and fair. If the judges, in deciding whether laws are constitutional are to be left free only to the admonitions of their own consciences why was it that the Founders gave us a written Constitution at all?"[44]

A year later the same issue faced the Court in a case from New York.[45] Kelly and others, New York City residents receiving financial aid under federally assisted Aid to Families with Dependent Children (AFDC) programs or under New

York's general Home Relief program, alleged that officials administering these programs terminated, or were about to terminate, the assistance without prior notice and hearing, thereby denying them procedural due process of law. The District Court held that pre-termination hearings would satisfy the requirements of due process and, in an opinion written by Justice William Brennan, Jr., the Supreme Court upheld the judgment of the lower Federal Court. The appellees must be given timely and adequate notice.

Black again dissented. He pointed out that the government was experimenting with the welfare state; it was a new public policy and "new experiments should not be frozen into our constitutional structure. They should be left, as are other legislative determinants, to the Congress and the legislatures that the people elect to make our laws."[46] The opinion of the majority, he wrote, read like a report of the House Committee on Education and Labor; as a legal opinion he found it "woefully deficient."

> I regret very much to be compelled to say that the Court today makes a drastic and dangerous departure from a Constitution written to control and limit the government and the judges and moves toward a Constitution designed to be no more and no less than what the judges of a particular social and economic philosophy declare on the one hand to be fair or on the other hand to be shocking and unconscionable.[47]

That same term Black joined in a dissent written by Chief Justice Earl Warren. The case dealt with a Connecticut law that established a one-year residency requirement before people could apply for welfare assistance. The District Court held such a plan to be an unconstitutional violation of the Due Process Clause and, in an opinion written by Justice Brennan, the Supreme Court upheld the lower court judgment and invalidated welfare residency requirements. Justice Warren said simply that the Constitution gave the Congress, acting under one of its enumerated powers, the right to impose minimal nationwide residence requirements (or authorize states to do so).[48]

> The era is long past (wrote Warren) when this Court under the rubric of due process has reviewed the wisdom of a congressional decision that interstate commerce will be fostered by the enactment of such regulations.[49]

In 1970, in one of his final opinions, Black again was forced to dissent from the opinion of the Court—this time disagreeing with Harlan's application of the "fundamental fairness" standard. Connecticut law did not provide indigent citizens who, in good faith sought judicial dissolution of their marriage, with a Court hearing because they were unable to pay court fees and costs. Indigents, because they had no money for the fees, were denied access to the Courts; this situation, to the majority of the Court, was a denial of fairness and therefore a procedure violative of the procedural due process guarantee in the Fourteenth Amendment. Hugo Black was the only dissenter.

Absent some specific federal constitutional or statutory provision, he argued, marriage is completely under state control, and so is divorce. Black maintained that there is a difference between criminal trials and due process guarantees and civil actions. The Bill of Rights safeguards against illegal governmental action against criminal defendants only; "in civil suits, government is neutral; there is no punishment depriving anyone of life, liberty, or property."[50] Natural Law concepts, Black explained, "lack any constitutional precision. (They) mark no constitutional boundaries and cannot possibly depend on anything but the belief of particular judges, at particular times, concerning particular interests which those judges have divined to be of 'basic importance.'"

> Such unbounded authority to use these words in any group of politically appointed or elected judges would be sufficient to classify our Nation as a government of men, not the government

> of law of which we boast. With a "shock the conscience" test of constitutionality, citizens must guess what is the law, guess what a majority of nine judges will believe fair and reasonable. Such a test willfully throws away the certainty and security that lies in a written constitution, one that does not alter with a judge's health, belief, or his politics. I believe the only way to steer this country toward its great destiny is to follow what our Constitution says, not what judges think it should have said.[51]

A few months later, Justice Black had occasion to chastize the Court for not acting consistently with its recently announced *Boddie* principle. Five cases were denied certiorari and in all five the issue was indigents denied access to civil courts because of their poverty. Black said that "if the decision in *Boddie* is to continue to be the law, it cannot and should not be restricted to persons seeking a divorce. It is bound to be expanded to all civil cases. Persons seeking a divorce are no different from other members of society who must resort to the judicial process for resolution of their disputes. Consistent with the Constitution, special favors cannot and should not be accorded to divorce litigants."[52]

Boddie, Black wrote, could "safely rest on only one crucial foundation—that civil courts belong to the people of this country and that no person can be denied access to those courts, either for a trial or for an appeal, because he cannot pay a fee, finance a bond, risk a penalty, or afford to hire a lawyer. In my judgment, *Boddie* cannot and should not be limited to either its facts or its language, and I believe that there can be no doubt that this country can afford to provide court costs and lawyers to Americans who are now barred by their poverty from resort to the law for resolution of their disputes."[53]

In *Boddie* and *Meltzer*, decided two months apart in the Spring of Black's last year on the Court, one sees the essential qualities of the man. Black dissented in *Boddie* because he felt that if changes were to be made in social and legal arrangements the people should initiate them, not the Court. The Court, however, did initiate changes in societal relations—based on a Natural Law formula. And *Meltzer* is an example of why Black was so untiring in his criticism of the use of such formulas—they were too flexible and imprecise. Meltzer involved a tenant who fought his eviction by resort to the courts, thereby risking, according to local statute, the penalty of *double the rent due* during the litigation if he lost. Using the formulas, that is, "shock the conscience," or "fundamental fairness," the Court *denied* certiorari in Meltzer yet reviewed the Connecticut ordinance and found it to be unconstitutional. How was this possible? Because, Black pointed out for thirty-four years, the judges were setting up "hierarchy of interests" based on their own beliefs, values, and prejudices. The solution for Black was simple and clear—the Courts belong to all the people and, whether the problem is marital, rental, bankruptcy, child guardianship, evictions, *all people* who are indigent (not just those whose "cause" attracts the eye of the majority of nine judges) must be able to use them. That was the only "crucial foundation" upon which the decision in *Boddie,* in Black's view, rested.

Trespass Laws and Social Protests

In Sir William Blackstone's *Commentaries,* trespass was defined by the eighteenth century legal scholar as follows: "Trespass signifies any transgression or offense against the law of society; whether it related to a man's person or his property....Every trespass is willful, where the defendant has notice, and is especially forewarned not to come on the land; as every trespass is malicious, though the damage may not amount to forty shillings, where the intent of the defendant plainly appears to be to harass and distress the plaintiff."[54]

Hugo Black readily accepted the legitimacy of general trespass statutes and he would have agreed with Blackstone's comment that "every man's land is, in the eyes of the law, inclosed and set apart from his neighbor's: and that either by a visible and material fence,...or by an ideal invisible boundary, existing only in the contemplation of law."[55] In some quite controversial cases in the 1960s, Justice Black sharply defended the trespass law and the individual owner's property rights defended by that law against the counter-argument put forward by social activists and judges that people have a right to protest against social policies, not inside the legislative assembly or through the ballot, but inside the premises of a person whose actions reflect the social policies the protesters disdain.

In a 1967 case dealing with labor protesters, Justice Black dissented from the majority view that local union picketers could protest on the private property of their enemy.[56] Weis' establishment, located in a private shopping center, had been peacefully picketed. The union men were enjoined by the Pennsylvania Court of Common Pleas because Weis' real property rights were being infringed. The Pennsylvania Supreme Court affirmed the decision and the Union appealed the decision to the Supreme Court. Justice Thurgood Marshall, speaking for the Court majority, held that the injunction was an unconstitutional interference with the First Amendment right of freedom of speech and assembly. Justice Black dissented.

Black's view of speech (as will be developed fully in Chapter Five) was an absolute one but it was one that distinguished speech from conduct. Conduct associated with free speech rights had to be "right conduct," that is, conduct that was consistent with the laws and the Constitution. In the *Logan Valley* case Black believed that the entire injunction was valid. "I believe that, whether this Court likes it or not, the Constitution recognizes and supports the concept of private ownership of property....These pickets," Black concluded, "do have a constitutional right to speak about Weis' refusal to hire union labor, but they do not have a constitutional right to compel Weis to furnish them a place to do so on its property."[57]

The conflict between trespass laws and social protesters took its sharpest outlines in the negro rights "sit-in" cases of the early 1960s. *Bell v Maryland*, in 1963, was a watershed case because in it one perceived basic differences of opinion, profound, substantive "meritorious" differences of opinion, developed by three judges: Goldberg and Douglas (both employing Natural Law standards to decide the issue) and Hugo Black who insisted, once again, that personal feelings of judges ought not to determine the outcome of constitutional cases.

In 1960 Robert Bell and others were convicted in a Maryland court for trespass as a result of their participation in a "sit-in" demonstration in a Baltimore restaurant. After entering the restaurant they were told by the hostess, on orders of the manager, that "solely on the basis of their color" they would not be served. Bell and the others did not leave; instead, they took seats and insisted that they be served. The arrests followed. The statute under which the arrests and convictions were made and obtained was the Maryland Criminal Trespass Law which made it a misdemeanor to "enter upon the premises or private property of any person or persons in this state after being duly notified by the owner or his agent not to do so."[58] The Maryland Court of Appeals affirmed the convictions. The appeal went to the Supreme Court and, on the last day of the 1963 term, Justice William Brennan announced the opinion for the Court majority. The opinion did not reach the merits of the constitutional conflict but instead vacated and reversed the judgments because of changes in Maryland law that raised the issue of abatement.

Justice Goldberg concurred because he felt that the constitutional issue should be discussed and resolved by the

Supreme Court. Due to Black's dissent he was "impelled to state the reasons for (his) conviction that the Constitution guarantees to all Americans the right to be treated as equal members of the community with respect to public accommodations."[59] The Fourteenth Amendment should not be read as a legislative code but "as the revelation of the great purposes which were intended to be achieved by the Constitution as a continuing instrument of government." Since the 1954 *Brown* decision, the Court has consistently applied "the constitutional standard of Equality to give real meaning to the Equal Protection Clause as the revelation of an enduring constitutional purpose."[60] The Maryland courts were not acting as neutrals; they were as "affirmative in effect as if the state had enacted an unconstitutional law explicitly authorizing racial discrimination in places of public accommodation....A state may not use its criminal trespass laws to frustrate the constitutionally granted right to equal access of public accommodation nor may it frustrate this right by legitimizing a proprietor's attempt at self-help."[61]

Echoing the Black concern for law and order, Goldberg said that the law must be preserved but differed as to the direction of "the weight and protective strength of law and order" in the instant case:

> In my view the Fourteenth Amendment resolved this issue in favor of the right of petitioners to public accommodations and it follows that in the exercise of that constitutionally granted right they are entitled to the law's protection.[62]

Goldberg concluded by saying that the "great purpose of the Fourteenth Amendment is to keep the free air of America free and equal. Under the Constitution no American can or should be denied rights fundamental to freedom and citizenship."[63]

Justice Douglas dissented because he felt the issue should have been decided on substantive grounds.

> No question preoccupies this country more than this one; it is plainly justiciable; it presses for a decision one way or another; we should resolve it. The people should know that when filibusters occupy other forums, when oppressions are great, when the clash of authority between the individual and the state is severe, they can still get justice in the courts. When we default, *as we do today,* the prestige of the law in the life of the Nation is weakened. For these reasons I reach the merits; and I vote to reverse the judgments of conviction outright.[64]

The real issue for Douglas was the nature of the modern corporation; "the corporation that owns this restaurant did not refuse service to these Negroes because 'it' did not like Negroes. The reason 'it' refused service was because 'it' thought 'it' could make more money by running a segregated restaurant."[65] Personal prejudice, then, was not the real issue. The corporate interest in making money was the real issue.

But Justice Black, he felt, raised a different question and Douglas responded to Black's dissent based on the notion of trespass. The restaurant, said Douglas, was not private property such as the home and is in no way exempt from the demands of the Constitution. "We live under a constitution that proclaims equal protection under law. Why then," asked Douglas, "even in the absence of a statute, should apartheid be given constitutional sanction in the restaurant field."[66] He agreed with Goldberg's view that the Fourteenth Amendment contained certain fundamental principles of equality and he condemned the action of the state enforcing a policy of segregation.

Justice Black, as expected, vehemently disagreed with the expressions of Brennan, Goldberg, and Douglas. In a dissent, in which Justices White and Harlan joined, Black stated that the crucial issue (apart from the rhetoric) was whether "the Fourteenth Amendment, *of itself,* forbids a state to enforce its trespass laws to convict a person who comes into a privately owned restaurant, is told that because of his color he will not be served, and over the owner's protest refuses to leave. We dissent," he said, "from the Court's refusal to decide that question....We feel that the question should be decided and that the Fourteenth Amendment does not forbid this application of a state's trespass laws."[67]

The trespass law was valid because it was directed against what Bell did and not what Bell said; Bell trespassed and "remaining on the grounds/premises of another after having been warned to leave is *conduct* which states have traditionally prohibited in this country."[68] Freedom of expression said Black does not "carry with it a right to force a private property owner to furnish his property as a platform to criticize the property owner's use of that property."

> The experience of ages points to the inexorable fact that people are frequently stirred to violence when property which the law recognizes as theirs is forcibly invaded or occupied by others. Trespass laws are born of this experience....The Constitution does not confer upon any group the right to substitute rule by force for rule by law. Force leads to violence, violence to mob conflicts, and these to rule by the strongest groups with control of the most deadly weapons....At times the rule of law seems too slow to some for the settlement of their grievances. But it is the plan our Nation has chosen to preserve both 'liberty and equality for all.' On that plan we have put our trust and staked our future. This constitutional rule of law has served us well. Maryland's trespass law does not depart from it. Nor shall we.[69]

Standing alone and in the absence of some cooperative state action or compulsion, the Fourteenth Amendment does not forbid property owners to practice racial prejudice. The criminal justice system allows "the worst citizen no less than the best" to use the laws to have wrongs committed against them vindicated in the courts. "We must never forget," he said, "that the Fourteenth Amendment protects 'life, liberty, and property' of all people generally, not just some people's 'life,' some people's 'liberty,' and some kinds of 'property.'"[70] To Goldberg and Douglas, Black said the following:

> We are admonished that in deciding this case we should remember it is a constitution we are expounding. We conclude as we do because we remember that it *is* a Constitution and that it is our duty to bow with respectful submission to its provisions....Our duty is simply to interpret the Constitution, and in doing so the test of constitutionality is not whether a law is offensive to our conscience or to the 'good old common law,' but whether it is offensive to the Constitution. Confining ourselves to the constitutional duty to construe, not rewrite or amend, the Constitution, we believe that Section one of the Fourteenth Amendment does not bar Maryland from enforcing its trespass laws so long as it does so with impartiality.[71]

Consistent with the First Amendment, Bell had the right to criticize the restaurant's policy and the owner's private racial views, but, reiterated Black, the owner did not have to supply Bell with a "platform or a pulpit."[72]

In a 1966 Florida case, *Adderly v Florida,*[73] Justice Black's dissent became the majority opinion of the Court. Florida A & M students, protesting the arrests of fellow students, congregated on a nonpublic jail driveway. They were told that they were trespassing on county property and were thereafter arrested when they refused to leave the driveway. They were convicted for violating the Florida trespass statute for "trespass with a malicious and mischievous intent." They appealed their convictions to the Supreme Court but, in a 5-4 opinion, the Court held that the trespass statute as written was not unconstitutionally vague.

There is nothing in the Constitution of the United States, declared Justice Black for the majority, that

> prevents Florida from even-handed enforcement of its general trespass statute against those refusing to obey the sheriff's order....The State, no less than a private property owner, has power to preserve property under its control for the use to which

it is lawfully dedicated....The United States Constitution does not forbid a state to control the use of its own property for its own non-discriminatory purposes.[74]

These and other "civil disobedience" cases raised,[75] beyond all issues of Federalism and "state action", an essentially normative question: could the positive law of the land be subject to evaluation based on a "higher law" and, if found to be "unjust," could that positive law be rejected as "no law at all."[76] Further, as a result of such a normative judgment, could "direct action" be taken by the allegedly aggrieved group to erase the law? Hugo Black was a staunch defender of the positive Rule of Law; he was a Benthamite who would have accepted Bentham's admonition—with respect to public policy-making and judicial activities—that the "season of fiction" is over (with respect to the belief in the existence of Natural Law, Divine Law, and all other forms of "higher law"). Hugo Black was opposed to lawlessness and violence entering the democratic political processes. The end, he said to a law-clerk, never can justify the means used to attain it. And so, in these social protest cases by the Southern Negro, Black put the emotional issue aside and examined the facts: was there peaceful picketing? was there a violation of a general, non-discriminatory law by these groups? This was all a judge should do, Black believed. To go beyond these basically legal questions, to determine that a law legally passed and not in conflict with the positive, written Constitution was somehow unwarranted and unjustified because it violated something called "Natural Law," was not a task for the judges. Legislators, if they wished, might use such a standard—but not judges. Certainly this posed a moral dilemma for Justice Black, for he had been a consistent supporter of equal opportunities and fair treatment of Blacks since his days as crusading county prosecutor in Alabama just after World War One. But, as a judge, he did not have, Black believed, the prerogative to act as he did as an elected official. And beyond that issue, he was concerned, terribly so, with the resort to lawlessness and violence and the threat posed to the Rule of Law. That Rule of Law "and the peaceful and judicial settlement of disputes" was what was at stake in these cases.[77] Given his commitment to law and orderly resolution of disputes, Black had to dissent in *Bell* and decide *Adderly* as he did.

Recapitulation

Social issues and constitutional questions surrounding such social legislation, as seen in this chapter, led to more "emotional rhetoric" by the judges then did economic issues *but* the basis for judicial response to the issues in both areas (by some Supreme Court justices) was a self-created formula. The formulas, those "excresences" on the law, were what Black continually decried and personally eschewed from using himself as a Justice of the Court. These were "concoctions" created by judges based on their own value systems; they lacked the clarity and the precision of the plain words of the Constitution; moreover, Black argued, it was not the judge's function to create such devices nor was it his function to remake the law–a consequence derived from using these devices.

"Due Process of Law" cannot be stretched to mean "fundamental fairness," "Conscience of mankind," or some other vague, subjective test. Judges, Black once said, "are as human as anyone and as likely as others to see the world through their own eyes and find the 'Collective Conscience of Mankind' remarkably similar to their own."[78]

Judges must not be advocates of causes; the Constitution does not contain, Black said, Keynes' economic theories, neither does it contain theories on birth control and teacher hiring and firing. Judges are judges of constitutional cases where the issue is whether a law is repugnant to what the

Constitution says, not whether the judges happen to like or dislike the law in question. If the law does not run afoul of a constitutional prohibition, if it had been passed in accordance with the democratic processes, then it was law, albeit bad, stupid, law—all judges' feelings of shock and outrage aside.

This notion of Black's, the very essence of his views on judicial behavior, led him to certain judicial conclusions in the latter years on the bench that upset those who saw Black as a "liberal" judge, especially, as this chapter has indicated, in the area of Negro rights where Black parted company with Douglas and other libertarians. But Black's views in *Harper, Griswold, Reitman, Hunter, James, Shapiro, Bell, Adderly, Cox, Palmer,* et al., were entirely consistent with his view that, even in cases involving Negro Rights—which was a most "worthy cause"—Judges were bound by the words of the Constitution and were not free to use their own notions of fairness in deciding constitutional cases and controversies. If any group, black or white, acted in a manner that was not protected by the Constitution, the state law that regulated that conduct could punish the members for violating the law and had to be adjudged legitimate. If a statute was challenged by Blacks, or any action of government for that matter, the closing down of swimming pools in Jackson, Mississippi for example, the Court had to determine, not the motives of the legislators, but whether that action came into conflict with a specific clause of the Constitution. The only reason for the Court invalidating a state law, regardless of the judges feelings about that enactment, was the constitutional reason. More than a "liberal," Hugo Black was a "literalist."

4

The Meaning of Procedural Due Process: "Fundamental Fairness vs "Incorporation"

Although Hugo Black differed with other Justices of the Court about the efficacy and wisdom of interpreting Due Process "substantively" with respect to economic and social legislation, both Black and his judicial opponents did agree that originally, historically, that clause was an important procedural "fence against wrongs" perpetrated by government against the people. However, operationalizing this procedural admonition in the Constitution, that no person shall "be deprived of life, liberty, and property without due process of law," in concrete cases and controversies was left to the men who had to interpret the Constitution.

In giving meaning to procedural due process, judges came into conflict and there was continuous philosophical conflict on the bench between two men who admired and respected each other, Felix Frankfurter and Hugo Black. For Black the controversy over the procedural meaning of Due Process was basically the war against substantive due process but fought on a different battlefield. The enemy, for the Justice from Clay County, Alabama, was still the same: judges, who have no right to make public policy, making policy judgments through the use of self-created and concocted standards of "Natural Law."

Frankfurter's Perception: The "Vague Contours" of Due Process

Justice Felix Frankfurter's view was that due process of law conceptually could not "be captured in a neat catch-all rule of thumb."[1] The Justice maintained that while procedural due process was "more elemental and less flexible than substantive due process,"[2] it was still imprecise enough so that its "vague contours" had to be illuminated and fleshed out via the construction of judge-made guidelines.

The guidelines for Frankfurter were those "canons of decency and fairness which express the notions of justice of English-speaking peoples." "Even toward those charged," concluded Frankfurter, "with the most heinous offenses."[3] He believed that judges could carefully scrutinize the legal and social history of the English-speaking people's notions of decency, fairness, and justice (while scrutinizing themselves to "avoid infusing into the vagueness of [that] Constitutional command one's merely private notions")[4] and be able to come up with objective guidelines which would then be employed by the judges in cases dealing with conflicts between the government and criminal defendants. The essence of these notions of decency and justice, for Frankfurter, was spelled out in the "English *sporting sense* of fair play."[5] Due process of law was adhered to, according to Frankfurter's parameters, if the governmental action was fair and did not shock the conscience of judges well versed in the sense of fair play.

Black's Perception: The Clear Contours of Due Process

Justice Black rejected this substantive interpretation of procedural due process. "The Natural Law concept," he said in an interview, "canons of decency and fairness, is not what due process is all about. It would permit judges to write the Constitution over from day to day, month to month, year to year, based on what best fits the times."[6] He could not "subscribe to such a loose interpretation of due process."[7]

The language of due process, he believed, had its origin in the Magna Carta, Section 29, which declared that "no free man shall be taken, outlawed, banished, or in any way destroyed, nor will we prosecute him, except by the lawful judgment of his peers and by the law of the land."[8] In that "law of the land" notion was the beginning of due process of law. Due process came to mean, for those who wrote the Constitution, that the people were assured that government would not take life, liberty, and property without a trial in accord with the law of the land that existed at the time the alleged criminal offense was committed:

> The clause thus gives all Americans, whoever they are and wherever they happen to be, the right to be tried by (1) independent and unprejudiced courts (2) using established and non-discriminatory procedures and (3) applying valid pre-existing laws. There is not one word of legal history that justifies making the term 'due process of law' mean a guarantee of a trial free from laws and conduct which the courts deem at the time to be 'arbitrary,' 'unfair,' or 'contrary to civilized standards.'[9]

In short, for Black, due process meant that a person had the right to a fair trial in accordance with "established and non-discriminatory procedures," that is, a "trial in accordance with the Bill of Rights."[10] In Black's view, the procedural guarantees within the Bill of Rights, the Fourth through Eighth Amendments, were absorbed or incorporated into the Due Process Clause. A former law clerk put Black's view in very simple language: "There were two facets of Justice Black's theory of due process...Facet No. 1 was that due process encompassed all the specific prohibitions of the Bill of Rights and the Constitution....The Second Facet, equally important, was that due process did not encompass anything else."[11] The task of the judges, in deciding criminal cases and controversies, was to determine whether the state attempted to go over or around these "fences against wrongs." If a defendant was denied a "speedy and public trial," or was denied "right to counsel," then, according to Black's parameters, he was not tried in accordance with the laws of the land, that is, he was being denied the constitutional guarantee of due process of law. If that were found to be the case—and no judicial "concoction" was needed to determine the issue (only facts)—the courts had a solemn obligation to nullify that action of the government.

The collision between Frankfurter's views (and, after his retirement, Harlan's views) and Black's perception of due process came soon after both men began functioning as Justices of the Court. The remaining sections of the chapter will focus on that judicial confrontation and its impact on the decision-making activities of the Court in the area of criminal justice.

The Clash of Conflicting Interpretations of Due Process, From *Palko* to *McGautha* (1937-1970)

Until the adoption of the Fourteenth Amendment in 1868, the Bill of Rights was seen by the Court as a set of limits solely upon the federal government.[12] The passage of the Civil War Amendments extended federal constitutional constraints over actions of the state governments and led to a basic question: what was the relationship between the Fourteenth Amendment's Due Process Clause limits on the states to the limits on the Federal government found in the first eight Amendments in the Bill of Rights. Due to the workload of the Court, the answer was only hinted at in cases before the 1930s: there were very few state criminal law cases that came before the Court. In those cases that were appealed to the Court regarding the applicability of the Bill of Rights to the states via the Fourteenth Amendment, the judges were of the opinion that there was not too close a connection between the federal guarantees and the Fourteenth Amendment.[13]

In the 1930s the Supreme Court's docket contained many more state criminal law cases and the justices of the Court had to closely examine the question. In so doing, the Court developed the "fundamental rights" standard that appeared initially as a judicial standard in 1932.[14] This interpretation of due process was essentially the standard Justice Felix Frankfurter adhered to as a member of the Court. As he said, "since the Fourteenth Amendment *encompasses only* 'fundamental' rights, and (grand-jury indictment, and common law juries in civil cases) are not 'fundamental,' they make no requirements on the states."[15] There are certain fundamental rights essential to a fair trial; these are based on the pervasive consensus of the people in the community and their historically verifiable standards of fair play. Due process, then, means basic fairness and though some of the provisions of the Bill of Rights may be of fundamental importance to this right of fairness, that Clause *must not be restricted* to the Bill of Rights alone.

Palko v Connecticut, a case decided barely two months after Black took his seat on the Court, reflected this basic interpretation of due process of the law, i.e., the "Fundamental Rights" interpretation. A Connecticut statute permitted the state to appeal a criminal case where the judge committed errors of law that were prejudicial to the state. Palko had been convicted of murder in the second degree; with the new trial, based on the statute, he was convicted of murder in the first degree and he was sentenced to death. He appealed his conviction on the grounds that the Due Process Clause of the Fourteenth Amendment absorbed the Fifth Amendment's guarantee against double jeopardy. His argument was refuted in an opinion written by Justice Benjamin Cardozo.

Cardozo rejected out of hand the total incorporation

interpretation of due process, saying simply: "There is no such general rule."[16] Prior cases have also turned aside partial incorporation of certain Bill of Rights guarantees. However, the Court had, in the past viewed certain other Bill of Rights protections as applying to the states.

> Due Process of the Fourteenth may make it unlawful for a state to abridge by its statutes the freedom of speech which the first amendment safeguards against encroachments by Congress.... Immunities that are valid as against the federal government by force of their specific pledges of particular amendments have been found to be implicit in the concept of ordered liberty and thus, through the fourteenth amendment, become valid as against the states.[17]

Which rights are implicit in this concept of ordered liberty? How does a jurist draw the "line of division" between the fundamental and the not-so-fundamental guarantees? "Reflection and analysis" on the part of the dispassionate jurist, Cardozo argued, would lead to the emergence of a "perception of a rationalizing principle which gives to discrete instances a proper order and coherence."[18] While jury trial, self-incrimination protection, and immunity from prosecution "may have value and importance, they are not of the very essence of a scheme of ordered liberty. To abolish them is not to violate a principle of justice so rooted in the traditions and conscience of our people as to be ranked as fundamental. They may be lost and justice still be done."[19]

> We reach a different plane of social and moral values when we pass on to the privileges and immunities that have been taken over from the earlier articles of the federal Bill of Rights and brought within the Fourteenth Amendment by a process of absorption. These in their origin were effective against the federal government alone. If the Fourteenth Amendment has absorbed them, the process of absorption has had its source in the belief that neither liberty nor justice would exist if they were sacrificed....This is true, for illustration, of freedom of thought and

> speech. Of that freedom one may say that it is the matrix, the indispensable condition, of nearly every other form of freedom. With rare aberrations a pervasive recognition of that truth can be traced in our history, political and legal. So it has come about that the domain of liberty, withdrawn from the encroachments by the states through the Fourteenth Amendment, has been enlarged by latter-day judgment to include liberty of the mind as well as liberty of action.[20]

With these thoughts enumerated, the question in *Palko* was whether the double jeopardy protection was so fundamental as to be rooted in the concept of ordered liberty. Is the double jeopardy "to which the statute has subjected him a hardship so acute and shocking that our polity will not endure it? Does it violate those fundamental principles of liberty and justice which lie at the base of all our civil and political institutions? The answer," concluded Cardozo, "surely must be 'no.'"[21]

Justice Black went along with the Cardozo opinion and holding; an attitude, however, which was to undergo major repairs within a very few years. "In Black's early years," a law-clerk of Black said to the author, "he had not yet formulated his views completely and perhaps was reluctant to dissent too frequently at first. Thus, for example, *Palko*. In later years, the judge came to regard *Palko* as one of the worst of all due process opinions.[22] The *Palko* interpretation was to become, in the next two decades, the standard employed by a majority of the judges when confronted with criminal law situations such as Palko's. Even Black, for one or two years, used the "fundamental fairness" yardstick in his opinions. But he did attempt, prior to rejecting that standard, to align it with specific prohibitions in the Bill of Rights.

Chambers v Florida, a 1939 decision of the Court, offers an illustration of Justice Black's confrontation with the *Palko* standard. Chambers and other blacks had been picked up by local police after the brutal death of an elderly white man.

For almost eight days the convicted blacks were questioned constantly—days and nights. The men were at no time during this period of questioning permitted to see or confer with counsel, family or friends. When questioned, each was surrounded by four to ten men. On the morning of the eighth day, the petitioners confessed. The convictions and death penalties were based on these confessions. For a unanimous Supreme Court, Justice Black voided the death sentences.

"The scope and operation of the Fourteenth Amendment have been fruitful sources of controversy in our constitutional history," Black wrote. "However, in view of its historical setting and the wrongs which called it into being, the Due Process Clause of the Fourteenth Amendment...has led few to doubt that it was intended to guarantee procedural standards adequate and appropriate, then and thereafter, to protect, at all times, people charged with or suspected of crime by those holding positions of power and authority."[23]

> A liberty loving people won the principle that criminal punishments could not be inflicted save for that which proper legislative action had already by the 'law of the land' forbidden when done. But even more was needed. From the popular hatred and abhorrence of illegal confinement, torture, and extortion of confessions of violations of the 'law of the land' evolved the fundamental idea that no man's life, liberty or property be forfeited as criminal punishment for violation of that law until there had been a charge fairly made and fairly tried in a public tribunal free of passion, prejudice, excitement and tyrannical power. Thus, as assurance against ancient evils, our country, in order to preserve the 'blessings of liberty,' wrote into its basic law the requirement, among others, that the forfeiture of the lives, liberties, or property of people accused of crime can only follow if procedural safeguards of due process have been obeyed.[24]

Due process, Black concluded, required the states to "conform to fundamental standards of procedure in criminal trials."

> We are not impressed by the argument that law enforcement methods such as those under review are necessary to uphold our laws. The Constitution proscribes such lawless means irrespective of the end. And this argument flouts the basic principle that all people must stand on an equality before the bar of justice in every American court....Under our constitutional system, courts stand against any winds that blow as havens of refuge for those who otherwise might suffer because they are helpless, weak, outnumbered, or because they are non-conforming victims of prejudice and public excitement. Due Process of law commands that no such practice as that disclosed by this record shall send any accused to his death. No higher duty, no more solemn responsibility, rests upon this Court, than that of translating into living law and maintaining this constitutional shield.[25]

In *Chambers* Black introduced the theme that was to lead to his break with Palko, the notion of 'law of the land.' In the 1939 case it was married to the 'fundamental fairness' standard enunciated by Cardozo but by 1941 Black seriously questioned the foundation of the *Palko* standard. His dissenting opinions in *Lisenba v California* and in *Betts v Brady* expressed his discontent.

Lisenba v California[26] dealt with a murder conviction (and subsequent death penalty) based on allegedly coerced confessions of an accomplice. Justice Roberts, for the Court majority, upheld the judgment of the jury and the verdict of the Court. "The aim of the due process requirement is not to exclude presumptively false evidence, but to prevent fundamental unfairness in the use of evidence, whether true or not."[27] In order for the Court to find a denial of due process "we must find that the absence of that fairness *fatally* infected the trial." The admission of the confessions in the instant case, Roberts concluded, were not so "fundamentally unfair, so contrary to the common concept of ordered liberty as to amount to a taking of life without due process of law."[28]

Black, perhaps himself shocked at the reasoning of the

Roberts opinion, dissented. The confession, he said, was the simple result of coercion and compulsion. It was not freely and voluntarily given. The facts spoke for themselves. The principle enunciated in *Chambers* was relevant, that is, the state action contravened the 'law of the land' and the procedural requirements in the Bill of Rights. Distinguishing, as Roberts did, one type of coerced confession from another (prolonged police interrogation from physical torture), saying that one is a denial of due process while the other is not, overlooks the commands of the Due Process Clause.[29]

Betts v Brady[30] dealt with the right to counsel question. In earlier cases the Court had indicated that the right to counsel in state cases involving capital crimes was a fundamental right.[31] Betts, however, raised the question of assigned counsel in cases involving lesser offenses. The defendant was convicted of robbery; he had asked for and was denied counsel by the state courts. He appealed the conviction on the grounds that he was denied due process of law. The Supreme Court held, in an opinion written by Justice Roberts, that the matter of appointing counsel in indigent cases was one for legislative determination, not judicial policy making. "We reject the notion that due process of law demands that in every criminal case, whatever the circumstances, a state must furnish counsel to an indigent defendant....That which may, in one setting, constitute a denial of fundamental fairness, shocking to the universal sense of justice, may, in other circumstances, and in the light of other considerations, fall short of such denial."[32]

> The Fourteenth Amendment prohibits the conviction and incarceration of one whose trial is offensive to the common and fundamental ideas of fairness and right, and while want of counsel in a particular case may result in a conviction lacking in such fundamental fairness, we cannot say that the Amendment embodies an inexorable command that no trial for any offense... can be fairly conducted and justice accorded a defendant who is

not represented by counsel.[33]

"I believe," said Black in dissent, "that the Fourteenth Amendment made the Sixth Amendment applicable to the states." Even under the *Palko* "fundamental standards" view, the Betts judgment below should be reversed.[34] "Denial to the poor of the request for counsel in proceedings based on charges of serious crime has long been regarded as shocking to the 'universal sense of justice' throughout this country," concluded Black.[35] The layman requires "the guiding hand of counsel at every step," said Black; "he faces the danger of conviction (without counsel) because he does not know how to establish his innocence," quoted Black from the 1932 Powell opinion of the Court. But because a majority of the nine judges felt as they did, the conviction stood. And it was these cases, in the 1941 term of the Court, that led Black to conclude that justice would better be served if judges did not have to employ their skills in "finding" communal norms called fundamental, fair, etc.

During the 1943 term, Justice Black's view of due process (still to be given final shape but by now openly disavowing the "fundamental standard" *Palko* formula) came into conflict with that held by Justice Frankfurter. Their differing approaches toward the essential purpose and meaning of due process can be seen in two cases decided that term, *Ashcraft v Tennessee* and *Feldman v United States.*[36] Ashcraft was charged with the murder of his wife and was questioned constantly by the police, at one point being grilled for thirty-six hours straight. "From 7:00 Saturday evening until 9:30 Monday morning," noted Black, the police, "in relays because they became so tired they had to rest," questioned Ashcraft. He finally confessed; the confession was the principal weapon of the prosecution in its case. He was found guilty and he appealed the conviction. Justice Black wrote the opinion for the Court majority. The conditions under which Ashcraft confessed, wrote Black, were inherently coercive: "if Ashcraft made a confession it was not voluntary but compelled."

> It is inconceivable that any court of justice in the land, conducted as our courts are, open to the public, would permit prosecutors serving in relays to keep a defendant witness under continuous cross-examination for thirty six hours without rest or sleep in an effort to extract a 'voluntary' confession. Nor can we, consistently with constitutional due process of law, hold voluntary a confession where prosecutors do the same thing away from the restraining influences of a public trial in an open court room. The Constitution of the United States stands as a bar against the conviction of any individual in an American court by means of a coerced confession.[37]

Justice Frankfurter dissented, joining in a dissent written by Justice Robert Jackson, who contended that that police action did not, in the words of Justice Roberts, exhibit "fundamental unfairness."

In *Feldman* it was Justice Black who dissented from the majority opinion written by Justice Frankfurter. Feldman was compelled to give testimony in New York state court and under the New York statute he received immunity from future prosecution in that jurisdiction. He was then indicted in federal court for federal mail fraud and was convicted based, in large part, upon the testimony he was compelled to give in the state court. Justice Frankfurter, for the Court majority, ruled that there was no violation of due process of law. "The immunity from prosecution, like the privilege against testifying which it supplants, pertains to a prosecution in the same jurisdiction. Otherwise, the criminal law would be at the hazard of carelessness or connivance in some petty civil litigation in a New York state court."[38] Black dissented.

> The founding fathers sought by these provisions (4th, 5th, 6th, and 8th Amendments) to assure that no individual could be punished except according to 'due process,' by which they

> certainly meant that no person could be punished except for a violation of definite and validly enacted laws of the land and after a trial conducted in accordance with the specifice procedural safeguards written in the Bill of Rights.[39]

The point of the matter, for Black, was not respect for "dual sovereignty," that is, respect for the sovereignty of state and federal procedures; it was that Feldman was being forced to incriminate himself in violation of the prohibition against such involuntary action within the Bill of Rights and within the meaning of due process of law.

This viewpoint was fully developed in Black's dissenting opinion in *Adamson v California.*[40] Adamson had been convicted in a California court of first degree murder and sentenced to death. At the trial, he had not taken the stand in his own defense and under California law, the trial judge and prosecutor were permitted to comment to the jury about the failure of Adamson to refute the testimony and evidence against him. He appealed his conviction, arguing that the Due Process Clause's guarantee against compulsory self-incrimination allowed him to remain silent and that the judge's comments, and those of the prosecutor, about Adamson's silence violated that Clause. (Inferences of guilt was present and drawn upon by the prosecutor by virtue of Adamson's silence.)

Justice Reed wrote the opinion for the majority. The trial procedure was upheld; due process was not denied the defendant. "We reaffirm the conclusion of *Twining* and *Palko* cases that protection against self-incrimination is not a privilege or immunity of national citizenship."[41]

> The due process clause of the Fourteenth Amendment does not protect, by virtue of its mere existence, the accused's freedom from giving testimony by compulsion in state trials that is secured to him against federal interference by the Fifth Amendment.[42]

Given the circumstances in Adamson's case, no fundamental

unfairness was perceived by Reed and therefore "a denial of due process does not emerge."[43]

Justice Frankfurter concurred in the judgment of the Court. His opinion was directed to the Black dissent; it was an attempt by Frankfurter to refute the "total incorporation" argument presented by his colleague from Alabama. Forty-three judges have sat on the bench since the Fourteenth Amendment was adopted, Frankfurter pointed out, and only one of these justices indicated a belief that it was "shorthand for the first eight amendments."[44] (And he was "what may be called an eccentric exception.") "Those reading the English language with the meaning which it ordinarily conveys, those conversant with the political and legal history of the concept of due process, those sensitive to the relation of some of the provisions of the Bill of Rights to the process of justice, would hardly recognize the Fourteenth Amendment as a cover for the various explicit provisions of the first eight amendments," he maintained.[45]

The important, "relevant," question for the Court in these cases is whether the criminal proceedings "offended those canons of decency and fairness which express the notions of English-speaking peoples even toward those charged with the most heinous offenses." These standards of justices, Frankfurter said, are "not authoritatively formulated anywhere as though they were prescriptions in a pharmacopeia."

> Due Process has a independent potency which neither comprehends the specific prohibitions (provisions) by which the founders deemed it appropriate to restrict the federal government nor is it confined to them.[46]

Judges, he concluded, "were not wholly at large. The judicial judgment in applying the Due Process Clause must move within the limits of accepted notions of justice and is not to be based upon the idiosyncrasies of a merely personal judgment."[47]

Black dissented from the judgment of the Court and in so doing formulated his alternative interpretation of due process of law. It was an alternative that, unlike the more amorphous *Palko* standard, incorporated the procedural guarantees of the Bill of Rights totally into the Due Process Clause. The majority and Frankfurter reassert a constitutional theory that "this Court is endowed by the Constitution with boundless power under 'Natural Law' periodically to expand and contract constitutional standards to conform to the Court's conception of what at a particular time constitutes 'civilized decency' and 'fundamental liberty and justice.'"[48] Such a theory of judicial activism "degrades the constitutional safeguards" of the Bill of Rights and simultaneously "appropriates for this Court a broad power which we are not authorized by the Constitution to exercise."

The "Natural Law" formula should be abandoned as "an incongrous excrescence on our Constitution," he said.[49] And, according to Black's examination of the debates surrounding the passage of the Civil War Amendments in Congress (and drawing upon his experiences as a legislator), the first section of the Fourteenth Amendment "was intended to make the Bill of Rights applicable to the states."[50] Incorporating the entire set of procedural guarantees of the Bill of Rights into the Due Process Clause would limit the ability of the Court to use in an unauthorized manner such "natural law" formulas because the meaning of due process would be determined by referring to the specific terms of the Bill of Rights.

> At the time Twining said state courts need not conform to specific provisions of the Bill of Rights, it consolidated the power that Court had assumed under the due process clause by laying even broader foundations for the Court to invalidate state and even federal regulatory legislation. For under the *Twining* formula, which includes non-regard for the first eight amendments, what are 'fundamental rights' and in accord with standards 'and

> canons of decency'...is to be independently ascertained from time to time by judicial action.[51]

"I cannot consider the Bill of Rights to be an outworn 18th century 'strait jacket' as the *Twining* opinion did," said Black. "Though its provisions may be considered outdated by some, they were written into the Fundamental Law in order to combat 'ancient evils.' But they are the same kind of human evils that have emerged from century to century wherever excessive power is sought by the few at the expense of the many....I fear to see the consequences of the Court's practice of substituting its own concepts of decency and fundamental justice for the language of the Bill of Rights as its point of departure in interpreting and enforcing that Bill of Rights."[52] Judicial review, Black admitted, did involve interpretation "and since words can have many meanings, interpretation obviously may result in contraction or extension of the original purpose of a constitutional provision, thereby affecting policy.

> But to pass upon the constitutionality of statutes by looking to the particular standards enumerated in the Bill of Rights and the parts of the Constitution is one thing; to invalidate statutes because of application of 'natural law' deemed to be above and undefined by the Constitution is another.[53]

The Black dissent was joined by Justices Wiley Rutledge, Frank Murphy, and Douglas; and this was the four man "high tide" of the total incorporation view. After *Adamson* in 1946 came a period of years where the two views, Frankfurter's and Black's, clashed but where neither of the views commanded a majority of the Court's allegiance. Black, as will be seen in the remaining sections of this chapter, continued to criticize Frankfurter and Harlan for their use of "Natural Law" formulas but, because his view of due process was unacceptable to the majority of the judges, "often joined in results in cases in which he felt the opinion did not reflect a correct statement of due process and would occasionally join in the opinion."[54] As Black stated in *Adamson*: "While I would extend to all people in the nation the complete protection of the Bill of Rights, if the choice must be between the selective process of *Palko* or the *Twining* Rule applying none of them, I would choose the *Palko* selective process."[55] (As will be seen in Part III of this chapter dealing with "Selective Incorporation," Justice Black, in the eleven major cases, voted five times with the majority, wrote three separate concurring opinions, and wrote three opinions for the Court. He did not dissent at all.)

Black also had, of course, the opportunity to dissent—as he did in the case of *Foster v Illinois,* decided shortly after *Adamson.*[56] Arrested and charged with burglary and robbery, the defendant had not been given counsel. Convicted of the charges, he appealed the verdict. In an opinion written by Frankfurter, the Court held that there was no denial of due process of law under the Fourteenth Amendment because the Sixth Amendment's right to counsel was not made applicable to the states through the Fourteenth. Black dissented, saying simply that "this decision is another example of the consequences which can be produced by substitution of this court's day-to-day opinion of what kind of trial is fair and decent for the kind of trial which the Bill of Rights guarantees. This time it is the right of counsel. We cannot know," he concluded, "what Bill of Rights provision will next be attenuated by the Court."[57]

Black's rejection of the "natural law" standards employed by Frankfurter and Harlan was total. He would continuously dissent from Court opinions whose judgment was based on such reasoning. (His dissents and concurrences in one area of constitutional litigation, search and seizures, will be dealt with separately in the last portion of this chapter.) In a double jeopardy case that came before the Court in 1958, for example, Black dissented from the Court opinion written by

Frankfurter.[58] Bartkus was acquitted in a federal court for robbery of a federally insured savings and loan association. He was then charged with the same criminal offense in a state court in Illinois, found guilty, and sentenced to life imprisonment. In a lengthy opinion, Justice Frankfurter again (1) rejected the "total incorporation" theory of Black's and (2) upheld the conviction, saying that "state and federal courts had for years refused to bar a second trial even though there had been a prior trial by another government for a similar offense."[59] (In an Appendix to the majority opinion, Frankfurter pointed out that "double jeopardy" was not a fundamental right essential to a system of ordered liberty.)[60]

"Fear and abhorrence of governmental power to try people twice for the same crime," wrote Black in dissent, "is one of the oldest ideas found in Western civilization."[61] Arguing as he did in *Feldman*, Black rejected the contention that the practice was "justified in the name of federalism. This, it seems to me, is a misuse and desecration of the concept....We should be suspicious of any supposed 'requirements' of 'federalism' which result in obliterating ancient safeguards."[62] (In *Waller v Florida,* 397 *US* 387 (1969), Chief Justice Burger noted that the Bartkus and Abbate "dual sovereignty" theory "is an anachronism.") For Black this case presented a classic picture of denial of due process of law. Bartkus had been forced to undergo a second trial for the same offense; that was a patent violation of the double jeopardy provision of the Fifth Amendment. To attempt to obliterate that patent violation by government (and the trial record clearly indicated that Federal prosecutors had handed over to state prosecutors all information about Bartkus that had been gathered by them) by indicating that double jeopardy was not a "fundamental right" and that, in any case, "federalism" allowed that type of situation, was to rob the people of a basic procedural "fence against governmental wrongs" clearly provided to them in the Constitution.

This debate between Black and defenders of the "fair play" notion of due process went on after Frankfurter's retirement; it ended, in reality, when Black left the Court. During the last decade of his Court tenure, Black was able to clearly formulate, in final draft form, his views of due process. He did so primarily in written debates with his colleague John M. Harlan, Jr. (These debates were a source of some concern to other justices on the Court, those who had adopted the middle road discussed in Part III of this chapter. In one case, Justice Brennan noted, acidly, that perhaps Justices Black and Frankfurter had not focused adequately on the "determinative question" in the case before the Court.)[63]

Given his thorough-going, intense commitment to the "total incorporation" view and his equally intense disdain for the nebulous standards employed by the Frankfurter/Harlan justices, Black lost no opportunity to express himself openly whenever he thought the Court majority was moving toward acceptance of the "Natural Law" theory of due process. One time, however, his intense views on the subject were the source of some laughter in the Courtroom itself. It took place during oral argument in the *Gideon* case (a case examined subsequently in this chapter).

> Justice Stewart asked whether he was right in his impression that Fortas (Abe Fortas had been appointed by the Court to defend Clarence Gideon before the Court and was soon to become a justice himself.) was not arguing the old proposition that the Fourteenth Amendment incorporated the Sixth Amendment as such. Fortas agreed—he was not. But the answer that pleases one judge may arouse another, and this one aroused the member of the Court who had been arguing for a generation that the Fourteenth Amendment incorporated the entire original Bill of Rights—Justice Black. He asked in a puzzled way why Fortas was laying aside that argument.
>
> 'Mr. Justice Black,' Fortas replied, 'I like that argument that

you make so eloquently. But I cannot as an advocate make that argument because this Court has rejected it so many times. I hope you never cease making it.'

Justice Black joined in the general laughter.[64]

Black was especially at his best in the following series of opinions, concurring and dissenting, attacking the "fundamental fairness" notion of procedural due process and can be seen as the essence of his thoughts on the subject at their zenith.

He dissented in *In Re Winship,* a case that raised questions about the nature of juvenile justice.[65] Relying upon the "preponderance of evidence" standard developed by New York state legislators to determine the guilt or innocence of juvenile defendants, a Juvenile Court found the defendant, twelve years of age, guilty of robbery. He appealed the decision (his lawyers did) arguing that there was a denial of due process of law in that the "guilt beyond a reasonable doubt" standard was not employed by the judge. The New York Court of Appeals upheld the conviction. On appeal to the Supreme Court, the judgment was overturned. Justice Brennan, speaking for the Court, said that "proof beyond a reasonable doubt" was required by due process in criminal trials and "is among the essentials of due process and fair treatment" required during the adjudicatory stage when a juvenile is charged with an act that would constitute a crime if committed by an adult.[66]

Justice Black dissented from this majority view which he felt expressed the old "fundamental fairness" theory of due process. "The only correct meaning of due process of law is that our government must proceed according to the 'law of the land'—that is, according to written constitutional and statutory provisions as interpreted by Court decisions."[67] The Due Process Clause does not give the Court "blanket authority" to govern the country "according to the views of at least five members of this institution....When this Court assumes for itself the power to declare any law—state or federal—unconstitutional because it offends the majority's own views of what is fundamental, our nation ceases to be governed according to 'the law of the land' and instead becomes one governed by the 'law of the judges.'"[68]

The New York State legislature passed the law concerning juvenile offenses and standards of guilt or innocence. "The people, through their representatives may be wrong in making those determinations, but the right of self-government that our constitution preserves is just as important as any of the specific individual freedoms preserved in the Bill of Rights. The liberty of government of the people, in my opinion, should never be denied by this Court except when the decision of the people as stated in the laws passed by their chosen representatives, conflicts with the express or necessarily implied commands of our Constitution."[69]

While "proof beyond a reasonable doubt" was a standard used/required in federal criminal trials and was used "almost universally" in the states (and due process "commands that every trial in *that* jurisdiction must adhere to that standard"), if a state, as New York, in this case, "decides to apply a different standard, then that standard, unless it is otherwise unconstitutional, must be applied to insure that persons are treated according to the 'law of the land.' The State of New York has made such a decision, and in my view nothing in the Due Process clause invalidates it."[70]

Black concurred in another case that came from the New York courts.[71] Baldwin had been charged with a misdemeanor in New York City's Criminal Court. He was tried without a jury in accordance with the city's Criminal Court Act. He asked for a jury trial, was denied one, and was found guilty and sentenced to one year in the city jail. The New York courts affirmed the judgment and Baldwin appealed to the Supreme Court. Justice White, writing for the majority, reversed the judgment. Defendants accused of "serious" crimes must, under the Sixth Amendment, be afforded the right to trial by jury. No offense is "petty," reasoned White, where imprisonment for more than six months is authorized by law.

Black agreed that the jury trial was needed; he disagreed, however, with the view expressed by White that the right to a jury trial "is determined by whether the offense charged is 'petty' or a 'serious' one. The Constitution guarantees a right of trial by jury," Black argued, "in two places (Article III, Section 2, Clause 3 and Amendment Six), but in neither case does it hint of any difference between petty offenses and serious offenses."[72]

> Such constitutional adjudication (by White), whether framed in terms of fundamental fairness, balancing, or shocking the conscience, amounts in every case to little more than judicial mutilation of our written constitution. Those who wrote and adopted the Constitution and the Bill of Rights engaged in all the balancing necessary. They decided that the value of a jury trial far outweighed its cost for "all crimes" and "in all criminal prosecutions." Until that language is changed by...Amendment, I cannot agree that this Court can reassess the balance and substitute its judgment for that embodied in the Constitution.[73]

In *Williams v Florida,* Justice Black, dissenting in part, would have invalidated a state law he felt came into conflict with the Due Process Clause.[74] A Florida rule of procedure was challenged by the defendant Williams. If a defendant was to rely on an alibi as part of his defense the procedural rule called for him to disclose to the prosecution the names of alibi witnesses. The prosecution, in turn, according to the rule, had to disclose to the defense the names of witnesses it was going to present to rebut the alibi. Williams complied with the rule and was subsequently convicted on the basis of an alibi witness' deposition being used to impeach the witness. He appealed the conviction on the grounds that his Fifth and Sixth Amendment rights had been abridged by

Florida (he had been tried by a six man jury). Justice White, for the Court, dismissed the Sixth Amendment contention and ruled that the notice-of-alibi rule did not violate the self-incrimination prohibition in the Fifth Amendment.

Justice Black disagreed with the White judgment of the Fifth Amendment appeal. "If words are to be given their plain meaning," he argued, "the self-incrimination provision, in my opinion, states that a criminal defendant cannot be required to give evidence, testimony, or any other assistance to the State to aid it in convicting him of crime....The Florida statute is a patent violation of that constitutional provision."[75] Under the American criminal justice process, Black reminded the judges, the defendant need not do any thing to defend himself and "certainly he cannot be required to help convict himself. Throughout the process, the defendant has a fundamental right to remain silent, in effect, challenging the state at every point to: 'Prove it!'"[76]

> There is a hint in the Court's opinion of the ever-recurring suggestion that the test of constitutionality is the test of fairness, decency, or in short, the Court's own views of what is best....This decision is one more step away from the written Constitution and a radical departure from the system of criminal justice that has prevailed in this country.[77]

In *Coleman v Alabama,* still another criminal law case heard by the Court in 1969, Justice Black again concurred in the judgment of the Court because he refused to accept the "fundamental fairness" standard employed by the Court majority.[78] Coleman had been convicted of assault with intent to murder. The basis for the conviction had been an in-court identification. He appealed the conviction stating that that identification was tainted by a prejudicial station-house line-up and because he had no appointed counsel at the preliminary hearings. The Alabama courts rejected his appeal and Coleman took the case to the Supreme Court. Brennan, speaking for the Court, vacated the conviction and remanded the case to determine whether the denial of counsel at the preliminary hearing was a harmless error or fundamentally deprived Coleman of a fair trial.

Black concurred. He believed that the preliminary hearing was a basic part or stage of a criminal prosecution in Alabama and that the Sixth Amendment's "plain language" required the assistance of counsel in Coleman's behalf. But Black was concerned about Brennan's slide into the "Natural Law" jargon that Black eschewed.

> While 'fair trial' is an appealing (term), neither the Bill of Rights nor any other part of the Constitution contains it. The pragmatic government-fearing authors of our Constitution and Bill of Rights did not, and I think wisely did not, use any such vague, indefinite, or elastic language....The explicit guarantees of the Constitution provide a full description of the kind of 'fair trial' the Constitution guarantees and in my judgment that document leaves no room for judges either to add to or detract from these commands.[79]

"For one," Black concluded, "I still prefer to trust the liberty of the citizen to the plain language of the constitution rather than to the sense of fairness of the judges."[80]

In *McGautha v California,* a case decided just a few months before Black's death, his literalist commitment to the Constitution once again forced Black to write a separate though concurring opinion in a criminal procedure controversy.[81] McGautha was convicted of first degree murder and was sentenced to death. Under California law, the penalty was left to the jury's absolute discretion, and punishment was determined in a separate proceeding following the trial on the issue of guilt. Certiorari was granted by the Supreme Court in order to determine whether McGautha's rights were infringed by permitting the death penalty without standards to govern its imposition. Justice Harlan, for the Court, held that McGautha's rights were not violated by the state procedure, that he had a fair trial, and that the policies of the privilege against self-incrimination were not offended when a defendant in a capital case yielded to the pressure to testify on the issue of punishment at the risk of damaging his case on guilt. The procedure, claimed Harlan, was not "fundamentally lawless" and therefore not violative of the Due Process Clause.[82]

> To identify before the fact those characteristics of criminal homicides and their perpetrators which call for the death penalty, and to express these characteristics in language which can be fairly understood and applied by the sentencing authority, appear to be tasks which are beyond present human ability. In light of history, experience, and the present limitations of human knowledge, we find it quite impossible to say that committing to the untrammelled discretion of the jury the power to pronounce life or death in capital cases is offensive to anything in the Constitution.[83]

Justice Black concurred. He maintained that the task of the Court was not to determine whether the trial was "fairly conducted." "The Constitution grants this Court no power to reverse convictions because of our personal beliefs that state criminal procedures are 'unfair,' 'arbitrary,' 'capricious,' 'unreasonable,' or 'shocking to the conscience.' Our responsibility is rather to determine whether petitioners have been denied rights expressly or impliedly guaranteed by our Constitution as written."[84] He agreed with the Court's conclusion that the California procedures did not violate due process of law.

> Likewise, I do not believe that petitioner has been deprived of any other right explicitly or impliedly guaranteed by the other provisions of the Bill of Rights. The Eighth Amendment prohibits (forbids) 'cruel and unusual punishment.' In my view, these words cannot be read to outlaw capital punishment because that penalty was in common use and authorized by law here and in the countries from which our ancestors came at the time the Amendment was adopted. It is inconceivable to me that the

> Framers intended to end capital punishment by the Amendment. Although some people have urged that this Court should amend the Constitution by interpretation to keep it abreast of modern ideas. I have never believed that lifetime judges in our system have any such legislative power.[85]

"I have never believed that lifetime judges in our system have any such legislative power," captures the essence of Black's philosophy and his critique not only of the use of "fundamental fairness" concoctions by judges in criminal procedure cases but also the basic understanding he had of the function of the judiciary in a democracy. Throughout his political and legal lifetime, Black was to, again and again, reject the "obnoxious" contention, implicit in the employment of subjective judicial devices, that judges could set themselves above the law-making agencies of the American political system. As pointed out in this section, Black's view placed great reliance upon the words of the Constitution and the Bill of Rights themselves. It was not a naive approach; rather, disregarding the self-deprecating words of the Justice himself that he was a "rather backward country fellow,"[86] it was an "extremely complex approach, with deep philosophical and jurisprudential roots."[87] His underlying thesis was that the "original meaning and objectives of the Constitution must constantly be applied to changing conditions."[88]

Applying this viewpoint meant that Black would not be bound by precedent. "By limiting the force of precedents his philosophy asks courts always to return to the principles of the document itself."[89] This aspect of the judge's thoughts is well brought out in the "selective incorporation" period of recent Court actions in the procedural due process area.

"Selective Incorporation": The Middle Road for the Supreme Court

In the decade of the 1960s, Justice Black, surrounded by

new men on the Court,* participated in a series of Supreme Court opinions that selectively incorporated specific prohibitions against state action found in the Bill of Rights into the Due Process Clause. (See *Table One*) True to his commitment to the words of the Constitution and Bill of Rights, and to his statement in *Adamson* that, faced with the choice of *Twining*'s absolute bar against incorporating provisions of the Bill of Rights or *Palko*'s incorporation of those provisions that were essential to a "scheme of ordered liberty," "I would choose *Palko*," Black adopted the latter, more pragmatic, approach to the issue of procedural due process. "Obviously," Black said in 1968, "I am not completely happy with the selective incorporation theory since it still leaves to the determination of judges the decision as to which Bill of Rights provisions are 'fundamental' and thus applicable to the states....But (it) does limit the Supreme Court in the 14th Amendment field to specific Bill of Rights' protections only and keeps judges from roaming at will in their own notions of what policies outside the Bill of Rights are desirable." (By the end of the decade, most of the twelve provisions in the Bill of Rights concerning criminal procedure were incorporated and, in substance if not in form, Black's view of procedural due process had become the "law of the land.")

While there were a handful of cases that did apply the selective incorporation standard prior to the decade of the sixties, *Wolf* in 1949 left a large gap in individual protections which was not rectified for over a decade and *In Re Oliver*, decided in 1948, did not use the terminology of the subse-

---

*In 1953, Earl Warren replaced Fred Vinson as Chief Justice; in 1956, William J. Brennan, Jr., replaced Sherman Minton; in 1958, Potter Stewart replaced Harold Burton; in 1962, Byron White replaced Stanley Reed, and, in that same year, 1962, Arthur Goldberg replaced an ailing Felix Frankfurter. Later in the decade, Abe Fortas would take Goldberg's seat and Thurgood Marshall would replace Tom C. Clark, 1965 and 1967 respectively.

quent cases. (*Oliver* and *Cole v Arkansas,* 333 *US* 196, both decided in 1948, only suggested that the Bill of Rights protections were incorporated. The Court majority, in the 1968 *Duncan v Louisiana* decision, cited *Oliver* for the first time as incorporating the right to a public trial. 391 *US* 145, 147. The *Cole* case dealt with the Sixth Amendment right to be "informed of the nature and cause of the accusation." *Wolf v. Colorado, Mapp v Ohio* and other cases dealing with the meaning of the search and seizure provision in the Fourth Amendment will, because of the complexity of that particular prohibition, be dealt with separately in the third section of this chapter.)

TABLE ONE

"Selective Incorporation" of Procedural Guarantees of the Bill of Rights into Due Process Clause of the Fourteenth Amendment

Particular Clause	*Name of Case*	*Black's Role*	*Date*
6th Amendment (Public trial)	*In re Oliver*	wrote opinion	1948
4th Amendment	*Wolf v Colorado*	concurred	1949
4th Amendment	*Mapp v Ohio*	concurred	1961
8th Amendment	*Robinson v California*	joined majority	1962
6th Amendment (Right to counsel)	*Gideon v Wainright*	wrote opinion	1963
5th Amendment (self-incrimination)	*Malloy v Hogan*	joined majority	1964
6th Amendment (Right of confrontation)	*Pointer v Texas*	wrote opinion	1965
6th Amendment (Speedy trial)	*Klopfer v N.C.*	joined majority	1967
6th Amendment (Right to compulsory process)	*Washington v Texas*	joined majority	1967
6th Amendment	*Duncan v Louisiana*	concurred	1968

Particular Clause	*Name of Case*	*Black's Role*	*Date*
(Right to jury trial)			
5th Amendment (Double jeopardy)	*Benton v Maryland*	joined majority	1969

Oliver,[90] an opinion written by Justice Black, dealt with the Sixth Amendment provision that "In all criminal prosecutions, the accused shall enjoy the right to a...public trial." The case came to the Supreme Court from the Michigan courts. Oliver was ordered to testify before a one man legislative committee behind closed doors of a judge's chambers. The judge, believing the testimony to be false, charged Oliver with contempt, convicted him, and sentenced him to sixty days for contempt of Court. All this was done in privacy and not in an open courtroom. He appealed the conviction and the Supreme Court reversed the judgment of the Michigan court.

Justice Black stated that the Due Process Clause of the Fourteenth Amendment meant "at least that a person cannot be tried secretly and sent to prison." The failure to afford Oliver the right, "reasonable opportunity," to defend himself was also a denial of due process.[91] "It is the 'law of the land,'" Black concluded, "That no man's life, liberty, or property be forfeited as a punishment until there has been a charge fairly made and fairly tried in a public tribunal. The petitioner was convicted without that kind of trial."[92]

Except for *Wolf,* decided in 1949, the Supreme Court did not really begin to "selectively incorporate" the Bill of Rights into the Fourteenth Amendment until the 1960s.[93] *Robinson v California,* was the first of seven watershed cases (not including *Mapp*) announced by the Court in that productive decade and it dealt with the Eighth Amendment's ban against "cruel and unusual punishment." In an opinion written by the recently appointed Potter Stewart (Black joined with the majority), the Court invalidated a California statute which made it a misdemeanor offense to be addicted to the use of narcotics. "We hold," he said, "that a state law which imprisons a person thus afflicted as a criminal, even though he has never touched any narcotic drug within the State or been guilty of any irregular behavior there, inflicts a cruel and unusual punishment in violation of the Fourteenth Amendment. To be sure, imprisonment for ninety days is not, in the abstract, a punishment which is either cruel and unusual. But the question cannot be considered in the abstract. Even one day in prison would be a cruel and unusual punishment for the 'crime' of having a common cold."[94]

The following term of the Court, Justice Black wrote an opinion for the majority of the Court which had to give him great pleasure. The opinion was *Gideon v Wainright*[95] and it overturned the *Betts v Brady* decision of the Court announced two decades earlier. (Speaking to a friend shortly after the *Gideon* opinion was announced, "Black said quietly: 'When *Betts v Brady* was decided, I never thought I'd live to see it overruled.'")[96] The case dealt with the Sixth Amendment's provision that "in all criminal prosecutions, the accused shall...have the Assistance of Counsel for his defense." In *Betts,* with Black writing a dissent, the Court had ruled that only in certain conditions and situations was the "Assistance of Counsel" required by the Due Process Clause of the Fourteenth Amendment and that the question of appointing counsel for indigent defendants in criminal prosecutions was one that legislatures, not judges, had to answer.

Gideon had been charged with larceny, certainly not a "special circumstance/capital offense" issue, and he defended himself because Florida law did not provide appointed counsel in non-capital offenses. He was convicted and his conviction was upheld by the Florida courts. He took his appeal to the Supreme Court of the United States. Writing for the Court, Justice Black stated that "reason and reflection require us to recognize that in our adversary system of criminal justice, any person haled into court, who is too poor to hire a lawyer, cannot be assured of a fair trial unless counsel is provided for him."[97]

Justice Black accepted an assumption made by the earlier Court majority in *Betts,* that a provision in the Bill of Rights which is essential to a fair trial is made obligatory upon the States by the Fourteenth Amendment. "We think the Court in *Betts* was wrong, however," he continued, "in concluding that the Sixth Amendment's guarantee of counsel is not one of these fundamental rights." Black concluded this important decision with the following words:

> The right of one charged with crime to counsel may not be deemed fundamental and essential to fair trials in some countries, but it is in ours. From the very beginning, our state and federal constitutions and laws have laid great emphasis on procedural and substantive safeguards designed to assure fair trials before impartial tribunals in which every defendant stands equal before the law....Twenty two states, as friends of the Court, argue that *Betts* was 'an anachronism when handed down' and that it should now be overruled. We agree.[98]

Gideon was decided shortly after Frankfurter left the Court and Black visited his old friend to tell him about the conference session conversation. "He had told the other members of the Court, Justice Black said to Frankfurter, that if Felix had been there he would have voted—faithful to his own view of due process—to reverse the conviction of Clarence Gideon and overrule *Betts v Brady.* Justice Frankfurter said: 'Of course I would.'"[99] Justice Harlan concurred in the *Gideon* judgment of the Court, but not with Black's reasoning. He agreed that *Betts* should have been overruled, "but considered it entitled to a more respectful burial than has been accorded."

The following term the Court dealt with the question of self-incrimination. The Fifth Amendment states, in part, that no person "shall be compelled in any criminal case to be a witness against himself." For years, with Black and Douglas dissenting (see his dissent in *Feldman*), the Supreme Court used the "dual sovereignty" notion of federalism, arguing that a second trial in another jurisdiction did not violate the Due Process Clause of the Fourteenth or the "self-incrimination" clause of the Fifth Amendment. In the 1963 term of the Court, in the cases of *Malloy v Hogan* and *Murphy v Waterfront Commission of New York Harbor,*[100] the Court overturned *Twining v New Jersey* and declared that the self-incrimination provision was essential to due process. (In addition to overturning *Twining,* the Court in these cases specifically overturned *Adamson v California, Feldman v U.S., U.S. v Murdock*, a 1931 decision that developed the "separate jurisdiction" standard, and *Knapp v Schweitzer,* a 1958 case where the petitioner Knapp sustained a state contempt of court conviction because he refused to answer questions for fear that it might subject him to subsequent federal prosecution. The Court upheld the contempt citation, with Black, Douglas and Warren dissenting. Black said that, with the Court ruling, a person "can be whipsawed into incriminating himself under both state and federal law even though there is a privilege against self-incrimination in the Constitution of both. I cannot agree that we must accept this intolerable state of affairs as a necessary part of our federal system of government.")

"The Supreme Court," said Brennan in *Malloy,* "has rejected the notion that the Fourteenth Amendment applies to the states only a watered-down subjective version of the individual guarantees of the Bill of Rights."[101] In *Malloy,* petitioner had refused to answer questions in a Connecticut gambling inquiry for fear that it would subject him to federal prosecution. Brennan overturned the conviction saying "We hold that the Fourteenth Amendment guaranteed the petitioner the protection of the Fifth Amendment's privilege against self-incrimination, and that under the applicable federal standard, the Connecticut Supreme Court of Errors erred in holding that the privilege was not properly invoked."[102] Four justices dissented: Stewart, White, Clark, and Harlan. The latter justice objected to "incorporating into due process without critical examination, the whole body of law which surrounds a specific prohibition directed against the Federal government." In *Murphy,* they (petitioners) were granted immunity from prosecution in New York and New Jersey. The petitioners, however, refused to testify because the answers might tend to incriminate them under the federal law—and the immunity granted them did not extend to that jurisdiction. They were cited for civil contempt and they appealed the judgment of the New Jersey courts affirming the judgments of contempt to the Supreme Court. Justice Goldberg, speaking for the Court majority, vacated the civil contempt judgments. "A state witness," he concluded, "may not be compelled to give testimony which may be incriminating under federal law unless the compelled testimony and its fruits cannot be used in any manner by federal officials in connection with a criminal prosecution against him."[103] Because the petitioners had "reasonable fears" that led them to refuse to testify, "fairness dictates that petitioners should now be afforded an opportunity to answer the questions."[104] Justice Black joined in both majority judgments.

The following term of the Court, 1964, Justice Black wrote the opinion for the Court majority that incorporated the Sixth Amendment provision that, "in all criminal prosecutions, the accused shall enjoy the right...to be confronted with the Witnesses against him." Pointer, the defendant, had been arrested and charged with robbery. He was indicted. Before the trial the primary witness against him moved to another state. At the trial, a transcript was introduced (made during the preliminary hearing) by the prosecution in which the now-absent witness identified Pointer as the culprit.

Convicted on the basis of this evidence, he appealed. The State courts upheld the conviction and the case went to the Supreme Court. In a short opinion, the Court held that "the Sixth Amendment right of an accused to confront the witness against him is a fundamental right and is made obligatory on the states by the Fourteenth Amendment."[105]

Justice Harlan concurred because he could not accept the "constitutional reasoning of the court," i.e., the incorporation doctrine. "For me this state judgment must be reversed because a right of confrontation is implicit in the concept of ordered liberty reflected in the Due Process Clause of the Fourteenth Amendment *independently* of the Sixth Amendment....The incorporation doctrines," he concluded, "whether full blown or selective, are both historically and constitutionally unsound and incompatible with the maintainance of our federal system on an even course."[106]

Two cases announced by the Court during the 1966 term of the Court incorporated two other provisions of the Sixth Amendment: *Washington v Texas* and *Klopfer v North Carolina.*[107] The former dealt with the part of the Amendment which guaranteed a person the right "to have compulsory process for obtaining witnesses in his favor," *Klopfer* dealt with the right "to a speedy trial." Chief Justice Warren wrote the opinions for the Court majority in these cases.

Washington dealt with a Texas statute that prohibited co-defendants in the same trial from testifying for each other–though they were not barred from testifying for the prosecution. Warren said that compulsory processes for obtaining favorable witnesses stands "on no lesser footing than the other Sixth Amendment rights," and "it is so fundamental and essential to a fair trial that it is incorporated in the Fourteenth Amendment."[108]

Klopfer presented a situation where the state prosecutor, after the jurors (petit jurors) had been selected and witnesses called, asked for and was granted a trial delay. The defendant appealed, arguing that he was denied due process of law because the constitutional guarantee of a "speedy trial" had been violated. Chief Justice Warren accepted the contention that that provision of the Sixth Amendment was essential to a fair trial and held that "the right to a speedy trial is as fundamental as any of the rights secured by the Sixth Amendment."[109] Justice Black joined in these opinions written by the Chief Justice.

In *Duncan v Louisiana,* Justice Black wrote an opinion concurring with the majority judgment written by Justice White. The case dealt with the Sixth Amendment provision that "in all criminal prosecutions, the accused shall enjoy the right to a speedy and public trial, by an impartial jury." Duncan had been arrested for simple battery, a misdemeanor offense punishable in the state by a maximum of two years imprisonment and a fine of up to three hundred dollars. Duncan was convicted without a jury trial and sentenced to sixty days and a fine of $150. He had asked for and was denied the jury trial. He appealed the conviction to the Supreme Court and that tribunal held, in the opinion written by White, that "the right to jury trial in serious criminal cases is a fundamental right and hence must be recognized by the states as part of their obligation to extend due process of law to all persons within their jurisdiction."[110] Earlier in the opinion, White said: "trial by jury in criminal cases is fundamental to the American scheme of justice." While not defining the precise boundary line between petty and serious offenses, the punishment in Duncan's case is serious enough to entitle him to a jury trial.

Justice Black was "very happy to support this selective process through which our Court has since the *Adamson* case held most of the specific Bill of Rights protections applicable to the same extent they are applicable to the Federal Government."[111] He concurred, however, in order to respond to the Harlan dissent in *Duncan,* a dissent "which makes a spirited and forceful defense of the now discredited (*Twining*) doctrine" (that none of the provisions in the Bill of Rights were enforcible as such against the states.)[112]

Harlan treated due process as "leaving judges free to decide at any particular time whether a particular rule or judicial formulation embodies an 'immutable principle of free government' or is 'implicit in the concept of ordered liberty' or whether certain conduct 'shocks the judge's conscience' or runs counter to some other similar, undefined and undefinable standard."

> Thus due process, to my brother Harlan, is to be a phrase with no permanent meaning, but one which is found to shift from time to time in accordance with judge's predilections and understandings of what is best for the country....It is impossible for me to believe that such unconfined power is given to judges in our Constitution that is a written one in order to limit governmental power.[113]

Such self-created tests, Black concluded, "depend entirely on the judge's idea of ethics and morals instead of requiring him to depend on the boundaries fixed by the Constitution. Nothing in the history of the phrase, 'due process of law,' suggests that constitutional controls are to depend on any particular judge's sense of values."[114]

Justice Harlan dissented, joined by Stewart. "I have raised my voice many times before against the Court's continuing undiscriminating insistence upon fastening on the States federal notions of criminal justice, and I do so again in this instance." The Fourteenth Amendment "was meant neither to incorporate nor to be limited to the specific guarantees of the first Eight Amendments." The only logical manner to approach these cases, said Harlan, was "to start with the words 'liberty' and 'due process of law' and attempt to define them in a way that accords with American traditions and our system of government." This approach "seeks to ascertain those immutable principles of free government which no member of the Union may disregard."

During the 1968 term, the Court announced its decision in the case of *Benton v Maryland.*[115] The Court dealt with the issue raised in *Palko,* that is, whether or not the Fifth Amendment's guarantee that no person "be subject for the same offense to be twice put in jeopardy of life and limb" was made applicable to the States through the Due Process Clause of the Fourteenth Amendment. Thurgood Marshall, writing for the Court's majority, overturned the *Palko* decision: "we find today that the double jeopardy protection of the Fifth Amendment represents a fundamental ideal in our constitutional heritage and that it should apply to the states through the Fourteenth Amendment....Palko represented an approach to basic constitutional rights which this Court's recent decisions have rejected."[116] Black joined in this judgment of the Court; Harlan sadly dissented. "Today," Harlan wrote, "*Palko* becomes another casualty in the so-far unchecked march toward 'incorporating' much, if not all, of the Federal Bill of Rights into the Due Process clause."[117]

At 85 years of age, Black had lived to see the Due Process Clause clearly come to possess the guarantees of the procedural guarantees of the Bill of Rights. While not completely happy, Black was able to live with "selective incorporation" and, indeed, to write some of the opinions for the majority using that standard, because it, unlike the Harlan/Frankfurter alternative, *specifically* inserted particular, identifiable, *written* provisions of the Bill of Rights into the contours of Due Process of the Law in the Fourteenth Amendment. The critical factor was that now, twenty years after *Adamson* was announced, the Court–using the middle road of "selective incorporation"–gave the Due Process Clause form and substance; the form and the substance of the provisions of the Bill of Rights. And after the process of selective incorporation ends, judges would no longer be able to somehow "find" the meaning of that Clause by looking to Natural Law, concepts of ordered liberty, etc. The "fences against wrongs," Black felt, would be in securer hands and less likely to be ripped aside if judges were restricted from "finding" due process. Due process, he was saying, is there for all to read: in the Bill of Rights.

There was, however, Black admitted, one situation that called for a greater degree of judgment on the part of Justices of the Court than normally the case. This was the special case of the meaning of "*unreasonable* searches and seizures." The next section of the chapter deals with this judicial controversy.

The Special Case of Unreasonable Searches and Seizures

The Fourth Amendment, in its entirety, reads as follows: "The right of the people to be secure in their persons, houses, papers, and effects, against unreasonable searches and seizures, shall not be violated, and no Warrants shall issue, but upon probable cause, supported by Oath or affirmation, and particularly describing the place to be searched, and the person or things to be seized." What made this constitutional protection against governmental wrongs unlike the other provisions of the Bill of Rights was that the judges were "required to determine reasonableness," wrote Justice Black.[118] In "search and seizure" cases, then, according to Black, it was appropriate for the judges to create and employ standards of "reasonableness" in order to determine whether or not a police action was constitutional or not. While he did accept this constitutional requirement to determine "reasonableness," he constantly maintained that it was a most limited task of the Court and that such an examination on the part of the Justices would in no way be "dependent on" the general language of due process. While Black eschewed such judicial exercises in general, given his "literalist" interpretation of the Constitution, he was forced to turn to history and traditions and customs in order to determine whether or not a search and seizure was reasonable or unreasonable.

In the 1886 case of *Boyd v United States,*[119] the Supreme Court came into initial contact with the meaning of the Fourth Amendment. *Boyd* raised the question of whether evidence obtained by an illegal search and seizure was admissible against the defendant in a federal criminal proceeding. The Court ruled that such evidence was inadmissible, not because of the Fourth Amendment protection but because the Fifth Amendment prohibition against self-incrimination did not allow the use of such "compelled" testimony.

In *Weeks v United States* (1914),[120] however, the Supreme Court modified the impact of *Boyd,* ruling that any evidence obtained by federal officials in violation of the Fourth Amendment's prohibition against unreasonable searches and seizures must be excluded from the federal prosecution. The Court maintained that the right of privacy, which the Fourth Amendment protected, would be of little or no practical value to citizens unless the use of such illegally seized evidence was barred from the criminal trial itself.[121] The *Weeks* decision left in the air whether the exclusionary rule was a fundamental constitutional command or whether it was simply an administrative rule established by the Court for the federal court system.

Wolf v Colorado,[122] a 1949 decision of the Court, dealt with that very important theoretical question. In reality the Court addressed itself to two questions: (1) whether the Fourth Amendment's provisions were made applicable to the states through the Fourteenth Amendment, and (2) whether evidence illegally seized by state officers was admissible in a state court. Wolf, a doctor, had been convicted as an abortionist on the basis of what the Court held to be illegally seized evidence (police had entered his office without a warrant and seized his records, which were used to convict Wolf at the trial). Justice Frankfurter, writing for the Court, sustained the conviction because the *Weeks* exclusionary rule was adminstrative in character and was not a constitutional command essential to the maintenance of the concept of ordered liberty.

Reaffirming the approach used by the Court in *Palko* and, more recently, in *Adamson,* Frankfurter stated that the security of one's privacy "is basic to a free society" and therefore implicit in the concept of ordered liberty. As such, the Fourth Amendment provision against unreasonable searches and seizures is enforceable against the states through the Due Process Clause.[123]

> Due Process exacts from the states for the lowliest and the most outcast all that is implicit in the concept of ordered liberty. Due Process thus conveys neither formal nor narrow requirements. It is the compendious expression for all those rights which the courts must enforce because they are basic to our free society.... Representing as it does a living principle, due process is not confined within a permanent catalogue of what may at a given time be deemed the limits or the essentials of fundamental rights. To rely on a tidy formula for the easy determination of what is a fundamental right,...may satisfy a longing for certainty but ignores the movements of a free society. It belittles the scale of the conception of due process.[124]

Justice Black concurred in the judgment of the Court. He would have been for reversal, Black argued, and would have joined his colleagues Douglas, Murphy, and Rutledge in dissent but for one thing: "the Fourth Amendment, of itself, did not bar the use of evidence so unlawfully obtained." Instead, he agreed "with what appears to be a plain implication of the court's opinion that the federal exclusionary rule is not a command of the Fourth Amendment but is a judicially created rule of evidence which Congress might negate."[125]

A few years later, however, in the case of *Rochin v California,*[126] the Court began to deal with certain exceptions to the *Wolf* ruling. Three deputy sheriffs went to Rochin's house because they suspected he was involved in the illegal selling of narcotics. They entered the house, forced open his bedroom door, and found him sitting on the bed. Rochin immediately swallowed two capsules that were on the night table. The police quickly took him to a local hospital where, much against Rochin's will, his stomach was pumped. He vomited up the two capsules which were later found to contain morphine. The capsules were admitted into evidence against Rochin and he was convicted in the California court of violating a state law forbidding the possession of morphine. Justice Frankfurter, who wrote the *Wolf* opinion, overturned the conviction in *Rochin,* arguing that such police conduct was so abusive of individual privacy as to shock the conscience. As such, the introduction of such illegally seized evidence violated due process of law. The conviction "offended those canons of decency and fairness which express the notions of justice of English-speaking peoples...so rooted in the traditions and conscience of our people as to be ranked as fundamental."[127]

> In each case 'due process of law' requires an evaluation based on disinterested inquiry pursued in the spirit of science on a balanced order of facts exactly and fairly stated, on the detached consideration of conflicting claims, on a judgment not ad hoc and episodic but duly mindful of reconciling the needs both of continuity and of change in a progressive society. We are compelled to conclude that the proceedings by which this conviction was obtained do more than offend some fastitious squeamishness or private sentimentalism about combatting crime too energetically. This is conduct that shocks the conscience.... They are methods too close to the rack and the screw to permit of constitutional differentiation.[128]

Justice Black acidly responded to the remarks of the former Harvard Law School professor in a biting concurring opinion. He concurred, not because his conscience was shocked, but because, said Black, the Fifth Amendment prohibited a person from being compelled against his will to incriminate himself. "I think a person is compelled to be a witness against himself not only when he is compelled to testify, but also when, as here, incriminating evidence is forcibly taken from him by a contrivance of modern science."[129] What Frankfurter holds, said Black critically, "is that the due process clause empowers this Court to nullify any state law if its application 'shocks the conscience,' 'offends a sense of justice,' or runs counter to the 'decencies of civilized conduct.'[130]

> If the Due Process clause does vest this court with such unlimited power to invalidate laws, I am still in doubt as to why we should consider only the notions of English-speaking peoples to determine what are immutable and fundamental principles of justice....Some constitutional provisions are stated in absolute and unqualified language, others...do require courts to choose between competing policies (the Fourth Amendment necessitates a judicial decision as to what is an 'unreasonable' search and seizure). There is, however, no express constitutional language granting judicial power to invalidate every state law of every kind deemed 'unreasonable' or contrary to the Court's notion of civilized decencies.[131]

Two years after the constitutional debate in *Rochin*, the Court was again faced with a constitutional case that dealt with an illegal search which led to a conviction in a state criminal proceeding: *Irvine v California.*[132] Petitioner Irvine was convicted of gambling offenses in part as a result of illegal searches and seizures of his apartment (police had made a key to his apartment, entered it a few times to drill holes and plant listening devices, and then move them around so that the voices could be clearly picked up on the devices). Speaking for the Court, Justice Robert H. Jackson admitted that such actions were trespass acts, and probably a burglary but that they did not constitute a situation that so shocked the conscience as to invalidate the conviction. "The police action," Jackson admitted, "was incredible if it were not admitted. Few police measures have come to our attention that more flagrantly, deliberately, and persistently violated the fundamental principle declared by the Fourth Amendment." But, he concluded, 'the Court's holding in *Wolf* would seem to control here."[133] *Rochin,* Jackson claimed, did not apply in the case because, "however obnoxious the facts before us, they do not involve coercion, violence, or brutality to the person, but rather a trespass to property, plus eavesdropping."[134] The Court must not upset a "justifiable conviction of this common gambler."

Justice Black, joined by his colleague Douglas, dissented. He argued, as he did in *Rochin,* that Irvine's Fifth Amendment right against compulsory self-incrimination, applicable to the states by being incorporated into the Due Process Clause of the Fourteenth Amendment, prohibited the introduction of the illegally seized information.

Perhaps, ironically, more indignant than Hugo Black was Felix Frankfurter, who (as vehemently as he could) dissented from the opinion of the Court majority. He claimed that his opinions in *Wolf* and in *Rochin* had been misunderstood by Jackson. The conviction, Frankfurter asserted, offended the sense of fundamental fairness. "We have here a more offensive and powerful control over Irvine's life than a single, limited physical trespass (as in Rochin's case)."[135] Black's substantive silence in this case, with respect to the standards employed by the Court majority in *Palko, Wolf,* and *Rochin,* could well be understood. Frankfurter's plaint pleas that Jackson had "misunderstood" and "misapplied" the "comprehending principle" of *Wolf* and *Rochin* echoed precisely the basic complaint of Black's about the dangers present when judges used such "evanescent standards." Justice Black's silence was thunderous.

Breithaupt v Abram,[136] decided in 1957, was the last of

the major "shock the conscience" cases that the Court heard prior to its 1961 decision in *Mapp v Ohio.* Breithaupt was a truck driver who was involved in a car accident in which three persons had been killed. An empty whiskey bottle was found in the cabin of his truck and, while he was unconscious, blood samples were taken from him by a competent medical technician. The blood sample was found to contain a high degree of alcohol content and that evidence was introduced at a trial in which he was found guilty of involuntary manslaughter. He appealed his conviction to the Supreme Court; but the Court, in an opinion written by Justice Tom C. Clark, did not reverse. The Court noted that the blood test, unlike the pumping of a person's stomach, was a fairly routine operation. "Taking the blood by a skilled technician is not conduct that shocks the conscience," Clark concluded. "Neither does it offend a sense of justice."[137]

Black joined in dissents written by Chief Justice Earl Warren and Justice Douglas. Warren argued that "Due Process means at least that law-enforcement officers in their efforts to obtain evidence from persons suspected of crime must stop short of bruising the body, breaking skin, puncturing tissue, or extracting body fluids whether they contemplate doing it by force or by stealth."[138] Douglas dissented, saying in part that "if decencies of a civilized state are the test (of reasonableness of the search), it is repulsive to me for the police to insert needles into an unconscious person in order to get evidence necessary to convict him, whether they find the person unconscious, give him a pill which puts him to sleep, or use force to subdue him."[139]

In these cases, decided between *Wolf* in 1949 and *Mapp* in 1961, the Court was truly operating in the subjective "shock the conscience" world of Felix Frankfurter. Evidence illegally seized by police officers could be introduced at the trial only if the admittedly illegal conduct of the law enforcement officers (admitted by the judges to be contrary to the spirit of the Fourth Amendment's protection), was so grossly offensive so as to shock the judges into voiding the convictions that resulted. Black, rejecting the use of that open-ended standard, instead employed the Fifth Amendment protection against compelled self-incrimination in order to determine whether the evidence seized violated due process of law. In the *Mapp* case, based on a reexamination of the constitutional issue, Black joined the two constitutional protections, the Fourth and the Fifth, to give him an alternative to the exclusionary rule standard he refused to use in *Wolf.*

Mapp v Ohio[140] was a decision of the Court born out of the frustration and disappointment of the Justices with the *Wolf* judgment and the ensuing "shock the conscience" judgments. Dolly Mapp's home was searched by police in Cleveland, Ohio, in 1957, who were looking for incriminating evidence linking her with a local numbers racket. In addition, they found obscene literature and photographs, which they seized. Acquitted of the policy numbers offense, Mapp was indicted for possession of the obscene materials which carried a criminal penalty of up to seven years imprisonment and up to a $2000 fine. Found guilty of that charge she was sentenced to an indeterminate term. She appealed her conviction to the Supreme Court and, in an opinion written by Justice Clark, the Court reversed. All evidence obtained by an illegal search and seizure, said the Court, is inadmissible in a state criminal trial. "It makes good sense to hold that the exclusionary rule is an essential part of the Fourteenth Amendment's Due Process Clause. There is no war between the Constitution and common sense."[141]

Black wrote a short opinion concurring in the judgment of the Court. Given his literalist reading of the Constitution, he was "still not persuaded that the Fourth Amendment standing alone would be enough to bar the introduction into evidence against an accused of papers and effects from him in violation of its commands."[142] Reflection on the problem, however, and on the past opinions of the court, led Black to conclude "that when the Fourth Amendment's ban against unreasonable searches and seizures is considered together with the Fifth Amendment's ban against self-incrimination, a constitutional basis emerges which not only justifies but actually requires the exclusionary rule."[143] (Justices Frankfurter, Whittaker, and Harlan dissented. "This Court," complained Harlan, has "simply 'reached out' to overrule *Wolf.*" In so overruling the Court, "in my opinion, has forgotten the sense of judicial restraint which, with due regard for stare decisis, is one element that should enter into deciding whether a past decision of this Court should be overruled.")[144]

Although *Mapp* resolved one troublesome question that had plagued the Court, it created new and difficult ones that are endemic to the nature of cases coming up to the Court dealing with searches and seizures. First, with *Mapp* as law of the land, thousands of state court cases would now be appealed to the Supreme Court dealing with the questions of search and seizures, probable cause, etc. And second, perhaps most important, *Mapp* left no standards—did not develop any standards—by which state searches and seizures could be evaluated. In Federal cases, there were Congressional statutes establishing parameters for federal officers' activities in law enforcement as well as judicial rulings by the Supreme Court as supervisory agency of the Federal judicial system. One basic question, in light of this "federal" problem, was whether the Court—as it did with respect to the "exclusionary rule" in *Mapp*—would distinguish between these federal statutory and supervisory restraints and guidelines and those standards, certainly much less precise, in the Fourth Amendment of the Constitution in deciding states cases.

As will be seen, the search and seizure area is perhaps the

most controversial and complex of the procedural due process provisions in the Bill of Rights. The cases called for judgmental decisions by the judges regarding issues such as "stop and frisk" police action, when is there "probable cause" for issuance of a search warrant, etc. Different justices have differed in these search and seizure cases because their estimate of "probability" "hot pursuit," facts in the affidavit for search warrant, etc. differed. "The use of the word 'unreasonable' in this Amendment means," Black wrote, "of course that not all searches and seizures are prohibited. Only those which are unreasonable are unlawful. There may be much difference of opinion about whether a particular search or seizure is unreasonable and therefore forbidden by this Amendment. But if it is unreasonable, it is absolutely forbidden."[145] In an attempt to clarify Justice Black's perception of the complexities of the Fourth Amendment's meaning, there will be an examination of a few of the more controversial areas. Searches incident to a lawful arrest, stop and frisk case, hot pursuit, probable cause conditions for issuance of a search warrant, and wiretapping/eavesdropping.

The Court had, prior to the 1969 case of *Chimel v California*, decided that certain situations allowed police to search without a search warrant, for example, moving vehicles,[146] "stop and frisk," and hot pursuit situations (both described below in the cases of *Terry, Sibron,* and *Warden v Hayden*). Regarding searches incident to a lawful arrest, the Court had established standards for evaluating such police activities: the Harris-Rabinowitz Rule. The cases, decided in 1948 and 1950,[147] allowed, as reasonable searches and seizures, police to comb the household of those they arrested. In *Chimel,*[148] the Court reexamined the "Rule" and overturned it. The search of an entire three bedroom house, a warrantless search, Justice Stewart announced for the Court was an unreasonable act. Police, making an arrest, he said, could legitimately search the area under the control of the person arrested. The search incident to a lawful arrest was not so much to find evidence but basically for police protection in case the person was armed or was within reaching distance of a dangerous weapon. The Court said that this type of search was done to prevent injury and/or escape; any other type of search needed a warrant. Justice White wrote a stinging dissent, criticizing the Court majority for hampering the actions of law enforcement officers. Justice Black, the old county prosecutor from Alabama, joined in the White dissent.

Just about the time the Court was limiting the police search incident to an arrest, it examined another controversial police practice: the difficult and troublesome issue of police on-the-street *stops* of suspicious persons. The question for the Court was whether or not this action of the police was a reasonable search and seizure and, if reasonable at all, when did it become unreasonable. The leading case was *Terry v Ohio,*[149] in which the Court, in an opinion written by Chief Justice Warren (Black joined in the judgment), found limited constitutional authority for the practice. "Where a police officer observes unusual conduct which leads him *reasonably* to conclude *in light of his experience* that criminal activity *may* be afoot and that the persons with whom he is dealing *may* be armed and presently dangerous; where in the course of investigating this behavior he identifies himself as a policeman and makes *reasonable* inquiries; and where nothing in the initial stages of the encounter serves to dispel his *reasonable* fear for his own or others' safety, he is entitled for the protection of himself and others in the area to conduct a carefully limited search of the outer clothing of such persons in an attempt to discover weapons which might be used to assault him."[150] The Fourth Amendment, he concluded for the Court, must be viewed as governing all intrusions upon personal security, "and to make the scope of the particular intrusion, in the light of all these exigencies of the case, a central element in the analysis of reasonableness." (my italics)

What Warren was saying was this: in all cases coming to the Court dealing with stop-and-frisk situations, the judges had to examine very carefully all the facts of the case–the experience of the policeman, the scope of the search, the conditions surrounding the initial observation–in order to determine whether the search was reasonable. As in *Chimel,* the search was primarily to protect the police officer and innocent bystanders. Of course, this meant that nine judges would have to read the facts and, in the light of their own past experiences, training, etc., come up with the determination. That this was not easy was seen in a companion case announced the same day in which Justice Black disagreed with the evaluation of the Court majority: *Sibron v New York.*[151] In *Sibron,* a policeman was monitoring the actions of Sibron, a known narcotics pusher in New York City, and, after a number of hours in a restaurant, approached the defendant. After some words, the policeman put his hands inside Sibron's pocket and found a quantity of narcotics. This led to his arrest and conviction for the possession of narcotics in the New York courts. Sibron appealed, arguing that there was no probable cause for the detective to search him; neither was there a search warrant produced prior to the search. The Court majority held that that search was an unreasonable stop and frisk. Other than the reputation of Sibron, there was no reasonable probable cause to search him. Justice Black dissented. He argued that, as soon as Sibron put his hand in his pocket, the police officer, for his own safety, had the right to enter the inner clothing. Looking at the facts that were in the record, he felt that it was a justifiable search. "We should not overturn state court findings of the facts of reasonableness and probable cause," Black said, "unless in the most extravagant and egregious errors. It seems fantastic to me even to suggest that this is such a case."[152] (This was essentially a basic point he was to make in most of these cases: if judges below have examined the facts and found reasonable grounds for permitting the search consistent with the Fourth Amendment, the Court should not burden itself needlessly by repeating this examination.)

What about a situation where the police, in "hot pursuit" of a suspect, chase him into a house. Can they search the premises and seize material found in it for use in the subsequent trial? The police, said Justice Brennan in *Warden v Hayden,*[153] may enter the premises without a warrant when they are in hot pursuit of a suspected criminal. In *Hayden,* police were informed that an armed robbery had taken place and that the suspect had entered the house five minutes before they reached it. The Court reasoned that delay in such circumstances (to get the warrant) would endanger the lives of the police and others; the "exigent circumstances" justified entry without notice and warrant. Inside the house, Brennan concluded, the police were justified in looking wherever the suspect may have been hiding and also (before his capture) for hidden weapons. Black joined in the opinion of the Court: he and the Court majority noted the emergency conditions that existed and concluded that, under these conditions, the search and seizure without a warrant was a reasonable one.

Still another quite controversial area of constitutional litigation concerns the second part of the Fourth Amendment statement that search warrants shall be issued upon showing of "probable cause." The Justices had to examine the common situation of a police request for a search warrant based on information received from police informants. In a series of cases handed down in the latter part of the 1960s, Justice Black disagreed vehemently with the standards established by the Court majority for determining whether probable cause existed for the granting of the warrant by a magistrate. The disagreement between Black and the Court majority focused on the amount of information necessary to convince the magistrate to issue the warrant. The Court, in *Aguilar,*[154] *McCray,*[155] and *Spinelli,*[156] had developed and elaborated upon a "two-pronged test" with respect to the validity of the informer's information and whether it was sufficient "probable cause" to issue the warrant. The magistrate had to be given information that showed the reliability of the informer by noting his past record, and the magistrate had to examine the underlying circumstances supporting the tip. Justice Black (along with Justice Clark) dissented in these cases because he felt the standards established by the majority were too restrictive.

In effect, Black argued, these standards amounted to a "little trial" before the magistrate. The Fourth Amendment, he pointed out, called for a search warrant to be issued upon probable cause; the standard used by the majority demanded almost prima facia evidence for the warrant rather than mere probability that persons or things were to be found in a certain place. Dissenting in *Spinelli,* he said that "Aguilar was bad enough....But the Court today expands Aguilar to almost unbelievable proportions. Nothing in our Constitution requires that the facts be established with that degree of certainty and with such elaborate specificity before a policeman can be authorized by a disinterested magistrate to conduct a carefully limited search."[157]

> The existence of probable cause is a factual matter that calls for a determination of factual questions....We must inevitably accept most of the fact findings of the...courts, particularly when, as here, both the trial and appellate courts have decided the facts the same way....It seems to me that this Court would best serve itself and the administration of justice by accepting the judgment of the two courts below; after all, they too are lawyers and judges, and much closer to the practical everyday affairs of life than we are.[158]

Justice Black also dissented in a case decided just months before his death.[159] A sheriff, acting on a tip, received a warrant from a magistrate. A police officer in another county in Wyoming heard the police broadcast describing the suspects and the car they were driving and, stopping the suspects, made a warrantless search of the car and arrest of the suspects. Based on materials seized by the officer, they were convicted. The Supreme Court, in an opinion written by Justice Harlan (who wrote the *Spinelli* opinion), decided that the petitioners' rights had indeed been violated due to the paucity of the informant's tip and the ensuing unreasonable search, seizure, and arrest.

Justice Black, joined by the new Chief Justice Warren Earl Burger, vehemently dissented. "With all respect to my Brethren," he began, "who agree to the judgment and opinion of the Court, I am constrained to say that I believe the decision here is a gross and wholly indefensible miscarriage of justice. For this reason it may well be classified as one of those calculated to make many good people believe our Court actually enjoys frustrating justice by unnecessarily turning professional criminals loose to prey upon society with impunity." There was certainly probable cause to arrest the man, said Black. The tip received by the sheriff was "persuasive," and of course the policeman making the stop and arrest had enough information from the sheriff to have probable cause to take the action. "There is not even a suspicion here," Black observed in concluding his criticism of the Court, "that this hardened criminal is innocent and I would let him stay in confinement and serve his sentence."[160]

If these situations arising before the Court relating to the meaning of the Fourth Amendment protection were not controversial enough, there was still the matter of wiretapping that led to violent dissents on the Court. Was wiretapping by the government limited by the parameters (however nebulous they might be) of the Fourth Amendment? In *Olmstead v United States* and *Goldman v US,*[161] the Court, in 1928 and 1942 respectively, stated and reaffirmed the fact that words "search and seizure" in that Amendment did apply only to tangible property and not to hearing and sight. In short, the Court's judgment was that wiretapping, unless Congress passed legislation to deal with that form of eavesdropping, was not the type of search and seizure the Fourth Amendment sought to prohibit if found to be unreasonable.[162]

However, in *Berger v New York,*[163] a 1967 opinion of the Court, conversations now fell under the protection of the Fourth Amendment. The Court, in *Berger,* invalidated a New York State statute authorizing official electronic eavesdropping ("bugging") pursuant to a Court order. Eavesdropping information had been used to convict Berger of conspiracy to bribe the Chairman of the New York State Liquor Authority. Justice Clark for the Court ruled that the New York statute was "too broad in its sweep, resulting in a trespassory intrusion into a constitutionally protected area," and therefore violative of the Constitution. Eavesdropping had to meet the same requirements that other searches and seizures faced: reasonableness, probable cause for a warrant, and a showing of "exigent circumstances" if no warrant was used.

Justice Black dissented. Only because the judges were hostile to eavesdropping and wiretapping, calling it an "ignoble and dirty business," was the statute struck down. But "neither these nor any other grounds that I can think of are sufficient in my judgment to justify a holding that the use of evidence secured by eavesdropping is barred by the Constitution." While eavesdropping "is not ranked as one of the most learned or polite professions, nor would the eavesdropper be selected by many people as the most desirable and attractive associate,"these are not sufficient grounds for denying the value of such operations and operatives in law enforcement work. "In time of a crime problem that threatens the peace, order, and tranquility of the people," concluded Black, "legislators and police agents, unless barred by an absolute prohibition, should be left free to pass laws about crime, rather than have judges interfere."[165]

The following year the Court, in *Katz v United States,*[166] with Black again dissenting, spelled out in detail the guidelines for this type of search and seizure situation. Katz had been convicted for using the telephone to transmit wagering information across state lines. He used a public telephone which was tapped by FBI agents. Justice Stewart wrote that the tap constituted a search and seizure and, in order for it to pass constitutional muster, it had to meet the standards of the Fourth Amendment. The Fourth Amendment, he said, protects people, not places and "What a person knowingly exposes to the public, even in his own home and office, is not the subject of the Fourth Amendment protection."[167] Justice Black dissented. The essence of his dissent will be examined in the following section for, in both *Berger* and in *Katz*, the Court had made a "major change in constitutional philosophy."[168]

Implicitly in *Berger* and openly in *Katz,* the Supreme Court extended the coverage and protection of the Fourth Amendment beyond "property" protections, that is, protection of tangible objects such as papers, effects, houses, to cover the individual's right of "privacy" from governmental intrusion. Under the *Olmstead* standard, search and seizure protections were violated if there was an unreasonable *physical trespass* upon the person's private tangible property. *Katz* repudiated this standard and introduced instead the notion that a person is protected against unreasonable searches and seizures which intrude upon that which the person reasonably expects to be private. In short, the decision eliminated the importance of a liberal, physical intrusion upon the physical property. The Fourth Amendment, the Court was now saying, protects people, not places.

Justice Black, the literalist judge, absolutely refused to accept this judicial tampering with the words and, more important, the intent of the founders of the Republic. He argued, in *Berger* and in *Katz,* that the men who wrote the Constitution and the Bill of Rights were aware of eavesdropping and that the Fourth Amendment, while it was open to judicial interpretation, was not to be so changed as to be amended by lifetime appointed judges. "I do not overlook the fact," he wrote in *Berger* "that the Court at present is reading the Amendment as expressly and unqualifiedly barring invasions of 'privacy' rather than merely forbidding 'unreasonable searches and seizures.'"[169] The language of the Fourth Amendment specifically refers to searches and seizures, "not to a broad undefined right to 'privacy' in general."

> To attempt to transform the meaning of the Amendment, as the Court does here, is to play sleight-of-hand tricks with it. It is impossible for me to think that the wise framers of the Fourth Amendment would ever have dreamed about drafting an Amendment to protect the 'right of privacy.'...Use of privacy as a keyword simply gives this Court a useful new tool as I see it, both to usurp the policy-making power of the Congress and to hold more state and federal laws unconstitutional when the Court entertains a sufficient hostility to them....I do not believe it is our duty to go further than the Framers did on the theory that the judges are charged with the responsibility for keeping the Constitution 'up to date.'[170]

His dissent in *Katz* echoed his remarks in *Berger.* Judges did not have the right to amend the Constitution and this was precisely what they had done in these cases. His objection was twofold: (1) the words of the Amendment cannot bear the meaning given them by the majority, (2) "I do not believe that it is the proper role of the Court to rewrite the Amendment in order to bring it in harmony with the times and thus reach a result that many people believe to be desirable."[171]

> Since I see no way in which the Fourth Amendment can be construed to apply to eavesdropping, that closes the matter for me. In interpreting the Bill of Rights I willingly go as far as a liberal construction of the language takes me, but I simply cannot in good conscience give a meaning to words which they have never before been thought to have and which they certainly do not have in common ordinary usage.[172]

Black could absolutely not accept the fact that conversations were tangible objects (which is solely what the Fourth Amendment referred to historically): conversations, words, "can neither be searched nor seized."[173] The Fourth Amendment, he reiterated, refers to tangible items but also to things "already in existence so it can be described" in order for a search warrant to be issued. And while Black complimented Stewart and the Court for their "good efforts,"[174] *he* could not, in good conscience, as a judge, amend the Bill of Rights.

In these various constitutional controversies that came to the Court dealing with the Fourth Amendment's meaning one can clearly understand why Justice Black strongly argued against the Frankfurter philosophy. When free to roam, without clearly defined prohibitions (and this, of course, was the case with the Fourth Amendment), judges will differ with each other and will, because power unleashed had a way of corrupting judges, inevitably lead to judicial amending of the basic law as in *Berger* and in *Katz.*

Recapitulation

The Frankfurter/Harlan view of due process of law was one that placed a tremendous burden on the shoulders of the judges. They had to be extremely qualified men in order to function fairly and consistently, for their view called for men who were dispassionate, scholarly, objective, scientific, and omniscient. Given these qualities, Frankfurter and Harlan argued, judges could, starting with the words "liberty" and "due process of law," (1) define them based on what accorded with America's traditions of fairness and justice and decency, and (2) employ the definition in a particular case or controversy that called for judicial resolution. The key, then, to this Frankfurterian process was the "disinterested inquiry" by the scientific judge. Eschewing permanent cataloging of the meaning of due process, Frankfurter and Harlan instead spoke of due process as a "living principle" not restricted by the confinements of the specific provisions of the Bill of Rights.

This Frankfurterian philosophy, said Black in one of his rare moods of anger, was simply "judicial mutilation" of the Constitution. To tell a judge to reach back into the great bulk of jurisprudence produced by English-speaking peoples "And somehow to make the law"[175] out of it was simply too great a task for any human being—and judges were human beings; what is more, the great mass of jurisprudence was simply not a clear enough guide for the judges. Consequently, the judges could "roam at will" under the Frankfurterian theory in the pursuit of standards of "civilized decency" or "fundamental fairness," or simply resort to their shocked "conscience." This approach would simply not do for Black because it gave a judge too much of an opportunity "to indulge his own subjective preferences instead of trying to read the language of the Constitution."[176]

Black's understanding of Due Process lay in the "plain words" of the Constitution and the Bill of Rights. If the judges stuck to the original intent of the Framers and the meaning of the words in the Bill of Rights, there would be no difficulty in resolving constitutional controversies dealing with governmental attempts to bridge the procedural "fences against wrongs" in that document. "In Black's view," wrote a commentator of the Court, "the framers of the Constitution made the decision to protect individuals from governmental repression, so a judge should not feel timid or self-conscious about doing so."[177] In such a situation, where the liberties of the citizens are threatened, the "plain language of the Constitution" is an infinitely far better source of protection than the "sense of fairness of the judges."[178]

Black's intense commitment to his conception of due process—that is, that the Bill of Rights procedural guarantees were the parameters of due process of law—was a consequence of his concern for the fate of liberty if left to the feelings of judges. Liberty, he was saying in these procedural due process cases, was too precious to be left to the determination of judges. Judges come in different shapes, sizes, and characters. Some are wise, decent, dispassionate (and Black thought this of his friends Frankfurter and Harlan) but other judges might not have been so detached and scholarly. As Black himself said, in 1968, he knew a Court far different than [the justices that comprised] the liberal Warren Court (with its substantive commitment to "fairness" and "equality") of the 1960s. And so, with this concern in mind, his approach to procedural due process was a literalist one. Black loved and cherished liberty and freedom too much to leave it in the hands of nine men roaming at will in search of some evanescent, Natural Law standards of justice and due process!

5

The Foundation of Democracy: First Amendment Freedoms

"Congress shall make no law respecting an establishment of religion, or prohibiting the free exercise thereof; or abridging the freedom of speech, or of the press, or the right of the people peacefully to assemble, and to petition the Government for a redress of grievances." So reads the First Amendment to the United States Constitution; it is, seemingly, an authoritative command that the governors pass no laws that would interfere with the people's right to acquire information and to express themselves on public and private issues. The Amendment is not phrased in mild, advisory language–it is a mandate that government *not act* in certain areas of human activity. For more than a century after these words were adopted by the people, the Supreme Court was "singularly free from any necessity" of considering the practical meaning of this noble constitutional ideal.[1] (The very first treason case to come before the Supreme Court, *Cramer v United States*, 135 *US* 1 (1945), occasioned Justice Jackson to comment: "We have managed to do without treason prosecutions to a degree that probably would be impossible except while a people was singularly confident of external security and internal stability.")

The ideals contained in the First Amendment did finally come under judicial observation and subsequent interpretation, however, because government *did* pass laws, that is, criminal legislation, that did prohibit certain types of expression and which punished those persons who violated these laws by speaking, printing, or assembling in a manner not allowed by the legislation. "The constitutional ideal of free speech had to be made a reality in constitutional practice," wrote C. Herman Pritchett, "and this was not easy."[2] Twenty years before Hugo Black took his seat on the Supreme Court that tribunal began the difficult task of resolving these constitutional cases and controversies that dealt with the basic freedoms of speech and press and assembly. In 1919 the Supreme Court faced the dilemma for the first time because Congress had passed criminal legislation during the World War–the Espionage Act of 1917 and the Sedition Act of 1918. (The Acts made it a crime for people to make or print false statements or to interfere with the war effort. The legislation, essentially, was directed at speech critical of the national war effort and national policies reflecting that war commitment.) The justification for these laws proscribing certain types of speech was that the public order and safety had to be preserved. And the essential question, really, for the Court was whether or not, consistent with the First Amendment's mandate, the laws were constitutional.

This intense, thorny question was complicated still more by the fact that the Supreme Court, in a 1925 case, incorporated the First Amendment freedoms into the Due Process Clause of the Fourteenth Amendment (See *Table Two*). "For present purposes," wrote Mr. Justice Sanford for the Court, "we may and do assume that freedom of speech and of the press–which are protected by the First Amendment from abridgment by Congress–are among the fundamental rights and 'liberties' protected by the Due Process Clause of the Fourteenth Amendment from impairment by the states."[3]* This selective incorporation of the First

---

**Palko v Connecticut*, decided twelve years after *Gitlow*, stated that the First Amendment was the "matrix" of the American system of "ordered liberty."

Amendment effectively broadened the scope of possible litigation dealing with the basic question and, from 1925 on, the Supreme Court had to examine the many state laws as well as the relatively few national criminal laws that punished certain types of speech and assembly and press and that were alleged to come into conflict with the First Amendment protection. Inherent, of course, in this constitutional problem for the Court was the fact that there simply were no judicially devised guidelines for such litigation. Until the World War One legislation by Congress there had been no debates in the Court on the meaning of the First Amendment! The Alien and Sedition Acts of 1798 had been effectively repealed by the Jefferson Administration and the Congress so that no litigation challenging their validity ever came to the Supreme Court. After the first early crisis of 1798 had been averted, "debates on the limits and the guarantees of the Amendment passed into a state of quiescence."[4]

TABLE TWO

"Selective Incorporation" of the Guarantees of the First Amendment into the Due Process Clause of the Fourteenth Amendment

Particular Clause	*Name of Case*	*Date*
Freedom of Speech	*Gitlow v New York*	1925
Freedom of Press	*Near v Minnesota*	1931
Right of Assembly	*DeJonge v Oregon*	1937
Freedom of Religion	*Cantwell v Connecticut*	1940
Establishment of Religion	*Everson v Board of Education*	1947
Right of Association	*Shelton v Tucker*	1960

This extended quiescent period ended, however, with the World War One free speech cases.[5] Standards were examined and, in a 1919 opinion written by Justice Oliver Wendell Holmes, Jr., *Schenck v United States,* the Court announced the first of four major statements on the meaning and the dimensions of the First Amendment protections. This was the "clear and present danger" standard which mapped out the following contours and standards for the First Amendment and for the Court justices to follow:

> The question in every case is whether the words used are used in such circumstances and are of such a nature as to create a clear and present danger that they will bring about the substantive evils that Congress has a right to prevent. It is a question of proximity and degree.[6]

Using this standard meant that the justices of the Supreme Court had to exercise very good judgment in determining whether or not the utterance was or would be immediately injurious to the public safety and order; that is, whether there "was reasonable ground to believe that the danger apprehended is imminent."[7] As could be expected, Justice Black was highly critical of this and all other judicially devised standards that made the constitutionality of laws rest on the justice's judgment, based on his personal beliefs, of the situation and his determination of the proximity and degree of the danger facing the nation by such speech, etc. If, in the estimate of the justices, there were reasonable grounds to suppose that particular speech posed a *clear* danger to the safety of the state, then the limitation on that speech was a legitimate one. As Holmes indicated, these constitutional issues in the free speech area were matters of proximity and degree for judges to resolve by careful dispassionate inquiry. The standard was simply a very flexible one, one given form and shape by the good (or bad) judgment of the nine men sitting on the Supreme Court at the time. As Chief Justice Vinson noted (in 1949) in *American Communications Association, CIO v Douds* (339 *US* 382) "The important question that came to this Court immediately after the First War was not whether, but how far, the First Amendment permits the suppression of speech which advocates conduct inimical to the public welfare."

A second standard developed by the Court was the "bad tendency"/"legislative reasonableness" test. By definition, this standard was narrower than "clear and present danger" because judges could legitimize legislation that restricted expression of ideas if and when, in the eyes of the judges, these ideas had a *tendency* to produce evil results and threaten the security and safety of the public order. Deferring to the wisdom of the legislators in determining what types of expression could possibly tend to endanger the security of the community. Justice Sanford wrote:

> It cannot be said that the state is acting arbitrarily or unreasonably when in the exercise of its judgment as to the measures necessary to protect the public peace and safety, it seeks to extinguish the spark *without waiting until it has kindled the flame or blazed into a conflagration.* It cannot reasonably be required to defer the adoption of measures for its own peace and safety *until the revolutionary utterances lead to actual disturbances of the public peace or imminent and immediate danger of its destruction*; but it may, in the exercise of its judgment, suppress the threatened danger *in its incipiency.*[8]

In sum, this second standard would allow legislative acts to stand if the justices were of the opinion that there was a dangerous situation that had to be nipped in the bud. To wait for the danger to be imminent or immediate (the "clear and present danger" measurement) was to wait too long; speech that tended to endanger the public safety had to be curtailed. And such curtailment was not inconsistent with the First Amendment.

Both the "clear and present danger" and the "bad tendency/legislative reasonableness" standards had been developed prior to Hugo Black's arrival on the Court. Two standards were discussed by Black and other new arrivals (Vinson, Frankfurter, and Harlan) after 1937; these were the "ad hoc balancing" standard of Vinson, et al. and the Black "absolutist" interpretation of the Bill of Rights.

The "Ad Hoc Balancing" Standard

This judicially devised guideline, outlined by Chief Justice Vinson in the *Douds* case, and further developed by Justices Frankfurter and Harlan in the 1950s and 1960s, essentially was a competition between the individual's rights under the First Amendment with the general powers of government to legislate for the general good. If the former's rights were outweighed by the latter, they must be subordinated to the government's competing interest in suppressing them.

> When particular conduct is regulated in the interest of public order, and the regulation results in an indirect, conditional, partial abridgment of speech, the duty of the courts is to determine which of these two conflicting interests demands the greater protection under the particular circumstances presented....In essence the problem is one of weighing the probable effects of the statute upon the free exercise of the right of speech and assembly against the congressional determination that (such action) are evils of conduct that (have to be proscribed by the government).[9]

The proponents of this standard, refusing to elevate the First Amendment guarantees to a "preferred status,"[10] argued that, after examining the evil the statute was addressed to and after weighing the merits of both sides, the Court could come up with an objective and fair judgment. "Our function," said Justice Harlan in a 1959 opinion, "is purely one of constitutional adjudication in the particular case and upon the particular record before us, and not to pass judgment upon the general wisdom or efficacy of the activities of this (House Un-American Activities) Committee in a vexing and complicated field....Where First Amendment rights are asserted to bar governmental interrogation, resolution of the issue always involves a balancing by the Courts of the competing private and public interests at stake in the particular circumstances shown."[11]

Justice Black's "Absolutist" Position

Hugo Black thoroughly rejected all three of these judicially devised standards; they were all based on the premise that there were no absolute mandates, prohibitions in the Constitution and that all constitutional questions were questions of reasonableness, proximity, degree, and balancing of public against private interests.[12] But for Justice Black there *were* absolutes in the Constitution, "declared to be beyond the reach of this government," and the First Amendment was the primary example of such firm mandates:

> My view is, without deviation, without exception, without any ifs, buts, or whereases that freedom of speech means that government shall not do anything to people, either for their views they have or the views they express or the words they speak or write.[13]

In Black's very last written opinion on the Court, *New York Times v United States,* he bitterly assailed the Nixon Administration's attempt to avoid the constitutional mandate in the First Amendment: "The First Amendment was offered to *curtail* and *restrict* (Black's emphasis) the general powers granted to the Executive, Legislative and Judicial branches."

The right to speak and write freely was, for Justice Black, the foundation upon which democracy rested, "the nation's true security,"[14] the "most precious privilege of citizens vested with power to select public policies and public officials,"[15] the "very foundation of constitutional government."[16] And courts, especially the Supreme Court, must never allow these First Amendment guarantees to be diluted one iota by governmental actions. For the courts, especially the Supreme Court, must *apply the law,* most especially the Fundamental Constitutional Law, not make it.

Creating "tests," standards of "reasonableness," in order to handle constitutional controversies dealing with alleged infringement of First Amendment freedoms were examples of judges making law rather than applying the law of the Constitution as written. The most dangerous of these standards of reasonableness was the so-called "Ad Hoc Balancing" test of Vinson, Frankfurter, and Harlan. It was dangerous because it ignored the "plain words" of the Constitution and because it had an "unlimited breadth" given to it by judges doing the balancing that was highly dangerous to the maintenance of these "paramount protections."[17] First Amendment guarantees are the bedrock of democracy, Black constantly and vigorously argued; they are not "irrelevant," they should not be "degraded" to the "rational basis level."[18] In *Smith v California* (361 *US* 147), Black said in 1949 that "The First Amendment, which is the supreme law of the land, thus fixed its own value of freedom of speech and press by putting these freedoms wholly 'beyond the reach' of federal power to abridge. No other provision of the Constitution purports to dilute the scope of these *unequivocal commands* of the First Amendment. Consequently, I do not believe that any federal agencies, including Congress and this Court, have power or authority to subordinate speech and press to what they think are more 'important' interests."

Because in Justice Black's words "free speech plays its most important role in the political discussions and arguments which are the lifeblood of any representative democracy,"[19] because in the "political offender" cases one sees the kernel of Black's thoughts concerning the essence of the First Amendment, and because to cover the entire range of First Amendment cases in a single chapter in a book which focuses on the beliefs of a single Justice would be extremely difficult, the remaining sections of this chapter will closely examine Justice Black's attitudes toward the First Amendment by viewing cases dealing only with anti-subversive legislation, congressional investigations, loyalty oaths, and finally, with Black's distinction between speech and conduct.

Free Speech and the Political Offender

Anti-Subversive Legislation (National and State)

The Smith Act, passed in 1940 by the Congress, was one of a handful of federal laws designed to protect the security of the society in time of war. In 1861, Congress had passed anti-insurrectionist and anti-conspiracy legislation; and World War I had seen the enactment of laws dealing with espionage and prohibiting the dissemination of subversive ideas.

Passed on the eve of the Second World War, the Smith Act was an attempt to punish those who advocated overthrowing the government by force or violence. Its most celebrated provision was Title One, which made it a crime

> (1) to advocate the duty, necessity, desirability or propriety of overthrowing or destroying any government in the United States by force or violence,
> (2) to print, publish, distribute, or issue any seditious materials with the intent of causing the overthrow or destruction of any government in the United States; and
> (3) to organize or help organize any society, group or assembly of persons or to become a member of such a group, committed to the destruction of this country's governmental institutions.

The Act was used two times during the war years, resulting in one conviction which the Supreme Court refused to review. The picture changed, however, after the War ended when Russia changed from wartime ally to cold-war antagonist. The government began employing the Smith Act against Communist Party members in the United States; and Congress began, in 1947, to pass new legislation that defined and punished political crimes;[20] and the Supreme Court was called on to examine the legitimacy of these laws passed by the Congress. The first case to raise the issue of the legitimacy of the Smith Act on the merits before the court was *Dennis v United States.*[21] The essential question, in the eyes of the judges, was whether this act, "embodying the first federal peacetime restrictions on speaking and writing by American citizens since the ill-fated Sedition Act of 1798,"[22] came into conflict with the First Amendment standing alone or as modified by either the "clear and present danger" or "bad tendency" tests.

In hearings before the House Un-American Activities Committee, Attorney General Tom C. Clark questioned the utility of the Act: "As you know, this act is aimed at the individual rather than the group or party. Adequate proof against the individual in this regard is most difficult to adduce....We have found it more practical, effective, and much more speedy to proceed under other federal statutes."[23]

In 1948, the Truman Administration's Justice Department began prosecution of the eleven top leaders of the American Communist Party. The indictment charged them with (1) willfully and knowingly conspiring to organize as the Communist Party a society or group of persons who teach and advocate the overthrow and destruction of the government by force and violence, and (2) knowingly and willfully teaching and advocating the duty and necessity of overthrowing the government by force or violence. "No overt revolutionary acts other than teaching and advocating were alleged" and the only real evidence introduced at the trial in New York, which lasted for nine tumultuous months, was the information contained in four books: Marx's *Communist Manifesto*, Lenin's *State and Revolution*, Stalin's *Foundations of Leninism,* and a 1939 history of the Communist Party of the Soviet Union.[24] Convicted in the District Court, their convictions were sustained by the Court of Appeals. (Judge Learned Hand wrote a new standard of "clear and present danger" to justify the conviction: "Whether the gravity of the 'evil,' discounted by its improbability, justifies such invasion of free speech as is necessary to avoid the danger.") The convicted Communists appealed to the Supreme Court and, in its 1950 term, the Court upheld the constitutionality of the Smith Act and affirmed the convictions. There were five opinions written by the justices, clearly indicating the cross current of opinion on the bench at the time. Only two of the justices dissented; they were Justices Black and Douglas.

Chief Justice Vinson, who announced the judgment of the Court, joined Justices Reed, Burton, and Minton. "The obvious purpose of the statute is to protect existing government, not from change by peaceable, lawful, and constitutional means, but from change by violence, revolution, and terrorism." The language of the act, Vinson continued, was aimed at advocacy, and not discussion. And, addressing himself to defenders of "clear and present danger" and to Black's "absolutist" view of the First Amendment, Vinson said "To those who would paralyze our government in the face of impending threat by encasing it in a semantic straitjacket we must reply that all concepts are relative."[25]

Arguing that the government need not wait "until the *putsch* is about to be executed, the plans laid, the signal awaited," Vinson saw the convictions as justificable attempts by the Justice Department to put down this incipient rebellion. "Action by the government is required."[26] In each case, Vinson said (borrowing Learned Hand's modification of Holmes' test), "the Courts must ask whether the gravity of the evil, discounted by its improbability, justifies such invasion of free speech as is necessary to avoid the danger."[27] Taking judicial notice of the world-wide Communist conspiracy, Vinson urged the necessity of the governmental actions. If the government was tied down by semantic bonds, the Communists "will strike when the leaders feel the circumstances permit."[28] The Smith Act was a legitimate exercise of the powers of the State; the convictions were consistent with the Constitution.

Justice Frankfurter concurred in the judgment of the Court. Rejecting the ideas of Black that "the Constitution is a wholly unfettered right of expression" because "such literalness treats the words of the Constitution as though they were found on a piece of outworn parchment" and because "the soil in which the Bill of Rights grew was not a soil of arid pedentry,"[29] Frankfurter called for a balancing of the competing views to determine whether or not the convictions would fall. "The demands of free speech in a democratic society," he intoned, "as well as the interest in national security are better served by candid and informed weighing of competing interests, within the judicial process, then by announcing dogmas too inflexible for the non-Euclidian problems to be solved."[30]

Congress, however, was the primary agency responsible for assessing these competing interests, Frankfurter argued. Courts must not be given full responsibility for that choice. The judges' best quality, he believed, was "detachment, founded on independence. History teaches that independence of the judiciary is jeopardized when courts become embroiled in the passions of the day and assume primary responsibility in choosing between competing political, economic and social pressures."[31] Surveying the various types of free speech litigation that came to the court, Frankfurter concluded that in all there was a distinction made between the statement of an idea "which may prompt its hearers to take unlawful action, and advocacy that such action be taken."[32] Were the Communist leaders on trial guilty of advocacy? Frankfurter, agreeing with the dissenters, did not see conspiracy to overthrow the government, but, he said, "it would be equally wrong to treat it as a seminar in political theory."[33]

In concluding that the Act was a reasonable legislative output based on that agency's weighing of interests of speech and security, Frankfurter, due to the paucity of the "facts found by the jury," took "judicial notice" of the fact that Communist doctrines "which these defendants have conspired to advocate are in the ascendency in powerful nations who cannot be acquitted of unfriendliness to the institutions of this country....In sum, it would amply justify a legislature in concluding that recruitment of additional members for the Party would create a substantial danger to the national security."[34] And, while mindful of the threats that this legislation posed to freedom of speech, "it is a sobering fact that in sustaining the convictions before us we can hardly escape restriction on the interchange of ideas,"[35] he voted to "sustain the power of Congress." He concluded by reminding the Court of the weakness of the Court: "The ultimate reliance for the deepest needs of civilization must be found outside their vindication in courts of law"; "the democratic process at all events is not impaired or restricted in this case. Power and responsibility remain with the people and immediately with their representatives. All the Court says is that Congress was not forbidden by the Constitution to pass this enactment and that a prosecution under it may be brought against a conspiracy such as the one before us."[36]

Justice Jackson also concurred in the Court's judgment. He too took judicial notice of the "fact" that the Communist Party was a "conspiratorial and revolutionary junta, organized to reach ends and use means which are incompatible with our constitutional system."[37] He rejected the use of the "clear and present danger" standard because this would "hold our government captive in a judge-made trap;" instead "we must approach the problem of a well-organized, nationwide conspiracy, as realistically as our predecessors faced the trivialities that were being prosecuted until they were checked with a 'rule of reason.' I think reason is lacking for applying that test to this case.

> I would save it, unmodified, for application as a 'rule of reason' in the kind of case for which it was devised. When the issue is criminality of a hot-headed speech on a street corner, or circulation of a few incendiary pamphlets, or parading by some zealots behind a red flag, or refusal of a handful of school children to

> salute our flag, it is not beyond the capacity of the judicial process to gather, comprehend, and weigh the necessary materials for decision whether it is a clear and present danger of substantive evil or a harmless letting off of steam....The test applies and has meaning where a conviction is sought and based on a speech or writing which does not directly or explicitly advocate a crime but to which such tendency is sought to be attributed by construction or by implication from external circumstances....But its recent expansion has extended unprecedented immunities to Communists.[38]

Since the authors of "clear and present danger" never thought of applying it in cases like the present one, the Court must not employ it. "If applied, it means that Communist plotting is protected during its period of incubation; its preliminary stages of organization and preparation are immune from the law; the Government can move only after imminent action is manifest, when it would, of course, be too late."[39] When the country is faced with such a conspiracy, it must be able to deal effectively with that cancer. "The Constitution does not make conspiracy a civil right."[40] While Jackson, a former United States Attorney General under Roosevelt, considered "criminal conspiracy" a dragnet device capable of perversion into an instrument of injustice in the hands of a partisan or complacent judiciary, he nevertheless admitted that "it has an established place in our system of law, and no reason appears for applying it only to concerted action claimed to disturb interstate commerce and withholding it from those claimed to undermine our whole government."[41]

Douglas dissented from these views. Dennis and others were convicted and their convictions were upheld, not because of what they did but because of what people thought they would do in the future. The Court upheld the convictions based on "judicial notice"; Douglas also took judicial notice but of the fact that as a political party communism was of "little consequence" in America and that the Communist leaders were "miserable merchants of unwanted ideas." Free speech, he concluded, "the glory of our system of government, should not be sacrificed on anything less than plain and objective proof of danger that the evil advocated is imminent."[42]

Justice Black vigorously rejected the majority contentions of his brethren. The petitioners, he asserted, were not charged with actual conduct; they were not charged "with overt acts of any kind; they were not even charged with saying anything or writing anything designed to overturn government. The charge was that they agreed to assemble and to talk and publish certain ideas at a later date." The indictment, "no matter how worded, is a virulent form of prior censorship of speech and press which I believe the First Amendment forbids."[43]

Believing that the First Amendment was the "keystone of our government, that the freedoms it guarantees provide the best insurance against destruction of all freedom," Black argued that the dangers entailed by such "unfettered communication of ideas" could be met by counterargument and persuasion. "To the founders of this Nation, the benefits derived from free expression were worth the risk."[44] The First Amendment is not "little more than an admonition to Congress," Black emphatically stated. It is a command, a mandatory command not to abridge the right of free speech, whatever the dangers of such speech, press, and assembly. But he concluded on a sad, resigned note, well aware of the prevailing sentiment of Vinson, Frankfurter, Jackson, the Congress, and the country as a whole toward the communist conspiracy.

> Public opinion being what it now is, few will protest the conviction of these Communist petitioners. There is, however, hope that in calmer times, when present pressures, passions, and fears subside, this or some later Court will restore the First

Amendment liberties to the high preferred place where they belong in a free society.[45]

In *Dennis* the Supreme Court did several important things. "It gave support to the assumption that it had accepted the principle of guilt by association; illegal conspiracy could be established by demonstrating activities–any kind of activities–in furtherance of the organizational work of the Communist Party."[46] It also encouraged the government to bring similar prosecutions up against other party leaders. (By the time of the *Yates* decision, during the 1956 term, the record was 6 jury acquittals and 108 convictions in 17 Smith Act trials.)

Until its grant of certiorari in the 1955 term in the Yates Smith Act trial, the Supreme Court had not reviewed the convictions in these cases. In *Yates v United States,*[47] the Supreme Court examined the conviction of fourteen California leaders of the Communist Party and, while not challenging the constitutionality of the Smith Act as established in the *Dennis* case, reversed the convictions of five of the fourteen on procedural grounds and remanded the other nine back to the lower Courts for new trials. With respect to the charge of "organizing," Justice Harlan pointed out that the Party was formed in 1945, and that the three year statute of limitations nullified that part of the indictment. The second part of the majority opinion criticized the judge's charge to the jury. The trial judge did not distinguish between advocacy of "abstract doctrine and advocacy directed at promoting unlawful action."[48] The former, "even though uttered with the hope that it may ultimately lead to violent revolution, is too remote from concrete action to be regarded as the kind of indoctrination preparatory to action which was condemned in *Dennis*."[49] Examining the evidence to determine whether the record was "papably insufficient" to warrant a new trial, Harlan found it to be "strikingly deficient" and on that basis five defendants were completely cleared. As for the others, there was some evidence in the record—meetings held in devious manners—that could lead to convictions under the Court's standards. These were remanded to the lower Court for a new trial, if the Justice Department so chose to act in that manner.

Justice Black concurred in part and dissented in part. He was of the opinion that the Smith Act was unconstitutional and that all fourteen defendants should be acquitted.

> I cannot agree with the Court majority when it says that persons can be punished for advocating action to overthrow the government by force and violence, where those to whom addressed are urged to '*do* something, now or in the future, rather than merely to *believe* in something.' Under the Court's approach, defendants could still be convicted simply for agreeing to talk as distinguished from agreeing to act. I believe that the First Amendment forbids Congress to punish people for talking about public affairs, whether or not such discussion incites to action, legal or illegal.[50]

These governmental prosecutions, Black maintained, were more in line "with the philosophy of authoritarian government" than with the philosophy of the First Amendment. This suppression of "causes and beliefs" was the antithesis of the Constitutional commands and ideals.

> Unless there is complete freedom for expression of all ideas, whether we like them or not, concerning the way government shall be run and who shall run it, I doubt if any views in the long run can be secured from the censors. The First Amendment provides the only kind of security system that can preserve a free government—one that leaves the way wide open for people to favor, discuss, advocate, or incite causes and doctrines however obnoxious and antagonistic such views may be to the rest of us.[51]

During the 1960 term of the Court, two cases were reviewed that concerned the membership clause of the Smith Act, *Scales v United States,* and *Noto v United States.*[52]

Junius Scales was a party organizer in North and South Carolina (who renounced his affiliation with the Communist Party prior to his conviction for knowing acquisition or holding of membership in any organization that seeks the overthrow by force or violence the government of the United States.)[53] The Supreme Court upheld, arguing, that his conviction for such knowing membership with intent to act in a manner proscribed by the Smith Act was not an infringement of any Constitutional rights. Harlan, for the narrow five judge majority, pointed out that, on statutory as well as evidentiary grounds, the conviction had to stand.

Black dissented. He gave four basic reasons for his action. First, the Internal Security Act of 1950 (more will be said of that Act later in the chapter) prohibited per se membership convictions of Communists. Second, the First Amendment "absolutely forbids Congress to outlaw membership in a political party or similar association merely because one of the philosophical tenets of that group is that the existing government should be overthrown by force at some distant time in the future, when circumstances may permit."[54] A third reason for dissenting was that the statute was itself "at best unconstitutionally vague and, at worst, ex post facto" by virtue of his being convicted on the basis of the Court's rewriting the statute to include the words "activity" and "specific intent." In short, claimed Black, Scales "has been denied his right to be tried under a clearly defined, pre-existing 'law of the land' as guaranteed by the Due Process Clause and I think his conviction should be reversed on that ground."[55]

His last reason for dissenting was fundamental disagreement with the balancing formula employed by the Court majority in the many cases that had been adjudicated by the Court.

> This case reemphasizes the freedom-destroying nature of the 'balancing test' presently in use by the Court to justify its refusal

> to apply specific constitutional protections of the Bill of Rights....Under this test the question is simply whether the government has an interest in abridging the right involved and, if so, whether that interest is of sufficient importance, in the opinion of a majority of this Court, to justify the government's action in doing so. This doctrine, to say the least, is capable of being used to justify almost any action government may wish to take to suppress First Amendment freedoms.[56]

In *Noto v United States,* the companion case, the conviction was reversed because, according to Harlan for the Court majority, the evidence was insufficient to prove that the Communist Party was currently advocating overthrowal of the government by force and violence. (Scales had been convicted for his activities in the late forties and early fifties when the Party was advocating such a violent overthrowal.) To support the conviction, there had to be evidence of a call to violence, now or in the future, which is sufficiently strong and pervasive to "lend color to an otherwise ambiguous theoretical material regarding Communist Party teaching; present advocacy is necessary to be shown in evidence to support the conviction."[57]

Black concurred in the result. The majority opinion, he argued, was in effect telling government "that, if it wishes to get convictions under the Smith Act, it must maintain a permanent staff of informers who are prepared to give up-to-date information with respect to the present policies of the Communist Party."[58]

> I cannot join an opinion which implies that the existence of liberty is dependent upon the efficiency of the government's informers. I prefer to rest my concurrence in the judgment of reversal of petitioner's conviction on what I regard as the more solid ground that the First Amendment forbids the government to abridge the rights of freedom of speech, press, and assembly.

(Until he was pardoned by President Kennedy on December 24, 1962, Scales was the only political prisoner in a federal penitentiary.)

In 1950 there was passed the first major postwar statute dealing with Communist subversion in the United States—the Internal Security Act. Based on congressional examinations of the menace of international Communism, its provisions aimed at the registration, restriction, and public exposure of the members, organs, and fellow travelers of the Communist organization in the country. A five member, presidentially appointed Subversive Activities Control Board was created and empowered to act to enforce the Internal Security Act by holding hearings to determine whether a particular organization was connected with the dreaded Party. If the group was found to be Communist, it had to register with the Board and it and its members were then subject to further restrictions with respect to travel, employment, naturalization, and denaturalization.

Communist Party v Subversive Activities Control Board,[59] was the Court's initial response to the allegation that the Internal Security Act was unconstitutional. The Board, in 1953, had found the Communist Party to be a "communist front" organization and ordered it to register as such under Section 7 of the Internal Security Act. The Party refused, arguing that the Act was a Bill of Attainder, that it violated the First Amendment to the Constitution, and that it forced the members of the Party to incriminate themselves in violation of the Fifth Amendment to the Constitution. The Court of Appeals affirmed the SACB's order and the Party appealed to the Supreme Court. Justice Frankfurter, for the Court majority of five, affirmed the judgment of the Court of Appeals. The order dealt with registration only; not with subsequent issues that might arise and therefore the questions raised are "prematurely raised." Courts, Frankfurter argued, cannot simply dismiss legislation based on a decade and a half of legislative inquiry. "We certainly cannot dismiss them as unfounded or irrational imaginings....And if we accept them, as we must, as a not unentertainable appraisal by Congress of the threat which Communist organizations pose, we must recognize that the power to regulate Communist organizations of this nature is extensive." Congress, he argued, balanced the free speech value with the necessity of public order. The Court must respect their judgment. More important, Congress was not proscribing speech and assembly of the Communist group, merely calling for it to register. The self-incrimination charge made by the Party was simply set aside by Frankfurter as being "premature at this time."[60]

Justice Black dissented from this judgment of the Court. "I do not believe that it can be too often repeated that the freedoms of speech, press, petition, and assembly, guaranteed by the First Amendment must be accorded to the ideas we hate or sooner or later they will be denied to the ideas we cherish. The first banning of an association because it advocates hated ideas—whether that association be called a political party or not—marks a fateful moment in the history of a free country. That moment seems to have arrived for this country."[61]

The assumption behind the Act, Black said, was a paternalistic view of government protecting poor, unenlightened voters from hearing public policies discussed. "It is based on the principle that our people, even when adequately informed, may not be trusted to distinguish between the true and the false."[62] Black had too much faith in the people's wisdom to accept that assumption. The Act was unconstitutional because it directly conflicted with the Fifth Amendment's Self-incrimination clause, because it was a Bill of Attainder, because it violated due process of law, and because it abridged the freedoms of speech, press, and association.[63]

Essentially, Black's dissent in the *Communist Party* case was his absolute and unwavering commitment to the power of truth to triumph over the falsehoods spoken by men.

> Under our system of government, the remedy for this danger of revolutionary talk is the same remedy that is applied to the danger that comes from any other erroneous talk–education and contrary argument. If that remedy is not sufficient, the only meaning of free speech must be that the revolutionary ideas will be allowed to prevail.[64]

The freedoms this country is noted for, argued Black, will better serve to defend against internal insurrection than any Internal Security Act would because the "affection of the people" for the governmental institutions is strengthened by allegiance to freedom of speech and press; more so than by "instilling fear in the people of the power of government."[65]

> I would reverse this case and leave the Communists free to advocate their belief in proletariat dictatorship publicly and openly among the people of this country with full confidence that the people will remain loyal to any democratic government truly dedicated to freedom and justice–the kind of government which some of us still think of as being 'the last best hope of earth.'[66]

After the decision, the Party was under a duty to register. The Party leaders elected, instead, to send a letter to the Attorney General, signed with the Party Seal, stating that its officers declined to register or submit the appropriate forms for fear of self-incrimination. The Party was convicted for this inaction and fined $120,000. The Court of Appeals set aside the conviction, accepting as valid the contention that to fill in and sign the forms was in violation of the Fifth Amendment. The Supreme Court denied certiorari, thereby upholding the Circuit Court's limitation on the powers of the SACB.[67]

In 1963, *Aptheker v Secretary of State* challenged the section of the Internal Security Act, Section 6, which provided that when a Communist organization is registered, or under final orders to register, it shall be unlawful for any member with knowledge and notice of that order to apply for or use a passport. Herber Aptheker, a leading theoretician of the American Communist Party, was refused a passport and he appealed this judgment of the State Department, arguing that it violated his constitutional rights of freedom to travel and of due process of law. The three judge court denied him relief and the Court heard the case shortly thereafter. Justice Goldberg, writing for the majority, declared that section to be unconstitutional on its face for it too broadly and indiscriminately transgressed the liberties guaranteed by the Fifth Amendment. "The right to travel is a basic aspect of liberty–section six contains an irrebuttable presumption that all members of Communist organizations will engage in activities endangering our security if given passports."[68]

Justice Black concurred in the judgment of the Court majority. "The whole act," he believed, "is not a valid law; it sets up a comprehensive statutory plan which violates the Federal Constitution because (1) it constitutes a Bill of Attainder, (2) punishes without giving appropriate benefit of a trial, according to Due Process, and (3) denies appellants freedom of speech, press, association, which the First Amendment guarantees."[69]

> This case offers another appropriate occasion to point out that the Framers thought and I agree that the best way to promote the internal security of our people is to protect their First Amendment freedoms and that we cannot take away the liberty of groups whose views most people detest without jeopardizing the liberty of others whose views, though popular today, may themselves be detested tomorrow.[70]

The following year Black dissented from a per curiam order of the Court in *American Association For Protection of Foreign Born v SACB.*[71] The SACB order calling for that group to register was based on evidence about the activities of one man who had died prior to the order, and the Court's per curiam order vacated the judgment of the Board in order to determine the current status of the petitioners. Black argued once again that the entire Act was unconstitutional.

> The Act has borrowed the worst features of old laws intended to put shackles on the minds and bodies of men, to make them confess to more, to make them miserable while in this country, and to make it a crime even to attempt to get out of it. It is difficult to find laws more thought-stifling than this one even in countries considered the most benighted....My vote is to hear the case now and hold the law to be what I think it is—a wholesale denial of what I believe to be the constitutional heritage of every freedom-loving American.[72]

While the Court majority did not adopt the absolute views of Black regarding the total unconstitutionality of the Internal Security Act, in subsequent years it did strike down various sections of the Act dealing with registration forms,[73] and employment in defense facilities.[74] (Section 5 of the Act prohibited members of Communist organizations from working at shipyards designated as 'defense facilities' by the government.) Black concurred in former case and joined the opinion written by Chief Justice Warren in the latter.

The Supreme Court had occasion to pass on the constitutionality of various congressional enactments affecting the status of aliens suspected of harboring attitudes and views thought to be un-American. Congress had long been recognized to have almost absolute power to admit aliens to the Country and the conditions upon which they can remain in America.[75] The question that Black and the Court were faced with was the extent to which the basic provisions of the Constitution and the Bill of Rights applied to aliens who were being held during investigations and prior to deportation. As will be seen in the following cases, the majority of the Court refused to discuss the substantive questions whereas Black and Douglas did challenge the essence of the legislation that allowed the government to expel aliens for their political beliefs and associations, uprooting them from their families, homes, jobs.

Carlson v Landon, District Director of Immigration and Naturalization Service,[76] was an early case dealing with this emotional situation. Under Section 20A of the Immigration Act as Amended by Section 23 of the Internal Security Act of 1952, the Attorney General was empowered to hold without benefit of bail, pending determination of their deportability, aliens who were Communist Party members, where there was reasonable cause to believe that their release on bail would endanger the safety and welfare of the United States. Carlson appealed this denial of bail judgment and, in an opinion written by Justice Reed, the Court held that the refusal of bail was not arbitrary or capricious or an abridgment of the Fifth Amendment. Justice Black dissented. "It clearly appears that these aliens are held in jail for no reason except that they had been active in the Communist movement," wrote Black. "They must be isolated from their families and communities and kept in jail solely because a bureau agent thinks that is where Communists should be."[77] Simply put, Black argued that they were denied Due Process of Law. "I think that condemning people to jail is a job for the judiciary in accordance with procedural due process," he wrote. Also, "to put people in jail for fear of their talk seems to me to be an abridgment of speech in flat violation of the First Amendment."[78]

> This belief of mine in the Absoluteness of the First Amendment may and I suppose does influence me to protest wherever I think I see even slight encroachments on First Amendment liberties. But the encroachment here is not small. True it is mainly those alleged to be present or past 'communists' who are now being jailed for their beliefs and expressions. But we cannot be sure more victims will not be offered up later if the First Amendment means no more than its enemies or even some of its friends believe it does.[79]

In *Shaughnessy, District Director of Immigration and*

Naturalization v United States ex rel Mezei,[80] heard the following year, the Court was faced with the following set of facts. Mezei, an alien resident in the country for over twenty-five years, was ordered permanently excluded from the country without a hearing. The information used to reach the decision was kept confidential but Mezei was not allowed to enter the country after having visited Hungary for nineteen months. His entry, it was announced, would be prejudicial to the public interest for security reasons. Other nations refused to accept him and he remained on Ellis Island for twenty-one months. A federal District Court directed conditional parole on bond within the United States and the Court of Appeals affirmed the order. The government appealed the parole order and the Supreme Court, in an opinion written by former Attorney General Tom C. Clark, overturned the lower federal court's actions. The Attorney General's continued exclusion of Mezei, stated Clark, without a hearing does not amount to an unlawful detention and courts may not temporarily admit him to the United States pending arrangements for his departure abroad.

Black again dissented from the judgment of the Court. This practice was oppressive. "Our founders," he argued, "abhorred arbitrary one-man imprisonment. Due Process means to me that no governmental official can put or keep people in prison without accountability to courts of Justice."

> It means that individual liberty is too highly prized in this country to allow executive officials to imprison and hold people on the basis of information kept secret. It means that Mezei should not be deprived of his liberty indefinitely except as a result of a fair open court hearing in which evidence is appraised by the Court, not the prosecutor.[81]

Black also dissented in 1954 when the Court, in *Galvan v Press,* upheld the section of the Internal Security Act of 1950 that required the deportation of any alien who at the time of his entry or any time thereafter was a member of the

Communist Party.[82] But during the 1957 term of the Court, the judges limited slightly the awesome power of the Attorney General when it said that the questions asked in deportation hearings had to be reasonable.[83] Black continuously attacked these actions of the Attorney General because they infringed basic guarantees found within the Bill of Rights, i.e., the First Amendment's Free Speech and Association protections, and the Due Process Clause in that they were not given a fair hearing in a *Court* of justice. "The core of our constitutional system." he wrote in one dissenting opinion, "is that individual liberty must never be taken away by short cuts, that fair trials in independent courts *must never* be dispensed with. The system is in grave danger."[84]

The basic device used by states to control and limit anti-American activities by subversive groups and/or individuals, in addition to the loyalty oaths (which will be discussed later in this chapter), was the general criminal syndicalism act. In 1927, the Supreme Court, in *Whitney v California,* upheld the validity of such state anti-sedition acts.[85] By the mid-1950s, 44 states had such legislation on their statutes. However, in *Pennsylvania v Nelson,*[86] Chief Justice Warren for the Court majority stated that the aggregate of Congressional legislation had "occupied the field of sedition" and therefore superseded Pennsylvania's anti-sedition statute. And, in a 1968 *per curiam* order, *Brandenburg v Ohio,*[87] the Court held that the Ohio Criminal Syndicalism Statute, under which the defendant, a Ku Klux Klan leader, was convicted for advocating the duty and propriety of unlawful methods of terrorism as a means of accomplishing industrial or political reform, punished mere advocacy and it therefore ran afoul of the First and the Fourteenth Amendments. The First Amendment freedoms of speech, press, and assembly do not permit a state to forbid advocacy of the use of force or of law violation except where such advocacy promotes lawlessness. "*Whitney v California*," concluded the *per curiam* opinion, "overruled."[88] Black and Douglas concurred, Black saying that, agreeing with Douglas, "the clear and present danger doctrine should have no place in the interpretation of the First Amendment."[89]

Legislative Investigations of Subversive Activities

Legislative investigations serving no purpose other than that of defaming individuals for their personal political beliefs was, for Justice Black, just as reprehensible and violative of First Amendment freedoms as were legislative acts that abridged these basic "unceded rights." The Court, prior to the Cold War period, had allowed Congress wide scope with regard to its investigative powers but did suggest, in a 1927 case, that (1) neither house of Congress "is invested with general power to inquire into private affairs and compel disclosures, and (2) a witness may "rightfully refuse to answer when the bounds of the power are exceeded or the questions are not pertinent to the matter under inquiry."[90] The Court did, however, conclude by saying that the power of inquiry is "an essential and appropriate auxiliary to the legislative function."

In 1938 the House created a special Un-American Activities Committee whose task it was to ferret out persons and groups unfriendly to the nature, organization, and goals of the American government. For over thirty years that Committee has been investigating the private beliefs of individuals;[91] its actions were challenged in the Courts in the 1940s (although unsuccessfully, for the Supreme Court did not hear the challenges on their merits).[92] However, in the same year, when the Supreme Court announced *Yates,* it handed down the *Watkins* and *Sweezey* decisions, rulings that for the first time limited the activities of Congressional and state legislative committee activities when questioning "political" witnesses. Chief Justice Warren wrote the majority opinions in these two cases, with Hugo Black joining in the judgments and reasoning.

Watkins involved a labor union official who had been called as a witness before the HUAC. He testified openly about his contacts with Communist party officials, but refused to tell whether he knew a number of persons to have been members of the Party. He was convicted of contempt of Congress for refusing to answer questions pertinent to the questions under inquiry. The Court reversed his conviction. Warren stated that Watkins was "not afforded a fair opportunity to determine whether he was within his rights in refusing to answer, and his conviction is necessarily invalid under the Due Process Clause of the Fifth Amendment."[93] A witness must have the right to have knowledge of the subject to which the interrogation is deemed pertinent, Warren reasoned. Watkins did not have this knowledge, therefore the conviction was not allowed to stand.

Sweezy, decided the same day as *Watkins*, dealt with a New Hampshire Attorney General who was empowered to hold one-man investigations of subversive persons and groups by the legislature. Sweezy had refused to answer questions about the Progressive Party and about lectures he had given at the University of New Hampshire. He argued that the questions were not pertinent to the inquiry and he was jailed for contempt. Although not reaching fundamental questions, Chief Justice Warren, for the Court, overturned the jail sentence, finding that "it cannot be stated authoritatively that the legislature asked the Attorney General to gather the kind of facts comprised in the subjects upon which petitioner was interrogated."[94]

These and other decisions of the Warren Court during the 1956 term of the Court elicited violent response within the Congress.[95] And, perhaps as a response to the congressional threats to limit the Court's appellate jurisdiction, in the 1958 term of the Supreme Court, the Court majority retreated from *Watkins* and *Sweezy.* The cases that brought about the judicial retreat were *Barenblatt v United States* (concerning a HUAC investigation) and *Uphaus v Wyman* (concerning the activities of the New Hampshire Attorney General). Justice Black dissented in both cases.

In 1954 a HUAC Sub-committee summoned Barenblatt, a Vassar College psychology professor, to testify on Communist infiltration into the field of education. The defendant refused to answer questions about his association with the Communist Party. For this, he was given a six-month jail sentence.[96] He appealed the contempt conviction and, in an opinion written by Justice John M. Harlan, the conviction was sustained.

In reaching this judgment, Harlan clearly rejected the Black view of the First Amendment's absoluteness and primacy in the constitutional pattern of government and governing. "The protections of the First Amendment...do not afford a witness the right to resist inquiry in all circumstances. Where First Amendment rights are asserted to bar governmental interrogation, resolution of the issue always involves a balancing by the Courts of the competing private and public interests at stake."[97] There was, Harlan concluded, a valid legislative purpose behind the actions of the subcommittee. The Communist Party was not an ordinary political party but one that threatened the preservation of the government. "To suggest that because the Communist Party may also sponsor peaceable political reforms the constitutional issues before us should now be judged as if that party were just an ordinary political party from the standpoint of national security, is to ask this Court to blind itself to world affairs which have determined the whole course of our national policy since the close of World War II."[98] As such, "an investigation of advocacy of or a preparation for overthrow certainly embraces the right to identify a witness as a member of the Communist Party."

Regarding the exposure-for-the-sake-of-exposure argument (developed by Black in his lengthy dissent), Harlan merely said that "so long as Congress acts in pursuance of its constitutional power, the judiciary lacks authority to intervene on the basis of the motives which spurred the exercise of that power."[99]

Justice Black, joined by Chief Justice Warren and Justice Douglas, vehemently dissented from this judicial retreat from its oath to support and defend the Constitution. The Court had to guard against "*every* encroachment" of government into the areas not ceded by the people to its governors. He offered three reasons for dissenting from Harlan's judgment: (1) Rule XI creating the HUAC and authorizing such a sweeping, unlimited, compulsory examination of witnesses in the fields of speech, press, assembly, and petition violated the procedural requirements of due process of law; (2) compelling an answer from Barenblatt abridged his freedom of speech and associaton; (3) HUAC proceedings were part of a program to stigmatize and punish by public identification and exposure all witnesses considered by the Committee to be guilty of Communist affiliation. This was a task specifically denied to Congress in the Constitution.[100] The activities of HUAC "do precisely abridge First Amendment freedoms through exposure, obloquy, and public scorn," argued Black as he, once more, rigorously rejected the "balancing" test:

> To apply the Court's balancing test is to read the First Amendment to say 'Congress shall pass no law...unless Congress and the Supreme Court reach the joint conclusion that on balance the interest of the government in stifling these freedoms is greater than the interest of the people in having them exercised.' This is closely akin to the notion that neither the First Amendment nor any other provision of the Bill of Rights should be enforced unless the Court believes it is *reasonable* to do so. Not only does this violate the genius of our *written* Constitution, but it runs

> expressly counter to the injunction to Court and Congress made by Madison when he introduced the Bill of Rights: 'Independent tribunals of justice will consider themselves in a peculiar manner the guardians of these rights; they will be an impenetrable bulwark against *every* assumption of power in the legislature or Executive; they will be naturally led to resist *every* encroachment upon rights expressly stipulated for in the Constitution by the declaration of rights.' Unless we return to this view of our judicial function, unless we once again accept the notion that the Bill of Rights means what it says and that this Court *must* enforce that meaning, I am of the opinion that our great charter of liberty will be more honored in the breach than in the observance.[101] (Black's italics)

As for the Communist Party and its members, Black recommitted himself to the proposition that free speech and association will allow the common people to reject their outlandish ideas. Government can preserve itself, he said, *only* by leaving the people the "fullest possible freedom to praise, criticize, or discuss, as *they* see fit, all governmental policies and to suggest, if they *desire* that even its most fundamental postulates are bad and should be changed."[102] The Constitution, he said, "assumes that the common sense of the people and their attachment to our country will enable them, after free discussion, to withstand ideas that are wrong."[103]

As for the actions of HUAC, while Black did not question "HUAC's patriotism and sincerity in doing all this (pitiless publicity and exposure)," he "merely felt that it could not be done by Congress under our Constitution." For such publicity is punishment "and the Constitution allows only one way in which the people can be convicted and punished...by court and jury after a trial with all judicial safeguards." A person in America must be protected from such arbitrary punishment or else the country cannot be distinguished from those societies "where drumhead courts and other similar 'tribunals' deprive the weak and the unorthodox of life, liberty and property without Due Process of Law. It is this same right which is denied to Barenblatt."[104]

In concluding his dissent, Black said that "ultimately all the questions in this case really boil down to one—whether we as a people will try fearfully and futilely to preserve democracy by adopting totalitarian methods, or whether in accordance with our traditions and our Constitution we will have the confidence and the courage to be free."[105]

(In *Uphaus v Wyman,* decided the same day as *Barenblatt,* the Court majority, in an opinion written by Justice Clark, upheld the conviction of the director of a summer camp in New Hampshire, World Fellowship, Inc., because he refused to produce the names of guests for the state's Attorney General who was investigating subversive activities in that state. The "nexus between the organization and subversive activities disclosed by the record justified investigation and is sufficiently compelling to subordinate the interest in privacy." Black briefly dissented because Uphaus' rights under the first were denied.[106])

His so very powerful faith in the "common sense and attachment of the people to the country" was once again reaffirmed by Justice Black during the 1960 term of the Court when two other actions of the HUAC were challenged in the Courts. Both cases, *Wilkinson v United States,* and *Braden v United States*, were based on the Harlan reasoning of Barenblatt, and in both, Justice Potter Stewart writing the opinions for a five-man majority, the Court affirmed the convictions for refusal to answer congressional committee inquiries regarding Communist infiltration into basic industries in the South and propaganda of the Communist Party in the South. Justice Black vehemently dissented.

Wilkinson, a member of the Citizens Committee To Preserve American Freedoms, was interrogated by the HUAC because he had been critical of its activities. That was the only reason for his being brought before the committee,

Black argued.

> In my view, the majority by its decision today places the stamp of constitutional approval on a practice as clearly inconsistent with the Constitution and indeed with every ideal of individual freedom for which this country has so long stood as any that has ever come before this Court. For...I think it clear that this case involves nothing more nor less than an attempt by the HUAC to use the contempt power of the House of Representatives as a weapon against those who dare to criticize it.[107]

The balancing test applied, once again by a Court majority unwilling to limit the powers of the government, meant to Black, that the HUAC "may engage in any inquiry a majority of this Court happens to think could possibly be for a legitimate purpose whether that 'purpose' be the true reason for the inquiry or not." If the trend continued, thought Black, good people would either be quiet or in jail and "government by consent will be replaced by government by intimidation because some people are afraid that this country cannot survive unless Congress has the power to set aside the freedoms of the First Amendment at will," Black could "only once again reiterate my firm conviction that these people are tragically wrong. This country was not built by men who were afraid and it cannot be preserved by such men."[108]

How can "Americanism" be protected? Not by "persecuting minorities, but by strict adherence to basic principles of freedom that are responsible for this nation's greatness.

> These principles are embodied for all who care to see in our Bill of Rights. They were put there for the specific purpose of preventing just the sort of governmental suppression of critics that the majority upholds here. Their ineffectiveness to that end stems, not from any lack of precision in the statement of principles, but from the *refusal of the majority* to apply those principles as precisely stated. (They are stated) in precise and mandatory terms, and unless they are applied in those terms, the

> freedoms of religion, speech, press, assembly and petition will have no effective protection. Where these freedoms are left to depend upon a balance to be struck by this Court in each particular case, liberty cannot survive. For under such a rule, there are no constitutional rights that cannot be 'balanced away.'[110]

Wilkinson was protesting the HUAC's questioning of Braden, an uncooperative witness who had been active in the Emergency Civil Liberties Committee and in the Southern Conference Educational Fund–organizations charged by HUAC as being connected with the Communist Party and with opposing the HUAC and its investigative activities. He had refused to answer certain questions and was convicted of contempt of Congress. The Supreme Court upheld the contempt conviction.

Black argued, in dissent, that the only reason why he was called before HUAC was because he was a white man with antisegregationist views who lived in Kentucky and who signed a petition calling for the Congress to repeal or veto proposed legislation that would have empowered states to pass antisedition statutes. For this reason he was called from Rhode Island to testify before the HUAC meeting in Atlanta, Georgia. The Court, using the balancing test and refusing to examine the motives for such HUAC actions, was destroying liberty in the United States, argued Black. "Liberty, to be secure for any, must be secure for all–even for the most miserable merchants of hate and unpopular ideas." The First Amendment, Black reminded the Court, was not a "mere admonition," and the liberties in it were not to be left "completely at the mercy of Congress and this Court whenever a majority of this Court concludes on the basis of any of the several judically created 'tests' now in vogue (balancing, shock the conscience, decencies of civilized conduct, concept of ordered liberty), that abridgment of those freedoms is more desirable than freedom itself."[111]

The foundation on which the governmental structure of this nation rests was the right of the people to be "wholly free" to speak out fearlessly for or against the officials and the laws or actions taken by the officials. "When the government begins to send its dissenters, such as Barenblatt, Uphaus, Wilkinson, and now Braden, to jail, the liberties indispensable to its existence must be fast disappearing."

> It is already past the time when people who cherish the qualities of freedom protected by the Bill of Rights can afford to sit complacently by while those freedoms are being destroyed by sophistry and dialectics. Since (1949), the forces of destruction have been hard at work. Much damage has already been done. If this dangerous trend is not stopped now, it may be an impossible task to stop it at all.[112]

Black would have overruled the contempt conviction; he would have also overruled Barenblatt, "its forerunners and its progeny, and return to the language of the Bill of Rights." The course the "balancing" Court majority was taking, Black thought, was just "too dangerous."[113]

In *Russell v United States,*[114] a new, procedural, basis for challenging HUAC contempt of congress convictions was sanctioned by the Court in the opinion written by Justice Potter Stewart. In *Russell* and six other companion cases, contempt citations were overturned because "in each case the indictment returned by the grand jury failed to identify the subject under congressional subcommittee inquiry at the time the witness was interrogated." The vice of these indictments, said Stewart, "is that they fail to satisfy the first essential criteria by which the sufficiency of an indictment is to be tested, i.e., that they failed to sufficiently apprise the defendant 'of what he must be prepared to meet.'" Clark and Harlan dissented. Black concurred.

Security Programs and Loyalty Oaths to Contain Subversive Activities

Parallelling legislative attempts to curb subversion through investigations and via the passage of laws punishing advocacy of political thoughts, press, and speech, President Truman issued Executive Order 9835 setting up a program of loyalty investigations of federal employees in 1947. This was quickly duplicated in the states and, by the end of the decade, cases were coming to the Court raising the fundamental question of whether the government could refuse employment to people whose loyalty to the government was questioned or who refused to sign a loyalty oath (and whether the government, both national and local, could dismiss employees who acted in a manner that was considered suspect with respect to national security). From the very first case heard by the Court dealing with the signing of such "anti-communist" affidavits to one of the last opinions he wrote that dealt with a New York Bar Admission procedure, Justice Black was adamantly opposed to these governmental intrusions into the realm of belief and thought. Certainly, he would argue again and again, *conduct* by lawyers, doctors, subway conductors, teachers, and all others (who were obliged to swear allegience to the constitutional form of government) could be restrained by the state. But the government could not, consistent with the Constitution, punish a person by dismissing him or denying him employment, because of the views he held and wrote, spoke, petitioned, and assembled peaceably about.

The very first of these cases to come to the Court was, ironically, the initial venture of the Court in the entire field of subversive activities and governmental responses to these alleged threats to the security of the country: *American Communications Association, CIO v Doud, Regional Director, NLRB,* decided during the 1949 term of the Court. The issue dealt with a section (9h) of the National Labor Relations Act, as amended, which denied the benefits of the NLRB to any labor organization whose officers did not file a "non-communist" affidavit (as required by the Taft-Hartley Act passed in 1947). Chief Justice Vinson, speaking for the Court majority, held the law to be constitutional. One purpose of the NLRA was to remove obstructions to the free flow of commerce resulting from "political strikes" instigated by Communists who had infiltrated labor unions. Section 9 was written to protect the public, not from Communist beliefs, but from Communist actions. The effects of the law on the free exercise of speech, Vinson argued, must be weighed against the Congressional determination that political strikes are evils of conduct which cause substantial harm to interstate commerce and that Communists are continuous threats to the public interest by holding positions of political power in unions.

> Speech may be fought with speech....But force may and must be fought with force. Section 9h is designed to protect the public not against what communists advocate and believe, but against what Congress has concluded they have done and are likely to do again....When the effect of a statute or ordinance upon the exercise of First Amendment freedoms is relatively small and the public interest to be protected is substantial, it is obvious that a rigid test requiring a showing of imminent danger to the security of the nation is an absurdity.[115]

Black dissented from this first of many dozens of balancing decisions of the Court. The First Amendment was added *after* the adoption of the Constitution "for the express purpose of barring Congress from using previously granted powers to abridge belief or its expression. Freedom to think is inevitably abridged when beliefs are penalized by imposition of civil disabilities."[116] To deny the Union the services of the NLRB because officers refused to sign the affidavit was governmental proscription of political belief. In a warning to the Court that was to be the basis of his continuing dissents in the future, Black wrote:

> The Court finds comfort in its assurance that we need not fear too much legislative restriction on political belief or association 'while this Court sits.' That expression, while felicitious, has no validity in this particular constitutional field. For it springs from the assumption that individual mental freedom can be constitutionally abridged whenever any majority of this Court finds a satisfying legislative reason.[117]

The cases that follow deal exclusively with loyalty oath situations that arose in the state courts. These are distinguished from the loyalty-security programs developed by the governments, both national and state, which established elaborate screening programs by which the government could dismiss employees because they were found to be, after being hired, "security risks."* Justice Black's attitude, seen in his dissents in *Barsky v Board of Regents of University of The State of New York,* 347 *US* 442 (1953) and *Beilan v Board of Education, Philadelphia,* 357 *US* 399 (1958), was that these security programs were bills of attainder, denied the defendants procedural due process of law by these agencies operating outside the ordinary safeguards of the law with "arbitrary power to decide, conceivably on the basis of suspicion, whim, or caprice, whether or not (these people) shall lose their (jobs)." In *Adler v Board of Education of City of New York,* 342 *US* 485 (1951), where the Court majority upheld the dismissal of a public school teacher who belonged to an organization which advocated violent overthrowal of the government, Black dissented, saying, in part, "This is another of those rapidly multiplying legislative enactments which make it dangerous—this time for schoolteachers to think or say anything except what a transient majority

*See, for example, *Bailey v Richardson,* 341 *US* 918 (1950), *Peters v Hobby,* 349 *US* 331 (1954), *Cole v Young,* 351 *US* 536 (1955), *Slochower v Board of Higher Education of City of New York,* 350 *US* 551 (1955).

happen to approve at the moment."* Perhaps Black's strongest criticism of the Federal program came in *Joint Anti-Fascist Refugee Committee v McGrath,* 341 *US* 123 (1950):

> In this day when prejudice, hate, and fear are constantly invoked to justify irresponsible smears and persecutions of persons even faintly suspected of entertaining unpopular views, it may be futile to suggest that the cause of internal security would be fostered, not hurt, by faithful adherence to our constitutional guarantees of individual liberty. Nevertheless,...it surely should not be amiss to call attention to what has occurred when dominant governmental groups have been left to give uncontrolled rein to their prejudices against unorthodox minorities.

One of the first loyalty oath cases to reach the Court was *Wieman v Updegraff.* An Oklahoma statute required each state officer and employee to take a loyalty oath, as a condition of employment, stating that he has not been for the preceding five years a member of any group on the Attorney General's list of subversive or communist front organizations. The statute excluded persons from employment solely on the basis of membership, regardless of their knowledge of the activities and true purposes of such groups. Holding that the Act violated due process of law because it did not distinguish between innocent and knowing membership, Justice Clark set aside the exclusion decision. Due process of law, he said for the Court majority, extends to

*But see Brennan's opinion for the Court (Black joins) in *Keyishian v Board,* 385 *US* 589 (1966), in which the New York statute was declared unconstitutional due to vagueness. For an understanding of the ways in which the President's Loyalty Security Program operated, see *Vitarelli v Seaton,* 359 *US* 535 (1959). See also, Leonard G. Miller, "Subversion and the Cold War," in C. Herman Pritchett and Alan F. Westin, *The Third Branch of Government,* New York, Harcourt, Brace and World, 1963, pp. 204-233.

public servants whose exclusion is "patently arbitrary and discriminatory." Justice Black concurred in the judgment of the Court, but not in its reasoning.

"Test oaths are notorious tools of tyranny," wrote the Justice. Governments have ample power to punish treasonable acts "but they do not have the power to punish thought and speech as distinguished from acts."

> Our own free society should never forget that laws which stigmatize and penalize thought and speech of the unorthodox have a way of reaching, ensnaring, and silencing many more people than first intended. We must have freedom of speech for all or we will in the long run have it for none but the cringing and the craven. And I cannot too often repeat my belief that the right to speak on matters of public concern must be wholly free or eventually be wholly lost.[118]

While it is seemingly "self evident" that all speech critical of the government is also dangerous to the "status quo," Black emphasized that "even the slightest suppression of thought, speech, press, or public association is still more dangerous."[119]

In California, failure to sign a loyalty oath meant that the non-signers would lose tax exemptions provided for veterans by the California Constitution. During the 1957 term of the Court, the judges were asked to determine whether the provision was constitutional. Justice Brennan, for the Court, held that the enforcement of the provision denied people freedom of speech without procedural safeguards. "To deny an exemption to claimants who engage in certain forms of speech is in effect to penalize them for such speech," he concluded.[120] Justice Black concurred.

The California provision, he maintained, has placed a tax on belief and expression. This was a novel attempt, but one that was "wholly out of place in this country." Black, in this opinion, took time to reflect on the history of these loyalty oath cases.

> This case offers just another example of a wide-scale effort by

> government to impose penalties and disabilities on everyone who is or is suspected of being a 'Communist' or who is not ready at all times and all places to swear his loyalty to state and nation....Government employees, lawyers, doctors, teachers, pharmacists, veterinarians, subway conductors, industrial workers—taxpayers, denial of unemployment insurance, public housing, oaths of hunters, fishermen, wrestlers, boxers, and junkdealers. I am convinced that this whole business of penalizing people because of their views and expressions concerning government is hopelessly repugnant to the principles of freedom upon which this nation was founded and which have helped to make it the greatest in the world....Loyalty oaths, as well as other 'security measures,' tend to stifle all forms of unorthodox or unpopular thinking or expression—the kind of thought and expression which has played such a vital and beneficial role in the history of this Nation. The result is a stultifying conformity which in the end may turn out to be more destructive to our free society than foreign agents could ever hope to be. The course which we have been following the last decade is not the course of a strong, free, secure people, but that of the frightened, the insecure, the intolerant...Loyalty must arise spontaneously from the hearts of people who love their country and respect their government. It can never be secured through the endless proliferation of 'loyalty oaths.'[121]

Another area affected by the loyalty craze of the 1950s alluded to by Black in his *Spieser* concurring opinion, and one that touched a vital chord within the minds of the judges themselves, was admission of persons to the bar of the various states. As a precondition to such admission to the bar and the subsequent practice of law, applicants had to undergo a series of investigations including the signing of oaths or the answering of questions pertaining to their political beliefs and their allegiance to the government of the United States. In three cases announced the same day during the 1960 term of the Supreme Court, the Court majority validated these various pre-admission loyalty examinations of prospective members of the bar: *Konigsberg v State Bar of*

California, In Re Anastaplo, and *Cohen v Hurley.* The first dealt with the legality of a California law which created a Commission of Bar Examiners whose task it was to check the loyalty of candidates for admission to the state bar. Konigsberg, the applicant, refused to answer questions and he was not certified. Harlan, for the Court majority, upheld the denial of admission. Konigsberg had obstructed the full investigation demanded by the law. "We reject the view that freedom of speech and association are 'absolutes,' not only in the undoubted sense that where the constitutional protection exists it must prevail, but also in the sense that the scope of that protection must be gathered solely from a literal reading of the First Amendment."[122] Using the balancing test that Black dreaded, Harlan concluded that "it has already been held that the interest in not subjecting speech and association to the deterrence of subsequent disclosure is outweighed by the state's interest in ascertaining the fitness of the employee for the post he holds and hence that such a question (concerning Communist Party membership) does not infringe constitutional protections....We regard the state's interest in having lawyers who are devoted to the law in its broadest sense, including not only its substantive provisions, but also its procedures for orderly change as clearly sufficient to outweigh the minimal effect upon free association occasioned by compulsory disclosure in the circumstances here presented."[123]

Anastaplo's situation was basically the same. He had been denied admission to the Illinois bar because he refused to answer questions about Communist Party affiliation. Harlan saw obstruction by the defendant and again pointed out that the state's interest in enforcing the rules "outweighs" any deterrent effect upon speech and association. In the third case, Cohen was disbarred for refusing to produce records and answer questions and his disbarment was upheld by the Court in an opinion written by Harlan who said that the state had a "substantial interest in conducting investigations of this type" that outweighed Cohen's Bill of Rights guarantee against self-incrimination. Justice Black vigorously dissented in all three decisions, essentially criticizing the Court's adherence to the "balancing" formula while rejecting the "literalist" interpretation of the First Amendment.

"I reject the 'balancing' doctrine for I believe that the First Amendment's unequivocal command that there shall be no abridgment of the rights of free speech and assembly shows that the men who drafted our Bill of Rights did all the 'balancing' that was to be done in this field."[124] In our society, Black argued, *all* ideas must be "allowed to enter the competition of the market" and that the creation of "tests" by judges meant that certain thoughts would not be heard and discussed. Society, if it is not to remain static, must allow the fullest interchange of ideas. This, he argued, was the essence of the First Amendment. The employment of tests by judges showed their fears and their prejudices; "their fear that the American people can be alienated from their allegiance to our form of government by the talk of zealots....I think this fear is groundless. The loyalty and patriotism of the American people toward our own free way of life are too deeply rooted to be shaken by mere talk or argument from people who are too wedded to totalitarian forms of government."[125] The judges were simply prejudiced against those who preached the Communist doctrine and, by using the balancing formula, were forcing their own values upon these men and women. The Bill of Rights, said Black, prohibits the judges from using their values to "outweigh the values most highly cherished by the Founders."[126] These tactics of the 'balancing' judges, if not checked, will lead to a society of the weak and the cringing; and this, for Black, was the basic criticism and error of those balancers:

> Too many men are being driven to become government-fearing and time-serving because the government is being permitted to

strike out at those who are fearless enough to think as they please and say what they think.[127]

We must return to the original language of the Bill of Rights, urged Black. As he so simply put it: "We must not be afraid to be free."[128]

In Justice Black's last year on the Court, the 1970 term, three cases were handled that dealt with the loyalty issue and admission to the bar: *Sara Baird v State Bar of Arizona, In Re Martin Stolar,* and *Law Students Civil Rights Research Council v Wadmond.* The first two, *Baird* and *Stolar,* dealt with Arizona and Ohio laws that prohibited admission to the bar if applicants refused to answer questions concerning their loyalty, association with the Communist Party, and other questions dealing with political beliefs. Justice Black wrote the *majority* opinions of the Court disallowing the state actions that barred the applicants from being admitted to the bar.

"The best way to handle (these cases)," wrote Black, "is to narrate its simple facts and then relate them to the 45 words that make up the First Amendment."[129] The First Amendment, concluded Black, protects Miss Baird and Mr. Stolar from questions "potentially so hazardous to (their) liberty." It gives the applicants freedom of mind as well as freedom of conscience. The state has not shown any legitimate interest that would allow it to interfere with their freedom of thought, speech, and association. "And whatever justification may be offered, a state may not inquire about a man's views or associations solely for the purpose of withholding a right or benefit because of what he believes."[130] "We hold," Black concluded, "that views and beliefs are immune from bar association inquisitions designed to lay a foundation for barring an applicant from the practice of law."

The central question in all these loyalty cases, said Black in *Stolar,* was to what extent does the Constitution "protect persons against governmental intrusion and invasion into private beliefs and views that have not ripened into any punishable conduct."[131] The First Amendment, reiterated Black in this Ohio case, prohibits the state "from penalizing a man solely because he is a member of a particular organization....We can see no legitimate state interest which is served by a question which sweeps so broadly into areas of belief and association protected against government invasion."[132] Miss Baird had refused to answer questions concerning membership in the Communist Party or any organization that advocates overthrow of the United States government by force or violence. Mr. Stolar had refused to answer three questions concerning membership in "any organization" advocating violent overthrow and listing names and addresses of these organizations.[133] The record in both cases indicates, concluded Black, upstanding young people who had answered questions and presented evidence of their moral fitness to practice law. In neither case was there any shred of evidence that they were not fit to practice law—other than their refusal to answer questions concerning their political beliefs. To refuse them admission to the bar because they declined to answer these questions was an outright denial of their First Amendment rights. (Justice Harlan dissented in *Baird* and *Stolar*, arguing that the questions should have been answered, that any applicant who believes in violent overthrowal of the government should not be admitted to the bar, "nor do I think that the questioning of candidates as to their beliefs in violent overthrow necessarily runs afoul of true First Amendment concerns.")

> I maintain that there is no constitutional barrier to denying admission to those who seek entry to the profession for the very purpose of doing away with the orderly processes of law, and that temperate inquiry into the character of their beliefs in this regard, which is all that is shown here, is a relevant and permissible course to that end.[134]

And so, a decade after *Konigsberg* and *Anastaplo* and in the last full year on the Court for both Justices Black and Harlan, they found their roles reversed. But the elation Black must have felt was dampened somewhat by the decision of the Court in the *Law Students Civil Rights Research Council* case, in which he had, once again, to dissent.

The group had challenged the New York State bar admission practice where a Committee on Character and Fitness would receive affidavits from people acquainted with the applicant and would have the applicant in for interviews and the filling out of a questionnaire including questions of a political nature. The group argued that the process had a "chilling effect" on the exercise of free speech and association by students while still in law school. A three judge District Court upheld the general validity of the questionnaire and the Supreme Court, in an opinion written by Justice Stewart, affirmed the judgment of the lower court. There was found no constitutional infirmity in the statute requiring that applicants for admission to the bar possess "the character and general fitness" requisite for an attorney and counsellor-at-law.[135]

Dissenting from this view, Justice Black argued that New York was attempting to deprive people of the right to practice law because the applicant "failed to prove his loyalty or refused to answer questions about his political beliefs. In my view, the First Amendment absolutely prohibits a state from penalizing a man because of his beliefs....*even if his membership* (in an organization that advocated the violent overthrow of the government) *was knowing and he shared the organization's aims.*" (my italics)[136] "The First Amendment," Black concluded, "was intended to make speech free from government control, even speech which is dangerous and unpopular....It therefore follows for me that governments should not be able to ask questions designed to identify persons who have belonged to certain political organizations and then exclude them from the practice of law. Asking about an individual's mental attitude toward the Constitution simply probes his beliefs, and these are not the business of the state. For these reasons I would reverse the judgment of the court below."[137]

The Separation of Speech from Conduct

"I draw the line between speech and conduct," said Hugo Black in 1968. "I am vigorously opposed to efforts to extend the First Amendment's freedoms of speech beyond speech, freedom of press beyond press, and freedom of religion beyond religious beliefs. [These provisions] do not immunize other conduct in addition to these particularised freedoms."[138] In all his opinions discussed in part one of this chapter, Black was condemning the anti-subversive legislation, the investigations, and the loyalty programs because they were, in his eyes, infringing upon speech, thought, assembly rights that were absolutely protected from such governmental encroachment. He never denied that the government had the right to preserve itself against overt conduct that threatened the safety of the society. Given his literal commitment to the Constitution, if the document had abridged Congress and the states from passing laws regulating conduct, then Black would say (as he did), "it's a terrible thing that it can't regulate any conduct."[139] And he would have voted to strike down any law that did attempt to do just that.

But the First Amendment does not prohibit Congress and the states from passing laws regulating conduct and, because of that, the Supreme Court has been faced with the difficult task of determining the boundary between "pure" speech and press, which is protected from infringement and conduct, allegedly intimately associated with "pure" speech such as picketing, demonstrating, burning draft cards and American flags, which is not so protected.[140] "Let me make absolutely clear," wrote Black in 1968 about cases involving conduct and speech, "that even laws governing *conduct* must be tested, though only by a balancing process, if they indirectly affect ideas....This kind of balancing should be used only where a law is aimed at conduct and indirectly affects speech; a law aimed directly at curtailing speech and political persuasion can, in my opinion, never be saved through a balancing process."

In an interview on national television, in 1968, Justice Black was asked about the difference or line that separated action from speech as protest. Pointing to the Mormon case of 1878, *Reynolds v US,* where a Congressional law prohibiting polygamy in the Territories was upheld by the Court, Black said:

> The Mormons had a perfectly logical argument, if conduct is the same as speech. They said, 'But this expresses our religious views (polygamy). We're protesting because the government is passing a law suppressing our right to have a dozen wives.' Well, the Court says, 'That won't do, that's conduct, that's not speech.' Of course, it involves speech—partially. Before you get to it, before you get a dozen wives, you've got to do some talking. But that doesn't mean the Constitution protects their right to have a dozen wives. The two are separate. Of course there are places where you cannot sharply draw a boundary.

This segment of the chapter will focus on Black's attempts to delineate as clearly as possible the boundary between protected speech and clearly unprotected speech plus conduct. (See Black's views on such situations in cases discussed earlier, i.e., *Giboney, Adderly,* and *Logan Valley Plaza.*)

In the early 1950s Justice Black dissented in two cases that illustrate the judgmental difficulty that pervades many of these First Amendment cases, *Feiner v New York* and *Beauharnais v Illinois.* In the former case, a young militant student was arrested, charged with breaching the peace by speaking in an inflammatory manner on the streets of Syracuse, and convicted. In the other case, a white segregationist was convicted for distributing in Chicago anti-negro leaflets in violation of an Illinois statute that made it a crime to exhibit in a public place any publication which by depicting deprivation or lack of virtue in any class of citizens of any race, color, creed, exposes them to contempt, derision, and obloquy. In both cases the Supreme Court, in opinions written by Chief Justice Vinson and Justice Frankfurter respectively, upheld the convictions. Black thought differently; certainly there was conduct—the movements of both Feiner and Beauharnais prior to their arrests. But essentially these were situations where the men were arrested and convicted for what they said or for what *others* were doing and *that* was not permitted by the Constitution.

Countering the argument made by Vinson in *Feiner* that the student was arrested, not for the content of his speech, but for the reaction which it actually engendered, Black simply said that the only disturbance, as the record indicated, came from a married man who, in front of his wife and children, told the arresting policemen to stop Feiner from speaking or else he would "kill the s-o-b." The record "convinces me," said Black, "that the petitioner, a young college student, has been sentenced to the penitentiary for the unpopular views he expressed on matters of public interest while lawfully making a street-corner speech in Syracuse, New York."[142]

"The conviction makes a mockery of the free speech guarantees of the First Amendment," stated Black. The upshot of this decision, he argued, was that now cities and states have a "readily available technique" which can with impunity subject all speeches "to the supervision and censorship of the local police. I can have no part or parcel," Black said, in a holding "which I view as a long step toward totalitarian authority."[143] He concluded by saying that he "regretted (his) inability to persuade the Court not to retreat from the principle that the liberties of free speech and press are essential to enlightened opinion and right conduct on the part of the citizens in a democracy."[144]

A year later, in the 1951 *Beaurharnais* case, Black dissented from the Frankfurter judgment that the Illinois statute was not violative of First Amendment rights. Frankfurter, said Black, justifies the Act by "acting on the bland assumption that the First Amendment is wholly irrelevant."[145] He was arrested for what he said, not what he was doing and how he was doing it, argued Black. "The Illinois Act sets up a system of state censorship which is at war with the kind of free government envisoned by those who forced the adoption of our Bill of Rights. The motives behind the state law may have been to do good. But the same can be said about most state laws making opinion punishable as crimes. History indicates that urges to do good have led to the burning of books and even to the burning of witches."[146]

If these cases were, for Black, clear-cut examples of "pure" speech being infringed by state action, the following cases clearly illustrate situations and conditions where the state, according to Black, had an obligation to act to restrain unprotected conduct: *Cox v Louisiana, United States v O'Brien, Tinker v Des Moines,* and *Street v New York.*

Cox was arrested and charged (and subsequently convicted) by Louisiana authorities with (1) breaching the peace, (2) obstructing public passage, and (3) courthouse picketing. Louisiana Statute Section 14:103.1 states:

> Whoever with intent to provoke a breach of the peace, or under circumstances such that a breach of the peace may be occasioned thereby: (1) crowds or congregates with others, providing however nothing herein contained shall apply to a bona fide legitimate labor organization or to any of its legal activities such as picketing, lawful assembly or concerted activity in the interest of its members..., in or upon a public street or public highway, or

upon a public sidewalk, or any other public place or building and who fails or refuses to disperse and move on, or disperse and move on, when ordered to do so by any law enforcement officer of any municipality, or parish, in which such acts or acts are committed, or by any law enforcement officer of the state of Louisiana, or any other authorized person...shall be guilty of disturbing the peace.

In two opinions (Number 24 dealt with the first two charges, Number 49 dealt with the courthouse picketing charge), Justice Goldberg writing for the Court majority overturned all three charges. Goldberg argued, in 24, that Louisiana deprived Cox of his First Amendment rights of free speech and assembly by drawing up a breach-the-peace statute that was unconstitutionally vague and overbroad.[147] The conviction for courthouse picketing was invalidated because it was a dragnet statute. A narrowly drawn, more specific statute regulating conduct as distinguished from speech and press does not infringe First Amendment rights, maintained Goldberg. The statute in question, however, was not so narrowly drawn. Therefore the conviction had to be set aside.[148]

Black concurred in the first judgment of the Court (Number 24) but dissented in the second, that is, the one that invalidated the conviction for courthouse picketing. "A state statute regulating conduct—patrolling and marching—as distinguished from speech, would in my judgment be constitutional.

The First and Fourteenth Amendments, I think, take away from government, state and federal, all power to restrict freedom of speech, press and assembly *where people have a right to be for such purposes.* (his italics) This does not mean, however, that these amendments also grant a constitutional right to engage in the conduct of picketing or patrolling, whether on publicly owned grounds or on privately owned property....Picketing, though it may be utliized to communicate ideas, is not speech and therefore is not of itself protected by the First Amendment.[149]

Paralleling his views about the danger of giving law enforcement officers discretionary censorship powers presented in *Feiner,* Black voted to set aside the breach of peace conviction. "Louisiana has by a broad, vague statute given policemen an unlimited power to order people off the streets not to enforce a specific, nondiscriminatory state statute forbidding picketing or patrolling, but rather whenever a policeman makes a decision on his own personal judgment that views being expressed on the street are provoking or might provoke a breach of the peace....This kind of statute provides a perfect device to arrest people whose views do not suit the policeman or his superiors while leaving free to talk anyone with whose views the police agree."[150]

Black also agreed that the second conviction, for obstructing public passages, be set aside for "while I have no doubt about a general power of Louisiana to bar *all* picketing on its streets," the statute in question was discriminatory because it allowed some to picket (labor organizations) while denying that right to others. Black, however, vehemently disagreed with the Court's judgment concerning the third charge and conviction for courthouse picketing.

The group, reasoned Black, was marching and picketing and patrolling the streets outside the Courthouse "for the express purpose of influencing the Courthouse officials in the performance of their official duties."[151] (Civil rights colleagues had been arrested earlier and they were going to trial the day the Cox march took place.) "The very purpose of a court system is to adjudicate controversies both criminal and civil in the calmness and solemnity of the courtroom according to legal procedures," Black said. (Black's view on this topic of Courtroom decorum were expressed in the important opinion, *Illinois v Allen,* 397 *US* 337 (1969): "Once lost (due to disruptive behavior), the right to be present can, of course, be reclaimed, as soon as the defendant is willing to conduct himself consistently with the decorum and respect inherent in the concepts of courts and judicial proceedings.") Justice, Black maintained, cannot be "rightly administered, nor are the lives and safety of prisoners secure, where throngs of people clamor against the processes of justice right outside the courthouse or the jailhouse.

> The streets are not now and never have been the proper place to adjudicate justice....And minority groups, I venture to suggest, are the ones who always have suffered and always will suffer most when street multitudes are allowed to substitute their pressures for the less strenuous but more dependable and temperate process of the law. Experience demonstrates that it is not a far step from what to many seems the earnest, honest, patriotic, kind-spirited multitude of today, to the fanatical, threatening, lawless mob of tomorrow. And the crowds that press in the streets for noble goals today can be supplanted tomorrow by street mobs pressing the courts for precisely opposite ends.[152]

While Black was "confident" that Cox acted under the mistaken notion that he and his followers had a constitutional right to picket the courthouse, the history of the past twenty-five years of Negro struggle "if it shows nothing else shows that his group's constitutional and statutory rights have to be protected by the Courts which must be kept free from intimidation and coercive pressures of any kind."[153] He concluded his dissent by underlining his belief that

> government under law as ordained by our Constitution is too precious, too sacred to be jeopardized by subjecting the Courts to intimidating practices that have been fatal to individual liberty and minority rights wherever and whenever such practices have been allowed to poison the stream of justice.

While *Cox* dealt with specific conduct, picketing and patrolling, a trio of cases that reached the Court in the late 1960s raised the question of whether conduct called "symbolic" speech had the protection of the First Amendment.

The idea that "speech" may also be nonverbal or "symbolic" had come before the Court in earlier years. See *Stromberg v California,* 283 *US* 359 (1931), *Board of Education v Barnette,* 319 *US* 624 (1943), *Brown v Louisiana,* a 1965 sit-in case where the Court stated that "First Amendment rights are not confined to verbal expression." Black dissented in the last case, arguing that permitting young blacks to stand-in in a library to protest public policies would lead to the destruction of the Rule of Law:

> I am deeply troubled with the fear that powerful private groups throughout the Nation will read the Court's action...as granting them a license to invade the tranquility and beauty of our libraries whenever they have some quarrel with some state policy....It is an unhappy circumstance in my judgment that the group, which more than any other needed a government of equal laws and equal justice, is now encouraged to believe that the best way for it to advance its cause, which is a worthy one, is by taking the law into its own hands from place to place and from time to time. Governments like ours were formed to substitute the rule of law for the rule of force....I say once more that the crowd moved by noble ideals today can become the mob ruled by hate and passion and greed and violence tomorrow. The peaceful songs of love can become as stirring and provocative as the Marseillaise did in the days when a noble revolution gave way to rule by successive mobs until chaos set in. The holding in this case today makes it more necessary than ever that we stop and look more closely at where we are going.

United States v O'Brien dealt with a young Vietnam war protestor who had burned his draft card to "voice" his discontent with the war policies of the Johnson Administration. In so acting he had violated a federal statute, 50 USC 462 (b), which made it a crime to "forge, alter, knowingly destroy, knowingly mutilate, or in any manner change any such (Selective Service Registration) certificate."

O'Brien argued that the statute was unconstitutional because it abridged his constitutional right of free speech and because it served no valid legislative purpose. Chief Justice Warren, in an opinion joined in by Justice Black, rejected both arguments and upheld the conviction. "This Court has held that when 'speech' and 'nonspeech' elements are combined in the same course of conduct, a sufficiently important governmental interest in regulating the nonspeech element can justify incidental limitations on First Amendment freedoms." The legislation was legitimate because Congress is responsible for raising and supporting an army and navy and, pursuant to this power, "Congress may establish a system of registration for individuals liable for training and service, and may require such persons within reason to cooperate with the registration system. The issuance of certificates indicating the registration and eligibility classification is a legitimate and substantial adminstrative aid in the functioning of the system. And legislation to insure the continuing availability of issued certificates serves a legitimate and substantial purpose in the system's administration."[154]

Tinker v Des Moines also raised the symbolic speech question but this time it was young schoolchildren wearing black armbands to protest the war in Vietnam. And the Court had again to consider whether this nonverbal conduct was protected, that is, whether "pure" speech was protected from infringement by, in this case, school authorities, the state. For wearing the armbands, the children were suspended from school; their lawyers sought an injunction from the Courts barring the school officials from enforcing the suspension. The District Court had dismissed the complaint and the Court of Appeals, sitting *en banc,* affirmed that decision by an equally divided Court. On appeal to the Supreme Court, that Court, in an opinion written by Justice Fortas, overturned the lower Court judgments. Wearing armbands in a quiet and passive way was conduct not disruptive of the rights of others and was within the protection of the free speech clause of the First Amendment.[155]

Black dissented. Conduct of this type was not protected by the First Amendment. Wearing of these armbands, Black argued, *did* disrupt classes and distract students from their normal school activities. Schools are not the place to protest; students should not "defy orders of school officials to keep their minds on their own school work." What the Fortas opinion reflected, wrote Black, was a return to the judicial application of the "reasonableness" test. What Fortas was saying was that the Court majority felt that the incident in the Des Moines school was a "reasonable" expression of free speech and that the school officials acted "unreasonably."

> I have many times expressed my opposition to the[se] concepts on the ground that it gave judges power to strike down any law they do not like. If the majority is resurrecting that old reasonableness-due-process test, I think the constitutional change should be plainly, unequivocally, and forthrightly stated for the benefit of the bench and bar. It will be a sad day for the country, I believe, when the present day Court returns to the McReynolds due process concept.[156]

The action by Iowa's public school officials was consistent with the general powers they have to educate the children. "Iowa's public schools are operated to give students an opportunity to learn, not to talk politics by actual speech, or by 'symbolic' speech.

> One does not need to be a prophet or the son of a prophet to know that after the Court's holding today some students in Iowa schools and indeed in all schools will be ready, willing, and able to defy their teachers on practically all orders.[157]

That same term Justice Black wrote a dissent in yet another such "symbolic" speech case, *Street v New York.* Upon hearing that James Meredith, a civil rights participant, had been shot and wounded in Mississippi while on a solitary march across that state to protest its segregationist policies, the defendant had run out into the street and burned the American flag. He was arrested and charged with malicious mischief for violating Section 1425 of the New York State Penal Law which made it a crime to publicly mutilate, defy, or cast contempt upon any American flag either by words or by actions. Convicted for violating the law, he appealed and, in an opinion written by Justice Harlan, his conviction was set aside.

Harlan reasoned that the application of the statute violated Street's rights because it permitted him to be punished for merely speaking defiant words about the flag. (The record indicated that he had shouted, according to the arresting policeman who heard the words, "We don't need no damned flag....If they let that happen to Meredith we don't need an American flag.") The conviction had to be set aside if it could have been based solely on his words. The record, indicated Harlan, was insufficient to eliminate the possibility that Street's words were the sole basis of his conviction. New York cannot, said Harlan, constitutionally inflict punishment upon one who ventures publicly to defy or cast contempt upon the flag by words.[158]

Black wrote a brief, blistering dissent. If he could agree with Harlan's interpretation of the record "as to the possibility of the conviction's resting on these spoken words," he "would firmly and automatically agree that the law is unconstitutional."[159] But he could not; instead, Black accepted the unanimous opinion of the New York Court of Appeals that

> the conviction does not and could not have rested merely on the spoken words but that it rested entirely on the fact that the defendant had publicly burned the American flag—against the law of New York State. It passes my belief that anything in the Constitution bars a state from making the deliberate burning of the American flag an offense. It is immaterial to me that words

> are spoken in connection with the burning. It is the *burning* of the flag that the state has set its face against....The talking that was done took place as an integral part of conduct in violation of a valid criminal statute against burning the American flag in public. (his italics)[160]

In *Gregory v Chicago* one finds the very core of Justice Hugo Black's concern about allowing conduct such as marching and picketing and patrolling to proceed without check—and also his devout commitment to the words of the Constitution even if it meant deciding a case that was quite contrary to his own personal beliefs. Dick Gregory had led a peaceful and orderly march down the streets of Chicago to the residence of Mayor Richard Daley to protest certain conditions in the city. The onlookers grew quite restless, and concern for the public safety led the police to ask Gregory to disperse his group (Gregory and the police had jointly planned the march). He refused to do so and was arrested and convicted for disorderly conduct. The Illinois Supreme Court affirmed the convicton and Gregory appealed to the Supreme Court. In a one-page opinion authored by Chief Justice Warren, the Court held that he had been denied due process since there was no evidence to support their convictions. They were convicted, Warren said, for demonstrating and not for refusing to obey the police orders to disperse. One could not be convicted, Warren concluded, for acts protected by the First Amendment.[161]

Black concurred. He agreed that the disorderly conduct conviction be set aside because the law on which the conviction was based was not a narrowly drawn one but instead "a meat-ax ordinance." The Chicago ordinance read as follows: "All persons who make, assist in making, any improper noise, riot, disturbance, or diversion tending to the breach of the peace, within the limits of the city; all persons who shall collect in bodies or crowds for unlawful purposes or for any purpose, to the annoyance or disturbance of other persons, shall be deemed guilty of misconduct." As he stated in *Feiner* and *Cox,* such loose laws, "having a multiplicity of meanings," give the policemen on the beat tremendous discretion in determining just who shall be arrested and who shall be safe from arrest. Such lawmaking is the responsibility of legislators elected by the people, not policemen on their beats.[162] Their duty is to enforce laws already in existence and to make arrests only for conduct already made criminal by the law. "To let a policeman's command become equivalent to a criminal statute comes dangerously near making our government one of men rather than of laws."[163]

Had the law been more carefully drawn, the action of Gregory could have resulted in a valid conviction.

> No mandate in our Constitution leaves States and governmental units powerless to pass laws to protect the public from the kind of boisterous and threatening conduct that disturb the tranquillity of spots elected by the people either for homes, where they can escape the hurly-burly of the ouside business and political world, or for public or other buildings that require peace and quiet to carry out their functions, such as courts, libraries, schools, and hospitals.[164]

While he agreed to the reversal of the convictions, he once more reminded Chicago that it could pass laws to restrict conduct—but that they had to be written clearly and narrowly to proscribe *only* conduct. "To say that the First Amendment grants those broad rights free from any exercise of governmental power to regulate conduct, as distinguished from speech, press, association, or petition, would subject all the people of the Nation to the uncontrollable whim and arrogance of speakers and writers, and protestors and grievance bearers."

> I believe our Constitution, written for the ages, to endure except as changed in the manner it provides, did not create a government with such monumental weaknesses. Speech and press are, of

> course, to be free, so that public matters can be discussed with impunity. But picketing and demonstrating can be regulated like other conduct of men. I believe that the homes of men, sometimes the last citadel of the tired, the weary, and the sick, can be protected by government from noisy, marching, tramping, threatening, picketers and demonstrators, bent on filling the minds of men, women, and children with fears of the unknown.[165]

Recapitulation

Hugo Black was raising a basic question in all these cases: "Do we have the courage to be free?"[166] "We must not be afraid to be free," exclaimed Black in *Anastaplo.* He believed strongly that his colleagues feared the consequences, for themselves and for the country, of inflammatory ideas. Because of their fears, they attempted to prohibit, by upholding governmental actions that punished certain types of speech, those inflammatory thoughts. They even created tests to justify their evasion of the "mandatory command" of the First Amendment. But, for Black, every idea was a possible incitement to action; there was no real basis for distinguishing between advocacy of abstract thought and advocacy of illegal action. Speech was speech; ideas were meant to compete with other ideas. The people, Black suggested, had enough common sense to distinguish correctly, then for the Justice the only "real meaning" of free speech must be that the revolutionary ideas accepted by the people will be allowed to prevail.

The acceptance of the judgment of the people was the meaning of courage and freedom in a democracy. Black had enough faith in the courage and the strength of the American people, as he thought the Founding Fathers also had the same faith in the people, to be perfectly content to allow all speech to circulate freely, uninhibitedly, and robustly. His brethren on the Court, however, did not share his optimism, his faith in the people. And this attitude, not only on the part of his fellow Justices, but on the part of legislators and Presidents as well, greatly concerned Black. For him, this lack of faith was the first step on the path toward an authoritarian, totalitarian society of leaders and the "cringing and the craven."

It was this fear of what would happen to the constitutional democracy he so loved if the good men and women were in prison that led Black to argue so fiercely that the First Amendment freedoms not be "diluted," "degraded," "balanced," or "weighed" away. No ifs, ands, buts, and whereases about it, Black said again and again: the First Amendment, taken literally, was beyond the reach of governmental attempts to breach it. Simply put, if government was allowed to halt speech, press, association, and petition rights because it did not like the ideas expounded by the groups, then the society would rapidly turn into a community of oppressed, meek, and afraid individuals with the stagnant air of "stultifying conformity" ever present.

If Black showed his faith in the people to act wisely when faced with new, novel, revolutionary ideas, he also showed his "protestant pessimism" in the speech plus conduct cases. Reading history, Black believed that tramping, singing, marching, demonstrating, picketing people with the most worthy of motives but acting outside the boundary of the law to achieve their goals would lead to counter-demonstrations, marches, tramping by their opponents. From this would flow disastrous consequences; passions aroused, reason would be overtaken and ultimately, irrevocably, the rule of law would be replaced by the rule of men. Order would give way to disorder. In the face of these disturbing reflections on human nature, Black argued that the states could enact legislation that prohibited conduct if that was seen by the state to endanger the public order and safety. These statutes had to be narrowly drawn, non-arbitrary/discriminatory statutes that, in effect, set off islands of security to which men, women, and children could retreat from the vicissitudes of life—economic and political. Certainly changes could be proposed by the people: that was the essence of representative government. But change had to come through the normal democratic processes and not via intimidation and coercion.

If Black feared the consequences of legislative and executive actions that infringed upon the people's absolute right to speak and write freely, he also feared the consequences of speech and press accompanied by conduct that was anarchic, that is, untroubled and unwilling to be bound by the procedures and processes detailed and enumerated in the Constitution of the United States. The former led to a totalitarianism and stifling conformity; the latter led to lawlessness, violence, and anarchy. Black rejected both conclusions. His actions on the Court, with respect to the First Amendment, were based on his literalist interpretation of that Amendment because, beyond the defenses of literalism already mentioned in earlier chapters, literally interpreting the First Amendment meant allowing total freedom of speech and thought (which would frustrate the move to an oppressive society) and also meant that conduct could be regulated by the state (which would blunt the tendency toward chaos and anarchism if the Amendment allowed all conduct connected with speech). Black did not fear ideas; he only feared the consequences of the breakdown of law. Freedom, for Black, was fragile: neither governmental actions nor street rioters must be allowed to destroy it.

While this chapter on the First Amendment focused on Black's response to governmental actions that infringed on the rights of individuals to hold and express radical and revolutionary political doctrines that the majority feared and hated, certainly his views of the "absoluteness" of "pure" religious freedom etc. were just as firm. The First Amendment allowed people to worship or not to worship as they saw fit, but prohibited the state to interfere with such practices or non-practices. There was a wall of separation between Church and state, he wrote in 1947, and the First Amendment prohibits the state from breaching that wall. In the 1952 case of *Zorach v Clauson,* 343 *US* 306 (dissenting opinion), Black wrote:

> Under our system of religious freedom, people have gone to their religious sanctuaries not because they feared the law but because they loved their God. The choice of all has been as free as the choice of those who answered the call to worship moved only by the music of the old Sunday morning church bells. The spiritual mind of man has thus been free to believe, disbelieve, or doubt, without repression, great or small, by the heavy hand of government.

Writing the opinion for the majority in the 1962 case, *Engel v Vitale,* 370 *US* 423, where a New York State-sponsored prayer had been nullified because it violated the separation of Church and state principle, Black wrote:

> Government in this country, be it state or federal, is without power to prescribe by law any particular form of prayer which is to be used as an official prayer in carrying out any program of governmentally sponsored religious activity....The Establishment Clause thus stands as an expression of principle on the part of the Founders of the Constitution that religion is too sacred, too personal, to permit its 'unhallowed perversion' by a civil magistrate....It is neither sacrilegious nor antisacrilegious to say that each separate government in this country should stay out of the business of writing or sanctioning official prayers and leave that purely religious function to the people themselves and to those the people choose to look to for religious guidance.

Black was just as insistent that the First Amendment gave the press an absolute right to publish even falsehoods and, in the 1964 *New York Times v Sullivan* case, he concurred in the judgment of the Court (written by Brennan which set aside libel judgments against the newspaper and southern

Negro leaders because "actual malice" was not shown) because the word "malice" was:

> an elusive, abstract concept, hard to prove and hard to disprove. The requirement of malice...does not measure up to the sturdy safeguard embodied in the First Amendment. Unlike the Court, therefore, I vote to reverse on the ground that the Times and the individual defendants had an *absolute, unconditional* right to publish in the Times advertisement their criticisms of the Montgomery agencies and officials.

As for the Court determining whether something was obscene (and hence not protected speech of the First Amendment variety), Black scoffed at the notion of nine old men, sitting as a supercensor of society's morals, being able to determine what was or was not obscenity. "This Court is about the most inappropriate Supreme Board of Censors that could be found," he wrote in dissent in 1959. Whenever such cases were being heard by the Court, Black would *refuse* even to screen the movie or read the book that was allegedly pornographic or obscene.

6

Justice Black
An Elemental Force in American Jurisprudence

The Magnificent "Backward Country Fellow"

How could a "backward country fellow," the son of a farmer in Clay County, Alabama, recipient of a skimpy education in the liberal arts and in the law;[1] a man accused of being anti-negro,[2] a confessed member of the hated Ku Klux Klan, called too "damn" common by a fellow Senator, called judicially intemperate by many at the time of his appointment,[3] turn into what one person termed him, after Hugo Black's death, "an elemental force in American Constitutional development."[4] The answer lay in the internal make-up of Hugo Lafayette Black: "In an age of commercial travelers," wrote Anthony Lewis, "Hugo Black was a man. He had the essential quality of a judge, the inner strength to be independent."[5]

Hugo Black had the strength and fortitude to be loyal to the Constitution, regardless of the ill winds that blew about him—on the Court itself, in the Congress, in the Executive branch. He had, as his colleague, Chief Justice Earl Warren said, an "unflagging devotion" to the Constitution. "That Constitution is my legal bible," wrote Black in 1968, "its plan of our government is my plan and its destiny my destiny. I cherish every word of it, from the first to the last, and I personally deplore even the slightest deviation from its least important commands."[6] On another occasion he said, I like to read what it says, I like to read the words of the Constitution. I'm a literalist, I admit it. It's a bad word these days. I know, but that's what I am." And this literal, not liberal, commitment to the Constitution and the plan of government outlined in it led Black to stand up against all attempts to weaken or subvert its guidelines during the thirty-five years he sat on the Supreme Court. "More than a faith," wrote a law clerk of Justice Black, "he had a true passion for the Constitution."[8]

Hugo Black's Basic Fears For the Country

He revered the Constitution and believed that, if followed literally, America would be blessed with a living, functioning democracy. There were, however, threats to the maintenance of the Rule of Law: three basic challenges were governmental actions that infringed the constitutionally protected areas of speech, thought, and protected actions; judicial tampering with the literal meaning of the Constitution through the creation of tests, doctrines, which enabled them to justify changes in the Fundamental Law; and violence and demonstrative activities of people that threatened the very essence of order and decorum and procedure in a democratic society.

Black firmly believed that the only form of government consistent with the Constitution was one that was strong enough to combat privilege and regulate the economic development of the society but weak enough so as to not be able to infringe upon and abridge human freedom. He thought it was "possible to make government positive while keeping it from becoming punitive."[9] And so he rejected, for example, the argument that the President of the United States had the inherent right to seize the steel mills during the Korean conflict. There was no apparent Congressional and Constitutional authority for the seizure; the Framers of the Constitution, "the Founders of this Nation entrusted the law making power to the Congress alone in both good and bad times."[10] If Congress delegated such a power to seize the mills to the President, said Black, then that would be constitutionally acceptable–but Congress did not and therefore the President could not, arbitrarily and unconstitutionally, seize them. The President had only those powers given to him in the Constitution and delegated to him by the Congress. There were no inherent powers of the President. He continued preaching this view through his last opinion in which he rejected the contention, presented by the Nixon Adminstration, that, in the interest of "national security," the President, with the assistance of the Courts, could censor the press.[11]

Power corrupts, Black believed, and justices of the Supreme Court are as corruptible as other human beings. Hugo Black's fears were based on the activities of the pre-1937 Supreme Court; a Court that had willfully blocked efforts by the national majority to introduce new economic and social legislation that would have improved the condition of life in the country. Even before his elevation to the Court, he opposed judicial interpretations of due process of law which gave the judges a veto-power over legislation passed by the representatives of the people. From his first days on the Court to the very last opinion he wrote, Black harshly condemned such judicial policy-making in the guise of judicial interpretation of the Constitution. For a judge of the Court to examine cases and controversies with a measuring tool such as "civilized standards of decency," "fundamental fairness," "shock to conscience," "clear and present danger," "balancing of interests," "without socially redeeming values," "right of privacy," etc., was the height of injudicious action. The judge's oath committed the man to an absolutely mandatory obligation to obey the Constitution; the oath did not give him the power to change it. And changing it, even for the best of motives, meant that judges were violating the Rule of Law. And if "good" judges sat on the Court today and made policy that pleased the majority, what would happen when bad judges, in different circumstances, sat on the Court? As Alan Dershowitz so perceptively put it in comparing Justice Black and Harlan after their retirements:

> Justice Black maintained that his was truly the philosophy of judicial restraint since it limited the power of the judge to the plain meaning of the Constitution. He criticized Justice Harlan's 'due process' approach which made everything a matter of degree, thus empowering the justices to use their judgment. If all justices were of the calibre and fairness of these two great figures, then there would be little question that Justice Harlan's approach would produce wiser results in the long run. But Justice Black's philosophy might well provide a surer protection against the tyranny of evil men in robes.[12]

Black clearly indicated such a fear of judicial policy-making in one of his last dissenting opinions written during the 1969-1970 term of the Court. Perceiving that the majority judgment was employing the McReynolds "substantive due process" formula to decide the case, he wrote:

> The Framers of our Constitution and Bill of Rights were too wise, too pragmatic, and too familiar with tyranny to attempt to safeguard personal liberty with words and phrases like 'fair trial,' 'fundamental decency,' and 'reasonableness.' Such stretchy, rubberlike terms would have left the judges constitutionally free to try people charged with crime under the will-o-the-wisp standards improvised by different judges for different defendants. Neither the Due Process Clause nor any other constitutional language vests any judge with such power. Our Constitution was not written in the sands to be washed away by each successive political wind that brings new political administrations into temporary power. Rather, our Constitution was fashioned to perpetuate liberty and justice by making clear, explicit, and lasting constitutional boundaries.[13]

His third concern and fear for the American constitutional pattern was his alarm at the growing violence and lawlessness and permissiveness that he saw in America. These tramping, singing, patrolling, wearing of armbands, burning of flags and draftcards, sit-ins, stand-ups, and lay-ins were reflections of a deeper malaise: the disenchantment with normal democratic processes and procedures for changing social and economic situations in the local, state, or national communities. Much as he placed his faith in the wisdom of the people, Black "believed strongly that greed is woven tightly into the fabric of man's being, and that people often dislike instinctively people who are different from them."[14]

While the Negro rights struggle was a "worthy cause," as Black stated in a dissenting opinion in 1965, and while he vigorously supported, in secret conference sessions and in the written opinions of the Court, the struggle of the black man for true equality,[15] and while "bigotry and racial prejudice were totally foreign to his nature because to him, as to Thomas Jefferson, all men were in fact created equal and common sense required that they be treated as such,"[16] Black nevertheless (to the chagrin of blacks and liberals) would not accept boisterous conduct on the part of Negro demonstrators who were beginning to grow impatient with the normal channels and procedures of change. Nor would Black, much to the chagrin and anger of civil libertarians, bend the Constitution to give added protection to Negro actions or to strike down state laws that were, while perhaps racially motivated, not in conflict with specific constitutional prohibitions such as the Fourteenth Amendment's "Equal Protection" Clause. (See, for example, his opinion for the Court in *Palmer v Thompson,* 403 *US* 217 (1970). This attitude was not, however, any different from the one that motivated Mr. Justice Black to write dissenting opinions in cases handed down in the 1937 term of the Court regarding the evils of "substantive" due process. Judges, whether the issue is economic or racial, ought not, *must not,* allow their own perceptions of right and wrong to color their constitutional judgment. The fundamental question, in *any* constitutional case or controversy, was whether the statute ran afoul of the Constitution and not whether or not it ran afoul of some judge's sense of fairness, rightness, or justice. Black did not change his attitude on this issue during the entire thirty-five year period of his judicial activity. What did change were the issues, the cases, that came to the Court.

Certainly this concern of Justice Black that the passions of men would overwhelm, in times of stress and tension and threat to their economic, physical, and social security, their good qualities that he admired so much, may have explained his opinion written for the majority of the Court in 1944, *Korematsu v United States.* In that opinion, for which Black was greatly criticized, he wrote that the military orders calling for the establishment of detention centers for Japanese aliens and citizens of Japanese heritage were, under the wartime circumstances, legitimate. "Exclusion from a threatened area," he wrote, "no less than curfew, has a definite and close relationship to the prevention of espionage and sabotage."[17] In 1967, Black wrote, about that decision, that "I would do precisely the same thing today, in any part of the country....We had a situation where we were at war. People were rightly fearful of the Japanese...they all look the same to a person not a Japanese. Had they attacked our shores...a lot of innocent Japanese would have been shot in the *panic. Under these circumstances,* I saw nothing wrong in moving them away from the danger area."[18] (my italics)

Because freedom was based on reason and the common sense of the man "behind the plow down on the farm," and because men were fallible creatures, Black always attempted to restrain impassioned leaders of movements and acted on the bench to marshall the Court to deny to lawless types the absolute protection of the First Amendment's freedoms. He would tolerate the most blasphemous of doctrines, political, religious, or economic; he would allow them to compete in the marketplace with other ideas. He had faith that the people would choose correctly—but they must be allowed to choose in an orderly manner. Mobs threatening people did not accomplish anything except intimidation and coercion and counteraction by rival mobs who hated the other side. Bloodshed would follow and ultimately, if the conditions for aroused passion were not removed, the Rule of Law would fall. And so, no matter how worthy the cause, Black absolutely rejected lawlessness. The state, he said, was not powerless to control these actions. For constitutional government to survive, it *had* to control these actions.

Black's Vision and His Dream

His actions as a Justice of the Supreme Court focused repeatedly on three essential dilemmas. To a large extent, Hugo Black was successful in changing the direction of the Court with respect to the power of state and national legislatures to act, in the economic and social arena, free of judicial interference via substantive due process. And in the area of procedural due process, Black's argument that due process of law did not extend beyond the specific protections of the Bill of Rights was ultimately accepted, albeit in piecemeal fashion through the "selective incorporation" process. With respect to Freedoms of Speech for political offenders, Black did see the Court modify some of its harsh judgments of the 1950s although of course the Court did not come to accept his "absolutist" view of the First Amendment. Hugo Black was a major force, an elemental force, behind the movement for more judicial responsibility and firmness with respect to personal and political freedoms in these past three decades. From his first days to his last, Black demanded that the Court defend the Constitution from attacks by governmental agencies and others who disdained the parameters that document created for political action and changes in the laws of the land.

His vision was that of the great men of the eighteenth century's Age of Enlightenment. A society where all people would participate in discussions about politics, in discussions that would affect the quality of their lives. A society where all ideas would be allowed to freely circulate, where sound trucks and amplifier systems as well as radio and television and newspapers could be used to circulate ideas of all types–religious and political.[19] A society where the people had adequate representation[20] and where legislators would reflect the interests of the people, rather than the interests of the special privileged few. A society where all or almost all would not deem it necessary to intimidate or coerce or hate or fear others; where there was respect for and loyalty and allegiance to the Rule of Law.

Hugo Black's dream? That this vision of a non-static but "advancing" good society be realized in the America that he dearly loved. "The proponents of the First Amendment, committed to this faith in an advancing society, were determined that every American should possess an unrestrained freedom to express his views, however odious they might be to vested interests whose power they might challenge."[21] He believed that the dream was being realized, but, like all dreams, it was fragile and could evaporate without constant vigilance. His life was devoted to protecting that fragile reality called constitutional democracy. "I have thoroughly enjoyed my small part in trying to preserve our Constitution," he wrote in 1968, "with the earnest desire that it may meet the fondest hope of its creators, which was to keep this nation strong and great through countless ages."[22] His desire, his dream, will continue only if the country is fortunate enough to have men with the courage, the intense convictions, and the love and the passion for the Constitution that Hugo Lafayette Black had. "No man alone makes a style, creates a mode. Even within the Court, Hugo Black has sat with others who faced the same way. Yet, when the list is made up of those men through whom has chiefly been worked out this nation's resolve to live greatly through law, to make a way by law for democracy to prevail, to use law for the increase of general happiness, and yet steadfastly to express through law a respect for the individuality of man, Hugo Black's name will surely be among a very few of highest honor."[23]

Notes

Notes to Chapter One

(1.) Quoted in Anthony Lewis, "Hugo Black–'An Elemental Force,'" *The New York Times*, September 26, 1971, p.1.

(2.) Wallace Mendelson, *Justices Black and Frankfurter: Conflict in the Court,* Chicago: University of Chicago Press, 1961, p. 13.

(3.) Hugo Black, "The Bill of Rights," 35 *New York University Law Review,* April 1960, pp. 880-881.

(4.) *Ibid.*

(5.) Lenore Cahn, ed., *Confronting Injustice: The Edmond Cahn Reader,* Boston: Little, Brown and Co., 1966, p. 103.

(6.) Correspondence with law clerk, 1969-1970 term.

(7.) John P. Frank, *Mr. Justice Black: The Man and His Opinions,* New York: Alfred A. Knopf, 1948, pp. 11-12.

(8.) Hugo L. Black, *A Constitutional Faith,* New York: Alfred A. Knopf, 1968, p. 14.

(9.) A. E. Dick Howard and George A. Freeman, "Perspectives: Hugo L. Black," *Richmond, Virginia Times Dispatch,* December 12, 1971, pp. 1,3. (Both are former law clerks of the late Justice Black.)

(10.) William O. Douglas, Jr., "Mr. Justice Black: A Foreword," 65 *Yale Law Journal,* No. 4, February 1956, p. 449.

(11.) See, with respect to fallibilism, Howard Ball, *The Warren Court's Conceptions of Democracy,* Rutherford: Fairleigh Dickenson University Press, 1971, Ch. 1, passim.

(12.) Cahn, *op. cit.*, p. 103.

(13.) *New York Times v United States*, 403 *US* 734, at 737. (1970).

(14.) Black, *op. cit.*, p. 43; *Milkwagon Drivers Union v Meadowmoor Dairy,* 312 *US* 287 (1941), at 301-302 (Dissent).

(15.) George L. Saunders, "Remarks," *Meeting of the Bar of the Supreme Court of the United States in Memory of Justice Hugo L. Black,* Washington, D. C., April 18, 1972, p. 5.

(16.) *Boddie v Connecticut,* 401 *US* 371,at 389(1970). Dissent.

(17.) Black, *op. cit.,* pp. 62-63.

(18.) Howard and Freeman, *op. cit.,* p. 3.

(19.) Daniel M. Berman, "Hugo L. Black at 75," X *American University Law Review,* No. 1, January 1961, p. 44.

(20.) Lewis, *op. cit.,* p. 1.

(21.) Correspondence with law clerk, 1969-1970 term.

(22.) Black, *op. cit.,* p. 12. *Constitutional Faith.*

(23.) Hugo L. Black, Introduction to Cahn, *op. cit.,* p. xii.

(24.) *Adamson v California,* 332 *US* 46 (1946), at 89 (Dissent).

(25.) Cahn, *op. cit.,* p. 96.

(26.) Edmond Cahn, quoted in Hugo L. Black, "Justice Black and First Amendment 'Absolutes': A Public Interview," *New York University Law Review,* June 1963, pp. 549-563, at page 550.

(27.) Black, *Constitutional Faith,* p. 45.

(28.) Cahn, *op. cit.,* p. 97.

(29.) *Lincoln Federal Labor Union v Northwestern Iron and Metal Company,* 335 *US* 525 (1949) at 536.

(30.) Vincent Barnett, Jr., "Mr. Justice Black and the Supreme Court," 8 *University of Chicago Law Review,* No. 1, December 1940, p. 20.

(31.) Berman, *op. cit.,* p. 46.

(32.) Frank, *op. cit.,* p. v. Charles Beard, introducing the volume, stated that "the greatest of all political issues confronting Black (is): How to maintain a government strong enough to defend society against external and internal foes and yet so organized as to protect, by Supreme law and its administration, the liberties of the people against oppressive actions by public agents or popular tumults."

(33.) Cahn, *op. cit.,* p. xii.

(34.) Black, *Constitutional Faith,* p. 20.

(35.) *Ibid.,* p. 9.

(36.) *Colegrove v Green,* 328 *US* 549 (1946), at 573-74. (Dissent).

(37.) Hugo L. Black, "Reminiscences," 18 *Alabama Law Review,* No. 1, Fall, 1965, p. 10.

(38.) See, for example, *McCart v Indianapolis Water Company,* 302 *US* 419 (1937) and compare with *Labine v Vincent,* 401 *US* 532 (1970).

(39.) Black, *Constitutional Faith,* p. 24.

(40.) Douglas, *op. cit.,* p. 449.

(41.) John M. Harlan, Jr., "Mr. Justice Black–Remarks of a Colleague," 81 *Harvard Law Review,* No. 1, November 1967, p. 2.

(42.) Black, *Constitutional Faith,* p. 11.

(43.) Black, "The Bill of Rights."

(44.) *Ferguson v Skrupa,* 372 *US* 726 (1963), at 730,732.

(45.) *Chambers v Florida*, 309 *US* 227 (1939), at 241. (Dissent).

(46.) Black, *Constitutional Faith,* p. 14.

(47.) *Dennis v United States,* 341 *US* 494 (1950), at 581. (Dissent).

(48.) *The New York Times v United States,* 403 *US* 734 (1970), at 737.

(49.) *Tinker v Des Moines School District,* 393 *US* 503 (1969), at 518.

(50.) A. E. Dick Howard, "Mr. Justice Black: The Negro Protest Movement and the Rule of Law," 53 *Virginia Law Review,* No. 5, 1967, p. 1052.

(51.) Paul A. Freund, "Mr. Justice Black and the Judicial Function," 14 *UCLA Law Review,* No. 1, January 1967, p. 473.

(52.) Cahn, *op. cit.,* p. 104.

(53.) *Marsh v Alabama,* 326 *US* 501 (1946), at 507-508.

(54.) Correspondence with law clerk, 1969-1970.

(55.) Correspondence with law clerk, 1970-1971.

(56.) Howard, "Mr. Justice Black," p. 1051.

(57.) *Ibid.,* p. 1052.

(58.) Correspondence with law clerk, 1961-1962.

(59.) Freund, *op. cit.,* p. 473.

(60.) Correspondence with law clerk, 1961-1962 term.

Notes to Chapter Two

(1.) Paul Anderson, *The Nation,* quoted in Irving Dilliard, ed., *One Man's Stand For Freedom: Mr. Justice Black and the Bill of Rights,* New York: Alfred A. Knopf, Inc., 1963, p. 21.

(2.) *Ferguson v Skrupa,* at 729.

(3.) *Ibid.*

(4.) Black, *Constitutional Faith,* p. 31.

(5.) 16 *Wallace* 36 (1873)

(6.) *Santa Clara County v Southern Pacific Railroad,* 118 *US* 395 (1886).

(7.) *Mugler v Kansas,* 123 *US* 623 (1887).

(8.) *Ibid.*

(9.) *Lincoln Federal Labor Union v Northwestern Iron and Metal Co.,* 335 *US* 525 (1949) at 536.

(10.) *Allgeyer v Louisiana,* 165 *US* 578 (1897).

(11.) *Lochner v New York,* 198 *US* 45 (1905).

(12.) *Adair v United States,* 208 *US* 161 (1905); *Coppage v Kansas,*

236 *US* 1 (1915).

(13.) See Justice Holmes' opinions for the Court in: *Chicago, B&O Railroad v McGuire* 219 *US* 549 (1911); *Sturges and Burn Manufacturing Company v Beauchamp,* 231 *US* 320 (1913), and *Miller v Wilson,* 236 *US* 373 (1915).

(14.) See, generally, Frank, *Mr. Justice Black.*

(15.) Freeman and Howard, "Perspectives," p. 1.

(16.) Leon Friedman and Fred Israel, editors, *Volume III. The Justices of the United States Supreme Court, 1789-1969,* New York: Chelsea House, 1969, p. 2326.

(17.) *Ibid.,* pp. 2327-28.

(18.) *Ibid.,* p. 2330.

(19.) Black, *Constitutional Faith,* p. 41.

(20.) Frank, *op. cit.,* pp. 11-12.

(21.) 72 *Congressional Record,* pp. 1239-1240 (1930).

(22.) *Northern Pacific Railroad v United States,* 556 *US* 1 (1957), at 4.

(23.) Charlotte Williams, *Hugo L. Black: A Study in the Judicial Process,* Baltimore: The Johns Hopkins Press, 1950, p. 97.

(24.) Strickland, *op. cit.,* p. 207.

(25.) Howard, "Mr. Justice Black and the Negro Protest Movement," p. 1057.

(26.) *McCart v Indianapolis Water Company,* 302 *US* 419 (1937).

(27.) at 428.

(28.) at 438, 441.

(29.) *Burford et al v Sun Oil Company,* 319 *US* 315 (1942).

(30.) at 327.

(31.) at 332.

(32.) *Connecticut General Life Insurance Company v Johnson,* 303 *US* 77 (1937), at 80.

(33.) at 84.

(34.) at 85, 87.

(35.) at 90.

(36.) *Quin, White and Prince, Inc v Henneford,* 305 *US* 434 (1938), at 449.

(37.) at 454.

(38.) at 455.

(39.) *Wood v Lovett,* 313 *US* 362 (1940)

(40.) at 372.

(41.) at 373.

(42.) at 373-374.

(43.) at 374.

(44.) *Northwest Airlines v Minnesota,* 322 *US* 292 (1943).

(45.) at 302.

(46.) *International Shoe Corporation v Washington,* 326 *US* 310 (1945), at 325-326.

(47.) *R.F.C. v Beaver County,* 328 *US* 204 (1946), at 210.

(48.) *Polk Company et al v Glover, County Solicitor,* 305 *US* 5 (1938), at 15.

(49.) at 16.

(50.) *Southern Pacific v Arizona,* 325 *US* 761 (1944), at 778.

(51.) at 784.

(52.) at 793.

(53.) *Morey v Doud,* 354 *US* 457 (1956). Black wrote that, "whatever one may think of the merits of this legislation, its exemption of a company of known solvency from a solvency test applied to others of unknown financial responsibility can hardly be called 'invidious.'" at 471.

(54.) *AFL v American Sash and Door Company,* 335 *US* 538 (1948). See also, Black's opinions for the Court in: *Traveler's Health Association v Virginia,* 339 *US* 643 (1949)–regulation of mail-order health insurance companies, and *Giboney v Empire Storage Company,* 336 *US* 490 (1948)–Missouri statute forbidding agreements in restraint of trade upheld.

(55.) *Lincoln Federal Labor Union v Northwestern Iron and Metal Company,* 335 *US* 525 (1949), at 534.

(56.) at 536.

(57.) *Ferguson v Skrupa,* 372 *US* 726 (1962), at 729.

(58.) at 730.

(59.) at 730-731.

(60.) at 732.

(61.) Strickland, *op. cit.,* p. 72.

(62.) *Ibid.,* at 71.

(63.) Black, *Constitutional Faith,* p. 9.

(64.) Strickland, *op. cit.,* p. 199.

(65.) Berman, *op. cit.,* p. 45.

(66.) *Ibid.,* p. 47.

(67.) *US v Southeastern Underwriters Association,* 322 *US* 533 (1944).

(68.) *US v Frankfort Distillers,* 324 *US* 293 (1945).

(69.) *AP v US,* 326 *US* 1 (1944).

(70.) *Timkin Roller Bearing Company v US,* 341 *US* 593 (1951).

(71.) *US v General Motors, Corporation,* 384 *US* 127 (1966).

(72.) *Silver v New York Stock Exchange,* 373 *US* 341 (1963).

(73.) *Fashion Originators Guild of America v FTC,* 312 *US* 457 (1940).

(74.) *US v Pabst Brewing Company,* 384 *US* 546 (1966).

(75.) *Fashion Originators,* at 465.

(76.) *Southeastern Underwriters,* at 552.

(77.) *AP v US,* at 14.

(78.) at 20.

(79.) *Northern Pacific Railway Company v US,* 356 *US* 1 (1957), at 4.

(80.) *Eastern Railroad Presidents Conference v Noerr Motor Freight Company,* 365 *US* 127 (1961).

(81.) *US v Weldon,* 377 *US* 95 (1964).

(82.) at 115.

(83.) *US v Bethlehem Steel Corporation,* 315 *US* 289 (1941).

(84.) at 309.

(85.) *FPC v Natural Gas Pipeline Company,* 315 *US* 575 (1941), at 606.

(86.) at 600.

(87.) *ICC v Inland Waterways, Inc.,* 319 *US* 671 (1942).

(88.) at 695.

(89.) at 696.

(90.) at 697.

(91.) at 701.

(92.) *NLRB v Waterman Steamship Company,* 309 *US* 206 (1939), at 208.

(93.) at 209.

(94.) *Tiller v Atlantic Coast Line Railraoad,* 318 *US* 54 (1942), at 58.

(95.) at 68.

(96.) *NLRB v Allis-Chalmers Manufacturing Company,* 388 *US* 175 (1966).

(97.) at 201.

(98.) at 202.

(99.) 398 *US* 235 (1969).

(100.) at 257.

(101.) at 258.

(102.) Interview on *CBS Reports: Hugo Black and the Bill of Rights,* December 1968.

(103.) Correspondence with clerk, 1969-1970 term of Supreme Court.

(104.) Correspondence with clerk, 1968-1969 term of Supreme Court.

Notes to Chapter Three

(1.) Norman Dorsen, "The Second Mr. Justice Harlan: A Constitutional Conservative," 44 *New York University Law Review,* No. 2, April 1969, 251, at 258.

(2.) Harlan, *op. cit.,* p. 2.

(3.) Black, *Constitutional Faith*, p. 9; *Griswold v Connecticut*, 381 *US* 479 (1964), at 510.

(4.) In an interview, Justice Black said: "I do not wish to have to pass on the laws of this country according to the degree of shock I receive!...I get shocked pretty quickly, I confess." In Black, "Justice Black and the First Amendment."

(5.) *Indiana v Brand,* 303 *US* 95 (1937), at 11-12.

(6.) at 117.

(7.) *Harper v Virginia Board of Elections,* 383 *US* 663 (1965), at 666.

(8.) at 675.

(9.) *Idem.*

(10,) at 674.

(11.) at 678.

(12.) *Williams v North Carolina,* 325 *US* 226 (1944), at 271.

(13.) at 274.

(14.) *Griswold v Connecticut,* 381 *US* 479 (1964).

(15.) at 484.

(16.) at 492.

(17.) at 493.

(18.) at 500.

(19.) at 507.

(20.) at 511.

(21.) at 519.

(22.) at 520.

(23.) *Levy v Louisiana,* 391 *US* 68 (1967) at 75.

(24.) at 76.

(25.) at 78.

(26.) *Lou Bertha Labine v Vincent,* 401 *US* 532 (1970) at 536-537.

(27.) at 538.

(28.) at 539.

(29.) *Reitman v Mulkey,* 387 *US* 369 (1966) at 391.

(30.) *Ibid.*

(31.) at 396.

(32.) *Hunter v Erickson,* 393 *US* 385 (1968).

(33.) at 396.

(34.) at 397.

(35.) *James v Valtierra,* 402 *US* 137 (1970).

(36.) at 141.

(37.) at 142-143.

(38.) In June of 1971, Justice Black wrote the opinion of the Court in the case of *Hazel Palmer v Thompson,* 403 *US* 217 (1970), in which the Court validated the action of the city of Jackson, Mississippi (closing of five municipal pools rather than desegregate). Finding no violation of the "Equal Protection" Clause, Justice Black wrote that "probably few persons, prior to this case, would have imagined that cities could be forced by five lifetime judges to construct or refurbish swimming pools which they choose not to operate for any reason, sound or unsound." at 226.

(39.) *Boddie v Connecticut,* 401 *US* 371 (1970). Black dissented.

(40.) *Sniadach v Family Finance Corporation of Bayview,* 395 *US* 337 (1968).

(41.) at 339.

(42.) *Ibid.*

(43.) at 344-345.

(44.) at 350-351.

(45.) *Goldberg, Commissioner of Social Services v Kelly,* 397 *US* 254 (1969).

(46.) at 279.

(47.) at 277.

(48.) *Shapiro v Thompson,* 394 *US* 618 (1969), at 634.

(49.) at 635.

(50.) *Boddie v Connecticut,* 401 *US* 371 (1970), at 382.

(51.) at 386.

(52.) *Meltzer v LeCraw,* 402 *US* 954 (1970). Certiorari denied. Justice Black dissented.

(53.) *Ibid.*, at 955-956.

(54.) J. W. Ehrlich, *Ehrlich's Blackstone, Part Two; Public Wrongs, Private Wrongs,* New York: Capricorn Books, 1959, pp. 129,133.

(55.) *Ibid.*, at p. 130.

(56.) *Amalgamated Food Employees Union Local 590 v Logan Valley Plaza, Inc.,* 391 *US* 308 (1967).

(57.) at 330, 333.

(58.) *Bell v Maryland,* 12 *L ed 2d* 824 (1963), at 825.

(59.) at 833.

(60.) at 834.

(61.) *Ibid.*, at 847.

(62.) at 848.

(63.) at 850.
(64.) at 869.
(65.) at 870.
(66.) at 874.
(67.) at 851.
(68.) at 855.
(69.) at 866-867.
(70.) at 855-856.
(71.) at 864-865.
(72.) at 867.
(73.) *Adderley et al v Florida,* 385 *US* 39 (1966).
(74.) at 47-48.
(75.) See the following cases: *Garner v Louisiana,* 368 *US* 157, (1961); *Taylor v Louisiana,* 370 *US* 154 (1961); *Edwards v South Carolina,* 372 *US* 229 (1962); *Peterson v City of Greenville,* 373 *US* 244 (1962); *Hamm v City of Rock Hill,* 379 *US* 306 (1964); *Cox v Louisiana,* 379 *US* 559 (1964).
(76.) Martin Luther King, Jr., *Why We Can't Wait,* 1963, p. 82.
(77.) Howard, *op. cit.,* p. 1038.
(78.) *Goldberg v Kelly,* 397 *US* 254 (1969), at 275, note 6.

Notes to Chapter Four

(1.) Mendelson, *op. cit.,* p. 64.
(2.) *Shaugnessy v United States ex rel Mezei,* 345 *US* 206 (1953), at 224.
(3.) *Malinsky v New York,* 324 *US* 401 (1945), at 417.
(4.) *Haley v Ohio,* 332 *US* 596 (1948), at 602.
(5.) Mendelson, *op. cit.,* p. 65.
(6.) Black, *Interview, CBS Reports,* 1968.
(7.) Black, *Constitutional Faith,* p. 24.
(8.) See *Murray's Lessee v Hoboken Land and Improvement Company,* 18 *Howard* 272 (1856), and Ehrlich, *Ehrlich's Blackstone, Part One,* pp. 48, 49, 53.
(9.) Black, *Constitutional Faith,* p. 33.
(10.) *Ibid.* Earlier, Justice Black had written that "the provisions of the Bill of Rights that safeguard fair legal procedures came about largely to protect the weak and the oppressed from the strong and the powerful." In Black, "The Bill of Rights," p. 880.
(11.) Correspondence with law clerk, 1961-1962.
(12.) *Barron v Baltimore,* 7 *Peter* 243 (1833).
(13.) See for example: *Walker v Sauvinet,* 92 *US* 90: "trial by jury

may be modified by a state or abolished altogether," *Twining v New Jersey,* 211 *US* 28 (1908), "The exemption against self-incrimination will fail if the state elects to end it," and, *Hurtado v California,* 110 *US* 516 (1884), where the grand jury indictment protection in the Fifth was not made applicable to the states.

(14.) *Powell v Alabama,* 287 *US* 45 (1932). Right to Counsel for indigents charged with a capital crime is a "fundamental right."

(15.) Felix Frankfurter, "Memorandum on 'Incorporation' of the Bill of Rights into the Due Process Clause of the Fourteenth Amendment," 78 *Harvard Law Review,* No. 4, February 1965, 746,749.

(16.) *Palko v Connecticut,* 302 *US* 319 (1937).

(17.) at 324-325.

(18.) at 325.

(19.) at 325.

(20.) at 326.

(21.) at 327.

(22.) Correspondence with law clerk, 1968-1969 term.

(23.) *Chambers v Florida,* 309 *US* 227 (1939), at 235.

(24.) at 236.

(25.) at 241.

(26.) *Lisenba v California,* 314 *US* 219 (1941). See also, Black's dissent in *Hysler v Florida,* 315 *US* 411 (1941), a case dealing with a "tainted confession" that the Court majority found to be not violative of due process, i.e., it was fundamentally unfair.

(27.) at 236.

(28.) at 238-239.

(29.) at 241.

(30.) *Betts v Brady,* 316 *US* 455 (1941).

(31.) *Powell v Alabama,* 287 *US* 45 (1932).

(32.) at 463-464.

(33.) at 471.

(34.) at 475.

(35.) at 476.

(36.) *Ashcraft v Tennessee,* 322 *US* 143 (1943); *Feldman v US,* 322 *US* 487 (1943).

(37.) *Ashcraft*, at 155.

(38.) *Feldman*, at 492.

(39.) at 501-502.

(40.) *Adamson v California,* 332 *US* 46 (1946).

(41.) at 53.

(42.) at 54.

(43.) at 58.

(44.) at 62.
(45.) at 63.
(46.) at 68.
(47.) at 68-69.
(48.) at 69.
(49.) at 75.
(50.) at 70-71.
(51.) at 82-83.
(52.) at 89.
(53.) at 90-91.
(54.) Correspondence with law clerk, 1961-1962 term.
(55.) *Adamson*, at 89.
(56.) *Foster v Illinois*, 332 *US* 134 (1946).
(57.) at 140.
(58.) *Bartkus v Illinois*, 359 *US* 121 (1958).
(59.) at 131. See also *Abbate v United States*, 359 *US* 187 (1958).
(60.) at 134. See Frankfurter, "Memorandum," *op. cit.*, p. 747.
(61.) at 151.
(62.) at 155.
(63.) at 142.
(64.) Anthony Lewis, *Gideon's Trumpet*, New York: Random House, 1964, p. 174.
(65.) *In Re Winship*, 397 *US* 358 (1969).
(66.) at 365-366.
(67.) at 382.
(68.) at 384.
(69.) at 385.
(70.) at 386.
(71.) *Baldwin v New York*, 399 *US* 66 (1969).
(72.) at 74.
(73.) at 75.
(74.) *Williams v Florida*, 399 *US* 78 (1969).
(75.) at 111.
(76.) at 112.
(77.) at 115.
(78.) *Coleman v Alabama*, 399 *US* 1 (1969).
(79.) at 12.
(80.) at 13.
(81.) *McGautha v California*, 402 *US* 183 (1970).
(82.) at 225.
(83.) at 225-226.
(84.) at 226.

(85.) at 226.
(86.) Howard, *op. cit.*, p. 1050.
(87.) Correspondence with law clerk, 1961-1962 term.
(88.) Charles Reich, "The living Constitution and the Court's Role," in Strickland, *op. cit.*, p. 154.
(89.) *Ibid.*, p. 155.
(90.) *In Re Oliver*, 333 *US* 257 (1947).
(91.) at 273.
(92.) at 278.
(93.) See *Mapp v Ohio*, et al., also Table One, pp 105-106.
(94.) *Robinson v California*, 370 *US* 660 (1961), at 667.
(95.) *Gideon v Waintright*, 372 *US* 335 (1962).
(96.) Lewis, *op. cit.*, p. 192.
(97.) *Gideon*, at 344.
(98.) at 345-346.
(99.) Lewis, *op. cit.*, pp. 221-222.
(100.) *Malloy v Hogan*, 378 *US* 1 (1963); *Murphy v Waterfront Commission of New York Harbor*, 378 *US* 52 (1963).
(101.) *Malloy*, at 10-11.
(102.) at 15.
(103.) *Murphy*, at 58.
(104.) at 59.
(105.) *Pointer v Texas*, 380 *US* 400 (1964), at 403.
(106.) at 408-409.
(107.) *Washington v Texas*, 388 *US* 14 (1966); *Klopfer v North Carolina*, 386 *US* 213 (1966).
(108.) *Washington*, at 17.
(109.) *Klopfer*, at 223.
(110.) *Duncan v Louisiana*, 391 *US* 145 (1967), at 152.
(111.) at 162.
(112.) at 163.
(113.) at 168.
(114.) at 169.
(115.) *Benton v Maryland*, 395 *US* 784 (1968).
(116.) at 794.
(117.) at 808.
(118.) Black, *Constitutional Faith*, p. 26.
(119.) *Boyd v US*, 116 *US* 616 (1886).
(120.) *Weeks v US*, 232 *US* 383 (1914).
(121.) See *Elkins v US*, 364 *US* 290 (1960). Repudiation of "silver platter" tactic whereby federal officials would use evidence seized illegally by state officials to convict in federal courts.

(122.) *Wolf v Colorado,* 338 *US* 24 (1948).
(123.) at 27.
(124.) at 27-28.
(125.) at 39.
(126.) *Rochin v California,* 342 *US* 165 (1952).
(127.) at 168-169.
(128.) at 172.
(129.) at 174.
(130.) at 175.
(131.) at 176.
(132.) *Irvine v California,* 347 *US* 128 (1952).
(133.) at 132.
(134.) at 137.
(135.) at 145.
(136.) *Breithaupt v Abram,* 352 *US* 432 (1957).
(137.) at 438.
(138.) at 442.
(139.) at 444.
(140.) *Mapp v Ohio,* 367 *US* 643 (1960).
(141.) at 657.
(142.) at 661.
(143.) at 662.
(144.) at 674.
(145.) Black, "The Bill of Rights," p. 873.
(146.) *Carroll v US,* 267 *US* 132 (1925).
(147.) *Harris v US,* 331 *US* 145 (1948); *US v Rabinowitz,* 339 *US* 56 (1950).
(148.) *Chimel v California,* 395 *US* 752 (1969).
(149.) *Terry v Ohio,* 392 *US* 1 (1968).
(150.) at 18-19.
(151.) *Sibron v New York,* 392 *US* 40 (1968).
(152.) at 82.
(153.) *Warden v Hayden,* 387 *US* 294 (1967).
(154.) *Aguilar v Texas,* 378 *US* 108 (1966).
(155.) *McCray v Illinois,* 386 *US* 300 (1967).
(156.) *Spinelli v US,* 393 *US* 410 (1969).
(157.) at 429.
(158.) *Whiteley v Warden,* 401 *US* 560 (1970), at 570.
(159.) at 575.
(160.) at 576.
(161.) *Olmstead v US,* 277 *US* 438 (1928); *Goldman v US,* 316 *US* 129 (1942).

(162.) But see, *Silverman v US,* 365 *US* 505 (1961), for an exception.

(163.) *Berger v New York,* 388 *US* 41, (1966).

(164.) at 71.

(165.) at 88-89.

(166.) *Katz v US,* 389 *US* 347 (1967).

(167.) at 351.

(168.) Ronald Degen, et al., "Criminal Justice," *Annual Survey of American Law, 1968, Part I,* NYU Law School, p. 123.

(169.) *Berger,* at 76.

(170.) *Berger,* at 77, 87.

(171.) *Katz,* at 364.

(172.) at 373.

(173.) at 365.

(174.) at 364.

(175.) Freeman and Howard, p. 3.

(176.) *Ibid.*

(177.) Lewis, *op. cit.,* p. 83.

(178.) *Coleman v Alabama,* at 13.

Notes to Chapter Five

(1.) C. Herman Pritchett, *The Political Offender and the Warren Court,* Boston: Boston University Press, 1958, p. 16.

(2.) *Ibid.,* p. 17.

(3.) *Gitlow v New York,* 268 *US* 652 (1925), at 655.

(4.) Arthur North, *The Supreme Court; Judicial Process and Judicial Politics,* New York: Appleton–Century-Crofts, 1966, p. 108.

(5.) *Schenck v United States,* 249 *US* 47 (1919); *Frohwerk v United States,* 249 *US* 204 (1919); *Debs v United States,* 249 *US* 211 (1919), but see, *Abrams v United States,* 250 *US* 616 (1919).

(6.) *Schenck v United States,* at 51.

(7.) Justice Brandeis, in *Whitney v California,* 274 *US* 357 (1927).

(8.) *Gitlow,* at 667.

(9.) *American Communications Association v Douds,* 329 *US* 382 (1950).

(10.) See *Murdock v Pennsylvania,* 319 *US* 105 (1943) for elaboration of the view that the First Amendment was on a high, preferred plane above all other guarantees in the Constitution. In *Murdock,* Frankfurter's criticism of that doctrine was sharp. He called it a "mischievous phrase" embracing the (false) idea that "any law touching communication is infected with presumptive invalidity."

(11.) *Barenblatt v United States,* 360 *US* 109 (1959).
(12.) Black, "Bill of Rights," p. 866.
(13.) Black, *Constitutional Faith,* p. 45.
(14.) Black, "Bill," p. 881.
(15.) Black, *Constitutional,* p. 43.
(16.) *New York Times v United States,* 403 *US* 734 (1970).
(17.) Black, *Constitutional,* pp. 48-52, passim.
(18.) *Beauharnais v Illinois,* 343 *US* 250 (1951), at 269.
(19.) Black, *Constitutional,* p. 49.
(20.) Taft-Hartley Act, 1947; Internal Security Act, 1950; Immigration and Naturalization Act, 1952; Communist Control Act, 1954.
(21.) 341 *US* 494 (1950). First challenge to Smith Act, *Dunn v US,* 320 *US* 790 (1943), certiorari denied.
(22.) Pritchett, *op. cit.,* p. 18.
(23.) "Hearings On Proposed Legislation to Curb or Control the Communist Party of the United States," House Un-American Activities Committee, Eightieth Congress, Second Session, (1948), p. 21.
(24.) Pritchett, pp. 18-20.
(25.) *Dennis,* at 501.
(26.) at 509.
(27.) at 510.
(28.) at 516.
(29.) at 521.
(30.) at 524-525.
(31.) at 525-526.
(32.) at 547.
(33.) at 548.
(34.) at 549.
(35.) *idem.*
(36.) at 556-557.
(37.) at 563.
(38.) at 567.
(39.) at 569.
(40.) at 572.
(41.) *idem.*
(42.) at 591.
(43.) at 579.
(44.) at 580.
(45.) at 581.
(46.) Pritchett, *op. cit.,* p. 21.
(47.) 354 *US* 298 (1956).
(48.) at 316.

(49.) at 319.
(50.) at 340.
(51.) at 344.
(52.) *Scales v US,* 367 *US* 203; *Noto v US,* 367 *US* 290 (1960).
(53.) See, "The Case of the Communist Who Was 'Too Active,'" in Barker and Barker, *Freedoms, Courts, and Politics,* Englewood Cliffs, Prentice-Hall, 1965, pp. 95-128.
(54.) *Scales,* at 259.
(55.) at 261.
(56.) at 262.
(57.) *Noto*, at 296-297.
(58.) at 301.
(59.) 367 *US* 1 (1960).
(60.) at 69-71.
(61.) at 137.
(62.) at 139
(63.) at 146.
(64.) at 147.
(65.) at 168.
(66.) at 169.
(67.) *Communist Party v United States,* 331 *F 2d* 807 (DC Cir, 1963), certiorari denied, 377 *US* 968 (1964).
(68.) *Aptheker v Secretary of State,* 378 *US* 500 (1963), at 511.
(69.) at 518.
(70.) at 519.
(71.) 380 *US* 503 (1964).
(72.) at 511-512.
(73.) *Albertson v SACB,* 382 *US* 70 (1965).
(74.) *US v Robel,* 389 *US* 258 (1967).
(75.) *Fong Yue Ting v US,* 149 *US* 698 (1893).
(76.) *Carlson v Landon,* 342 *US* 524 (1951). See also, Black's dissent in *Ludecke v Watkins,* 335 *US* 160 (1948).
(77.) *Carlson,* at 551.
(78.) at 554-555.
(79.) at 556.
(80.) 345 *US* 206 (1952).
(81.) at 217-218.
(82.) *Galvan v Press,* 347 *US* 522 (1954).
(83.) *US v Witkovich,* 353 *US* 194 (1957).
(84.) *Jay v Boyd,* 351 *US* 345 (1956).
(85.) *Whitney v California,* 274 *US* 357 (1927).
(86.) Pennsylvania v Nelson, 350 US 497 (1956).

(87.) *Brandenburg v Ohio,* 395 *US* 444 (1968).

(88.) at 447.

(89). at 449-450.

(90.) *McGrain v Dougherty,* 273 *US* 135 (1927).

(91.) See, Eric Bentley, ed., *Thirty Years of Treason: Excerpts from Hearings Before the House Committee on Un-American Activities, 1938-1968,* New York, Viking Press, 1971.

(92.) See *US v Josephson,* 333 *US* 838 (1947); *Barsky v US,* 334 *US* 843 (1948), both: certiorari denied.

(93.) *Watkins v US,* 354 *US* 178 (1956).

(94.) *Sweezy v New Hampshire,* 354 *US* 234 (1956).

(95.) See, for example, Walter Murphy, *Congress and the Court,* 1962, and C. H. Pritchett, *Congress versus the Supreme Court,* 1961.

(96.) He was also fined $250. The questions he refused to answer were: "Are you now a member of the Communist Party? Have you ever been a member of the Communist Party? Did you know Francis Crowley as a member of the Communist Party? Were you ever a member of the Haldane Club of the Communist Party while at the University of Michigan? Were you a member while a student of the University of Michigan Council of Arts, Sciences, and Professions?"

(97.) *Barenblatt v US,* 360 *US* 109 (1958), at 126.

(98.) at 127.

(99.) at 131.

(100.) at 136.

(101.) at 143-144.

(102.) at 145-146.

(103.) at 146.

(104.) at 159-161.

(105.) at 162.

(106.) *Uphaus v Wyman,* 360 *US* 72 (1958), at 108.

(107.) *Wilkinson v US,* 365 *US* 399 (1960).

(108.) at 417.

(109.) at 420-421.

(110.) at 422-423.

(111.) *Braden v US,* 365 *US* 431 (1960), at 422.

(112.) at 444.

(113.) at 446.

(114.) *Russell v US,* 369 *US* 749 (1961); See also *Gojack v US,* 384 *US* 702 (1965).

(115.) *American Communications Association, CIO v Douds,* 339 *US* 382 (1949) at 396-397.

(116.) at 446.

(117.) at 449.

(118.) *Wieman v Updegraff,* 344 *US* 183 (1952) at 193. In 1943, Black had written that "words uttered under coercion are proof of loyalty to nothing but self-interest. Love of country must spring from willing hearts and free minds." *W. VA. Bd of Ed v Barnette,* (1942).

(119.) at 194.

(120.) *Speiser v Randall,* 357 *US* 513 (1957), at 518.

(121.) at 531-532.

(122.) *Konigsberg v State Bar of California,* 366 *US* 36 (1960), at 49.

(123.) at 52.

(124.) at 61.

(125.) at 77-78.

(126.) at 75.

(127.) *In Re Anastaplo,* 366 *US* 82 (1960), at 115-116.

(128.) at 116. The third case was *Cohen v Hurley,* 366 *US* 117 (1960) which was overturned in *Spevak v Klein,* 385 *US* 511 (1966).

(129.) *Baird v Arizona,* 401 *US* 1 (1970), at 4.

(130.) at 7.

(131.) *In Re Stolar,* 401 *US* 23 (1970), at 25.

(132.) at 30.

(133.) See *Baird,* at 45, and *Stolar,* at 25-27.

(134.) *Stolar,* at 35-36.

(135.) *Law Students Civil Rights Research Council v Wadmond,* 401 US 154 (1970), at 156.

(136.) at 174-175.

(137.) at 176.

(138.) Black, *Constitutional Faith*, pp. 53, 44-45.

(139.) Black, CBS-TV interview, 8 December 1968, transcribed on tape.

(140.) "I do not believe the First Amendment grants a constitutional right to engage in conduct of picketing or demonstrating, whether on publicly owned streets or privately owned property." Black, *Constitutional Faith,* p. 54.

(141.) CBS-TV interview.

(142.) *Feiner v New York,* 340 *US* 315 (1951), at 321.

(143.) at 323.

(144.) at 329.

(145.) *Beauharnais v Illinois,* 343 *US* 250 (1951), at 269.

(146.) at 274.

(147.) *Cox v Louisiana,* 379 *US* 536 (24), 559 (49), 1966.

(148.) at 562-564.

(149.) at 577-578.

(150.) at 579.

(151.) at 583.

(152.) at 584-585.

(153.) *idem.*

(154.) *US v O'Brien,* 391 *US* 367 (1967) at 373-374.

(155.) *Tinker v Des Moines Independent Community School District,* 393 *US* 503 (1968) at 507.

(156.) at 520.

(157.) at 523-525.

(158.) *Street v New York,* 394 *US* 576 (1968) at 590.

(159.) at 609.

(160.) at 610.

(161.) *Gregory v Chicago,* 394 *US* 111 (1968), at 112.

(162.) at 118-120.

(163.) at 120.

(164.) at 118.

(165.) at 124-125.

(166.) *Barenblatt v United States.*

Notes to Chapter Six

(1.) According to his biographer, John P. Frank, *Mr. Justice Black: The Man and His Opinions,* New York: Alfred A. Knopf, 1948, pp. 46-47, Black was not formally educated in the liberal arts and, between the time he first entered the Senate and his elevation to the Court, 1926-1937, he read the works of Franklin, Adams, Jefferson, Madison, the records of the Federal Constitutional Convention, Charles Beard, Greek, Roman, European, and English and American history and philosophy, Milton, Shakespeare, Hawthorne, Thoreau, Twain, Montesquieu, Rousseau, Locke, Bryce, Mill, Marx, Spencer, Veblen, Aristotle, Spinoza, James, Dewey, et al.

(2.) See Frank, *op. cit.,* and Williams, *op. cit.,* for discussions of the charges levelled against Black at the time of his appointment to the Court in 1937. See also Daniel Berman, "The Persistent Race Issue," in Strickland, *op. cit.,*

(3.) See footnote 2 above. In 1967, in an interview with the *New York Times,* under agreement not to publish it until after his death, Black said "with a boyish grin: 'You want to know the main reason I joined the Klan?' I was trying a lot of cases against corporations, jury cases, and I found out that all the corporation lawyers were in the Klan. A lot of the jurors were too, so I figured I'd better be even-up." *The*

New York Times, September 26, 1971, p. 76.

(4.) Anthony Lewis, *New York Times*, September 26, 1971, p. 1.

(5.) *Ibid.*

(6.) Black, *Constitutional Faith*, p. 66.

(7.) Black, *New York Times interview, op. cit.*

(8.) Correspondence with law clerk, 1968-1969 term.

(9.) Berman, *American University Law Review*, p. 46.

(10.) *Youngstown Sheet and Tube Company v Sawyer*, 343 *US* 579 (1951), at 589.

(11.) *The New York Times v United States*, 404 *US* 1 (1970).

(12.) Alan Dershowitz, "Two Choices," *The New York Times*, Spetember 26, 1971.

(13.) *Turner v United States*, 396 *US* 398 (1969), at 426.

(14.) Berman, *American Law*, p. 43.

(15.) See, for example, his activities in conference sessions of the Court before the watershed *Brown v Board of Education of Topeka* decision of 1954 as described in S. Sidney Ulmer, "Earl Warren and the *Brown* Decision," 33 *Journal of Politics* August 1971, pp. 689-702. It is, of course, not without a bit of irony that a man branded as viciously anti-negro became–immediately–a defender of the political and human rights of the negro minority. See Berman, "The Persistent Race Question."

(16.) Saunders, *op. cit.*, p. 1.

(17.) *Korematsu v United States*, 323 *US* 214 (1944), at 219.

(18.) *New York Times interview*, published September 26, 1971, p. 76.

(19.) See his opinion in *Kovacs v Cooper*, 336 *US* 77 (1949). "There are many people who have ideas that they wish to disseminate but who do not have enough money to own or control publishing plants, newspapers, radios, moving picture studios, or chains of show places.... To tip the scales against transmission of ideas through public speaking (through amplifying systems on sound trucks) is to deprive the people of a large part of the basic advantages in the receipt of ideas that the First Amendment was designed to protect."

(20.) See his dissenting opinion in *Colegrove v Green*, 328 *US* 549 (1946), where he argued that depriving the people of fair representation based on reapportionment plans based on population deprived the people of basic constitutional rights the Courts were obligated to protect.

(21.) *Feldman v United States*, 322 *US* 487 (1944), at 507.

(22.) Black, *Constitutional Faith*, p. 66.

(23.) Strickland, *op. cit.*, p. xii.

Index of Cases

Ball, Howard, 1937-
The vision and the dream of Justice Hugh L. Black: an examination of a judicial philosophy. [By] Howard Ball. University, University of Alabama Press, [1975]
vii, 232p. 22cm.

Includes bibliographical references and index.

1.Black, Hugo Lafayette, 1886-1971. 2.U.S. Supreme Court-Biography. 3.Judges-Biography. I.Title.